CHAPTER ONE

CHAPTER

ONE

AN IRISH FOOD STORY

ROSS LEWIS

WITH PHOTOGRAPHY BY BARRY McCALL

GILL&
MACMILLAN

DEDICATED TO MY PARENTS, MAGGIE AND GETHIN, AND TO MY WONDERFUL FAMILY, JESSICA, MOLLY, EABHA AND SHEANA. THANK YOU FOR ALL YOUR SUPPORT.

GILL & MACMILLAN

Hume Avenue, Park West, Dublin 12
with associated companies throughout the world
www.gillmacmillanbooks.ie

© Text, Ross Lewis 2013
© Photography, Barry McCall 2013
© Cover illustration, Graham Thew 2013

978 0717 5787 7

Publisher	Nicki Howard
Production Director	Mairead O'Keeffe
Managing Editor	Deirdre Rennison Kunz
Design and Page Layout	Graham Thew
Editor, Project Manager and Concept Consultation	Ross Golden-Bannon
Recipe Editor	Orla Broderick
Copy Editor	Aoife O'Kelly
Indexer	Grainne Farren
Printed by	Printer Trento Srl, Italy

This book is typeset in 10pt Onserif on 12pt.

CHAPTER ONE RESTAURANT

18–19 Parnell Square
Dublin 1
Ireland
Tel +353 (1) 8732266
info@chapteronerestaurant.com

CONTENTS

FIRST COURSE

MUSHROOM CONSOMMÉ with SMOKED POTATO and BUTTERMILK EMULSION 25

RICH ONION BROTH with BROCCOLI RABÉ and ORGANIC CELERIAC BAKED in SALT, JERUSALEM ARTICHOKE EMULSION and CULTIVATED MUSHROOMS 28

PEARL TAPIOCA and KNOCKDRINNA SHEEP'S CHEESE with SUMMER PEAS, BROAD BEANS and BLACK GARLIC 30

ARDSALLAGH GOAT'S CHEESE PARFAIT with SPRING VEGETABLES and APPLE BALSAMIC VINEGAR GEL 33

SPICED CHESTNUT SOUP with HAZELNUT CREAM and WHITE TRUFFLE 15

WARM BLACK TRUFFLE JELLY with SWEETCORN PURÉE 16

FETA CHEESE MOUSSE with SALT BAKED BEETROOT, CAPER SPROUT PURÉE, with MARINATED RED ONION and PICKLED CUCUMBER 18

WINTER PICKLED VEGETABLE SALAD with MARINATED GREEN RAISINS and CAPER SPROUTS, BEURRE NOISETTE and FRESH SALTED HAZELNUTS 20

CARROT and BUTTERMILK SOUP with ROASTED CARROTS and DILL OIL 2

TOMATO PLATE with SMOKED BUFFALO MOZZARELLA 6

FRENCH BEAN SALAD, FENNEL and MINT DRESSING with SALTED PEACH and SMOKED ALMONDS 8

FRESH CHERRY TOMATO JELLY and WILD STRAWBERRIES with BASIL and TOMATO CREAM 11

A HISTORY of CONVIVIALITY 45

CURED SALMON with BURREN SMOKED SALMON CREAM and LEMON BALM JELLY, HORSERADISH and WILD WATERCRESS, KILKENNY ORGANIC COLD PRESSED RAPESEED OIL 47

BROWN CRAB with PICKLED RED DULSE SEAWEED, CUCUMBER with SUMMER PEAS and CORIANDER OIL 50

DUBLIN BAY PRAWN, SMOKED BACON and BASIL SPRING ROLL with RED PEPPER ESCABÈCHE PURÉE 53

VINE RIPENED CHERRY TOMATO, AVOCADO and CLAM COCKTAIL 54

CARPACCIO of VEAL HAUNCH POACHED in MILK with BLACK OLIVES from THASSOS ISLAND and PICKLED GREEN TOMATO, TUNA EMULSION and CAPER SPROUTS 56

SECOND COURSE

PIG'S TAIL STUFFED with FINGAL FERGUSON'S BACON and RAZOR CLAMS, BASIL PURÉE with LAND CRESS and MUSTARD LIME FRUIT 83

POACHED CHILLED ROCK OYSTERS with a SMOKED RED DULSE JELLY, OYSTER CREAM and WILTED BABY GEM LETTUCE with SMOKED BACON CRACKERS 84

SCALLOP with a WHITE BEAN and RAZOR CLAM STEW, PUMPKIN PURÉE FLAVOURED with SMOKED BACON CREAM, BASIL OIL and PICKLED CROWN PRINCE PUMPKIN 89

CARPACCIO of SPICED BEEF with CREAMED SHALLOTS and HORSERADISH, MATURE WEST CORK GOUDA and SHAVED BABY VEGETABLES, PICKLED KING OYSTER MUSHROOMS and APPLE BALSAMIC CREAM 90

PICKLED MACKEREL with PEAR and HORSERADISH RELISH, SMOKED POTATO and CRÈME FRAÎCHE 60

CHARCUTERIE TROLLEY 63

CHAPTER ONE WHITE PUDDING with PARSNIP, BRAMLEY APPLE and HORSERADISH COMPÔTE 66

CURED and SMOKED IRISH RED DEER VENISON with FOIE GRAS, MADEIRA JELLY, ICEWINE VERJUS and GRILLED ONION BREAD 69

GAME TERRINE of SNIPE and WOOD PIGEON with MUSTARD QUINCE PURÉE and SMOKED PEAR 70

GOOSE and OATMEAL SAUSAGE with PICKLED CHERRIES, SHAVED PEAR and CELERIAC PURÉE 75

BRAISED PRIME HEREFORD OXTAIL with MACARONI and ROOT VEGETABLES COOKED in ROCK SALT 78

WARM SMOKED CURED CLARE ISLAND SALMON with CURED PORK JOWL and BRAISED SQUID with FRESH PEAS 105

BUTTER POACHED ATLANTIC LOBSTER with a LIGHT POTATO EMULSION and MALTED VINEGAR SAUCE, BROAD BEANS and SUMMER CABBAGE 108

CHARGRILLED GREEN ASPARAGUS with RAVIOLI of 36 MONTH OLD PARMESAN and GARLIC LEAF 99

OX TONGUE with SAUTÉED SPRING LAMB SWEETBREADS, BURREN WILD MUSTARD and WATERCRESS PURÉE with PICKLED and DEEP-FRIED SHALLOT 102

CONSOMMÉ of DUCK and SPRING VEGETABLES with DUMPLINGS of FOIE GRAS and SESAME, SMOKED DUCK FAT 95

CITRUS DRESSED SMOKED HADDOCK with ROPE MUSSELS and PICKLED CARROT, CELERIAC CREAM and SEAWEED 96

MAIN COURSE

HOTPOT of HEREFORD PRIME BEEF with JELLIED CONSOMMÉ and SPRING VEGETABLES 171

ROASTED SQUAB PIGEON with PICKLED BABY SHIITAKE and MUSHROOM KETCHUP, ROASTED WHITE ASPARAGUS with ROCKET JUICE and ROCKET OIL 174

ROASTED SKEAGHANORE DUCK with BLOOD ORANGE and GLAZED SALSIFY, CONFIT WING and GIZZARD with PURPLE SPROUTING BROCCOLI 177

STEAMED CORNED MUTTON and CAPER PIE with a WHITE ONION PURÉE and MUSTARD CREAM SAUCE with GREEN VEGETABLES 180

PORK CHEEK GRATINATED with JOWL, POTATO DUMPLINGS and BRANDON BAY COCKLES with CHARGRILLED WILD GARLIC 185

STEAMED WILD SEA BASS with ORGANIC CELERIAC, ROPE MUSSELS in a CRAIGIES CIDER DRESSING and TARRAGON JUICE with ROASTED JERUSALEM ARTICHOKE 188

POACHED GUINEA HEN with a SET SWEETCORN CREAM and SAGE JUICES, WHITE PUDDING and ROASTED VEAL SWEETBREADS 142

BRAISED TOP RIB of PRIME HEREFORD BEEF and SKERRIES NATIVE POTATOES with BUTTERMILK and SAVOY CABBAGE, RICH RED WINE and SHALLOT SAUCE 147

ROASTED WOODCOCK with RED CABBAGE, SMOKED POTATO and WILD MUSHROOM GRATIN with SMOKED BACON COOKED in YEAST 151

BRAISED STUFFED HARE with a LIGHT RED WINE SAUCE and GRATINATED CAULIFLOWER with TRUFFLE 154

BREAST of PHEASANT with a LIGHT MORTEAU SAUSAGE STUFFING and LEG GLAZED with a BLACK PUDDING and a WALNUT CRUST, FRIED CABBAGE and a BURNT ONION STUFFED with CRUSHED JERUSALEM ARTICHOKE, PHEASANT SAUCE and SAGE JUICE 159

CONFIT HALIBUT with JAPANESE SPICES and CITRUS FRUIT, ROASTED WHITE ASPARAGUS and SPIDER CRAB 163

TURBOT COOKED with CITRUS SALT, BROCCOLI PURÉE and FRIED POLENTA, CRAB and YUZU DRESSING with DILL OIL 166

UNFOLDING CHAPTERS 117

RIB of SLANEY VALLEY BEEF, OX CHEEK and TONGUE with SMOKED CHAMP POTATO and FRIED SPRING CABBAGE, NEW SEASON BROAD BEANS and CARROTS with PICKLED GARLIC and WILD GARLIC LEAF 118

CHARGRILLED JOHN DORY with LOBSTER and SORREL, VEGETABLES COOKED in PARCHMENT 122

ACHILL ISLAND BLACK FACED LAMB PLATE 127

LOIN of RABBIT STUFFED with a LIGHT PATA NEGRA FARCE, CARROT and BROWN BUTTER PURÉE with BLACK CUMIN, TOASTED SEEDS with BEE POLLEN and RABBIT SAUCE BROKEN with CARROT OIL 130

RARE BREED PORK PLATE 132

CHARGRILLED BLACK SOLE with CASTLETOWNBERE SHRIMP, CHASSELAS GRAPES and CAULIFLOWER with CHANTERELLE MUSHROOMS and LEEKS 136

PEPPERED SIKA VENISON LOIN with CEP PURÉE and ROOT VEGETABLES, CONFIT SPROUTS and CHESTNUTS with PARSNIP PURÉE and a RICH GAME SAUCE 139

NÍ NEART GO CUR LE CHÉILE. THERE IS NO STRENGTH WITHOUT UNITY.

Good cooking starts with good produce, and when you have the richness of the Irish larder to choose from, there is an opportunity to really soar. What you see on a plate in Chapter One is an expression of many artisans, various landscapes and hardworking talent. All that happens long before we've even started cooking. Many of our specialist growers and artisan producers have been supplying us since the earliest days in the nineties. Our Northside Dublin location was a notoriously difficult place to trade in, yet people who cared about food came and suppliers who were passionate about their uniquely Irish produce came too – integrity of produce was what united us.

They inspired me and my cooking. The landscape and the seasons inspired me too. The new Irish artisans were like a palette of flavours and textures to play with. A path had already been carved out for them by the artisan cheese sector and by people like Veronica Steele and Myrtle Allen, but I'd always wanted Chapter One to be an Irish restaurant with an international standard. I spent some time in Ferran Adrià's El Bulli in Catalonia in 1996. He is possibly the most influential chef of the last 50 years and his genius helped me develop a new way of thinking about food. This was a radical change for me but one inspired by my own landscape, raw materials, artisan producers and craftspeople. On short trips to Brittany I met Olivier Roellinger who owned a three-starred Michelin restaurant in Cancale and now devotes his life to the promotion of spices in cuisine through his spice shops Epices Roellinger in Paris and Saint-Malo. He opened up a world of spices for me, which have a very real and historical relevance to British and Irish food.

Since the beginning of Chapter One, I have tried to look at food with an open mind and coloured in the pictures of flavour and texture through a slow progression of self-development. Today our food is part of a story that is still unfolding, but it will always reflect honesty and integrity because these elements are the very soul of our food.

In creating this book I wanted to strike a balance between an official record of the many thousands of hours of talent that helped build Chapter One and wanting to share my food knowledge with the wider world. Inevitably there is a point where these two hopes do not meet. The home cook, no matter how talented or determined, is not blessed with a hardworking and talented brigade of chefs as I am, so it will be difficult to reproduce many of the recipes in full in a domestic kitchen. However, that doesn't mean this book is solely for professional chefs. Most of the dishes can be broken down to simpler versions of perhaps just two or three elements from a recipe. Also, each recipe states the season it stems from and draws attention to a small palette of flavours and inspirations that led to the creation of the dish. These small palettes could easily be used by the home chef to start their own journey creating recipes from those combinations and from the rich harvest our country has to offer.

Traditionally spring starts in Ireland on 1 February, St Brigid's Day, so if you think a dish is really late-winter rather than spring, this quirk of Celtic optimism might explain it to you. Then again, as most chefs know, the seasons stretch and shrink depending on weather conditions. The simple rule is: cook what has just been harvested because that is what is in season.

A few things to consider when working in a domestic kitchen: we've very hot ovens in Chapter One so you might need to cook and roast things a little longer than indicated. Also, a professional kitchen has sections where each chef might specialise in one particular area of a dish. This partly explains the layout of the recipes and it can be used to your advantage if you decide to tackle a major dish. Check which elements can be made in advance and stored or possibly frozen, and then simply assemble all the elements on the final day. Where possible, we've converted measurements into teaspoons and tablespoons, but we do weigh everything very precisely to ensure consistency and a digital scales is invaluable for this. We use a wide range of specialist equipment, much of it a far cry from the traditional batterie de cuisine, so we've offered some alternatives where we can.

This book was created throughout the autumn and winter of 2012 and into the spring of 2013. Therefore, there is an inevitable bias towards autumnal and winter flavours as we worked with the seasons. The design colours reflect this to a certain extent, but the palette we used also reflects the colours of the restaurant which in turn echo the colours of the Irish landscape, from purple heathers to rich green herbage and deep blue waters of the Irish lakes and coast.

MARTIN CORBETT, PROPRIETOR AND MAÎTRE D' EXTRAORDINAIRE.

FIRST COURSE

CARROT *and* BUTTERMILK SOUP *with* ROASTED CARROTS *and* DILL OIL

I love the way the acidity
of the buttermilk interplays
with the sweet texture of the
carrot soup, which is the last
flavour to leave your palate.

FOR THE SOUP
250 g onions, sliced
15 g garlic cloves, finely sliced
125 g butter
100 ml rapeseed oil
200 ml white wine
875 g carrots, thinly sliced
150 g beurre noisette (page 276)
750 ml water
1 litre chicken stock (page 285)
3 star anise
¼ tsp coriander seeds
2 black cardamoms
¼ tsp black cumin
¼ tsp ground cinnamon
30 g sugar
a little yuzu salt

FOR THE CARROT CRISPS
2 medium carrots, peeled
vegetable oil, for deep-frying

FOR THE CHARGRILLED CARROTS
100 g baby carrots, scrubbed clean
50 g butter
1 fresh dill sprig
a little olive oil

TO SERVE
240 ml Cuinneog buttermilk
100 ml cream, softly whipped
10 ml dill oil (page 281), in a small squeezy bottle

SERVES 8

SOUP

Sweat the onions and garlic in the butter and rapeseed oil
in a large pan over a medium heat until very soft but not
coloured. Add the wine and reduce by half, then add the
carrots and continue to cook. Add the beurre noisette along
with the water, stock, spices and sugar. Return to the boil
and simmer for 20 minutes until the carrots are tender.
Drain the carrot mixture through a colander into a clean
pan. Reduce the liquid by half, then purée the carrots in
a blender, adding back to the reduced liquid to make the
soup. Season with the yuzu salt and a pinch of salt, and
then pass through a fine chinois.

CARROT CRISPS

Preheat a deep fat fryer to 140°C. Using a mandolin, finely
slice the carrots, then deep-fry until crisp. Drain on kitchen
paper and season with salt.

CHARGRILLED CARROTS

Place the carrots in a pan with the butter and dill. Add
enough water to cover and simmer for about 40 minutes,
until the liquid has almost evaporated and the carrots are
cooked through and nicely glazed, tossing occasionally at
the end to prevent them from catching. Preheat a griddle
pan and brush with olive oil, then add the carrots and
chargrill on all sides. Cool, season and cut into 5 mm slices.

SERVING

Preheat the oven to 160°C. Reheat the chargrilled carrots in
a roasting tin for 3–4 minutes until just warmed through.
Heat 1.2 litres of the soup in a pan and when hot stir in the
buttermilk. Blend the soup with a hand blender, adding
the softly whipped cream. Divide the chargrilled carrots
among warmed serving bowls and pour 180 ml of the soup
over each one. Finish with a tablespoonful of the cream, the
carrot crisps and dots of dill oil.

DERMOT CAREY, PASSIONATE ORGANIC
GROWER FROM COUNTY DUBLIN, WAS ONE
OF THE CURATORS OF THE CARTY-LISSADELL-
LANGFORD HERITAGE POTATO COLLECTION,
PROTECTING VARIATIONS OF OUR NATION'S
TRADITIONAL STAPLE. HE HAS A COLLECTION
OF ALMOST 200 VARIETIES OF HERITAGE
POTATO.

TOMATO PLATE *with* SMOKED BUFFALO MOZZARELLA

This dish is quite simply summer on your plate. The different tomatoes are pickled, smoked, seasoned and dried, allowing their many varying flavours and textures to shine. The buffalo mozzarella acts as a creamy, soft backdrop while the yuzu salt unites the umami notes.

FOR THE PICKLED CHERRY TOMATOES
150 g cherry tomatoes
40 ml water
25 ml white wine vinegar
35 g sugar
20 g fresh basil leaves

FOR THE SMOKED TOMATO EMULSION
500 g ripe plum tomatoes
150 ml extra virgin olive oil
½ tsp fresh thyme leaves
2 garlic cloves, finely sliced
100 g organic tomato ketchup
25 g fresh basil leaves
a little thickener (glossary)

FOR THE SEASONED TOMATOES
8 large Marinda tomatoes
2 tsp extra virgin olive oil

FOR THE SMOKED MOZZARELLA
240 g Toonsbridge buffalo mozzarella

TO SERVE
6 tbsp caper sprout purée (page 283), in a small squeezy bottle
8 tbsp red onion relish (page 284)
24 semi-dried tomato pieces (page 287)
375 g tomato jelly (page 277)
100 g brioche croûtons (page 277)
a little rapeseed oil
20 ml chive oil (page 281), in a small squeezy bottle
20 ml basil oil (page 281), in a small squeezy bottle
handful fresh rocket flowers and micro herbs
a little yuzu salt
fennel pollen, optional

SERVES 8

PICKLED CHERRY TOMATOES

Blanch the cherry tomatoes in a pan of water for 1 minute and then transfer to a bowl of iced water. Cool and peel off the skins. Bring the water, vinegar and sugar to the boil, then drop in the basil. Remove from the heat, and when at room temperature, add the tomatoes, ensuring they are fully submerged. Leave to cool in the pickle for one day before using.

SMOKED TOMATO EMULSION

Slice 250 g of the tomatoes in half and dress in a bowl with 25 ml of the olive oil, the thyme, half a teaspoon of salt and a good pinch of black pepper. Spread in a smoker (page 294) and smoke for 10 minutes on a medium heat, and when ready, chop roughly. Heat the rest of the oil in a pan and fry the garlic for 2–3 minutes without browning. Meanwhile, roughly chop the rest of the plum tomatoes and add to the garlic with the smoked tomatoes and ketchup. Simmer gently for 1–2 hours, stirring occasionally and adding the basil for the last 20 minutes. Blitz in a blender to a purée and pass through a chinois. Season with salt and black pepper, and thicken with thickener, a pinch at a time, until it is a thick and creamy consistency. Put into a squeezy bottle and chill until needed.

SEASONED TOMATOES

Cut the tomatoes into 8 thick slices, discarding the ends. Arrange on a tray and sprinkle with half a teaspoon of salt, a good pinch of black pepper and the olive oil. Leave in a warm place for 30 minutes.

SMOKED MOZZARELLA

Smoke the mozzarella in a smoker (page 294) filled with applewood chips for 3–4 minutes over a medium heat. Leave to cool with the lid closed, then tear into 8 pieces.

SERVING

Place a slice of the seasoned tomato on each large, cold serving plate, then pipe a teaspoon of the caper sprout purée onto the tomato slices and top this with the red onion relish followed by the smoked mozzarella. Place 3 pieces of semi-dried tomato on each plate along with 2 pickled cherry tomatoes, then pipe dots of the smoked tomato emulsion in the gaps on the plate. Use a teaspoon to put pieces of the jelly around the tomatoes and add the same amount of brioche croûtons. Drizzle the plates with a generous amount of rapeseed oil. Dot around generous amounts of the herb oils so that they start to combine with the rapeseed oil. Finish with the rocket flowers, micro herbs, bronze fennel, sprinkling of yuzu salt and fennel pollen if using.

FRENCH BEAN SALAD, FENNEL *and* MINT DRESSING *with* SALTED PEACH *and* SMOKED ALMONDS

The fennel dressing here is a beautiful counterpoint to the fruit with the twist of mint. It also lifts the flavour of the beans, and when you combine it with the salted, sweet peach and smoky almond, you get a wonderful flavour combination. Fresh almonds work well here too.

FOR THE FENNEL DRESSING
100 g fennel purée (page 283)
50 g crème fraîche
squeeze of lemon juice
4 fresh mint sprigs

FOR THE FRENCH BEANS
400 g French beans, trimmed

FOR THE SALTED PEACHES
4 peaches, ripe but firm
1 tsp sea salt flakes

TO SERVE
4 fresh mint leaves, finely sliced
handful smoked almonds (glossary)
small handful fennel fronds
¼ tsp fennel pollen

SERVES 8

FENNEL DRESSING

Combine the fennel purée with the crème fraîche in a bowl and add the lemon juice, then season with salt and black pepper. Add the mint sprigs and leave to infuse in the fridge for at least 2 hours or overnight. Strain out the mint and use as required.

FRENCH BEANS

Blanch the French beans in a pan of boiling salted water until tender. They should be past al dente with a little give to ensure the bean flavour. Drain and refresh in a bowl of iced water. Pull apart and chill until needed.

SALTED PEACHES

Cut the peaches in half, removing the stone, and then cut each half into 6 × 1–2 mm slices. Sprinkle with a little salt and set aside for 10 minutes.

SERVING

Place the French beans in a bowl with the mint and enough of the fennel dressing to coat, then season with salt and black pepper. Place a small mound of beans in the middle of each serving plate. Arrange 4 slices of the salted peach over each mound of beans and sprinkle over some of the smoked almonds. Finish with a few of the fennel fronds. Dot a little more of the fennel dressing around each plate and add a sprinkling of the fennel pollen.

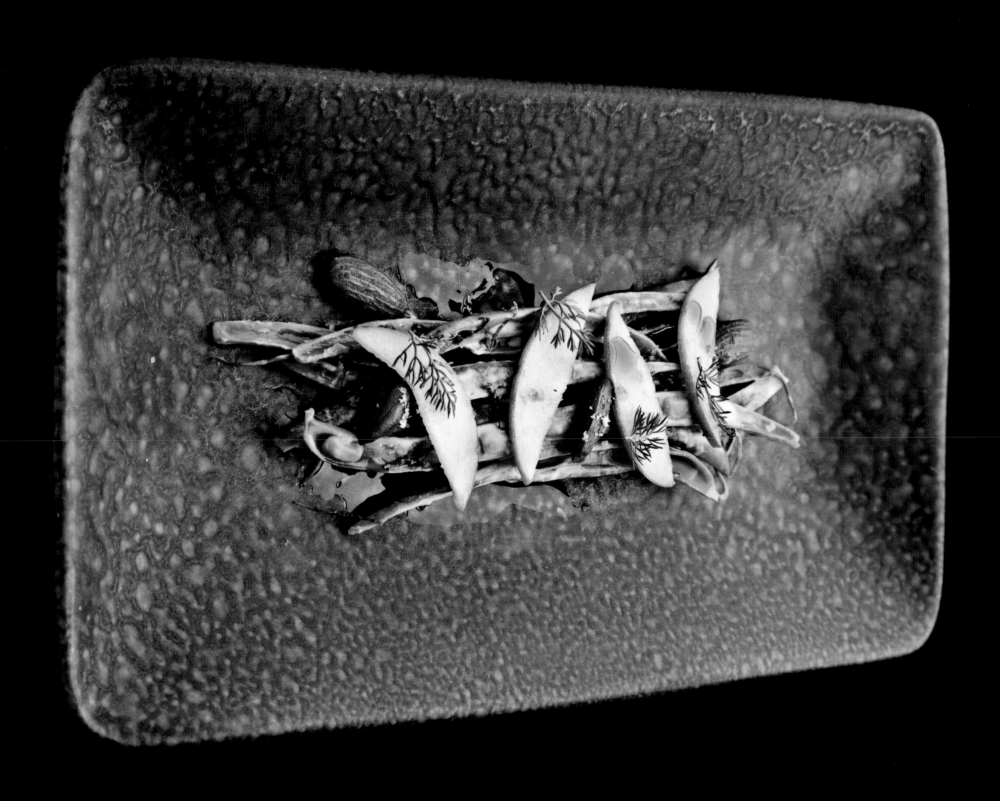

FRESH CHERRY TOMATO JELLY *and* WILD STRAWBERRIES *with* BASIL *and* TOMATO CREAM

FOR THE TOMATO CRÈME FRAÎCHE
150 ml tomato consommé (page 277)
100 g crème fraîche

FOR THE CHERRY TOMATO HEARTS
8 cherry tomatoes

TO SERVE
8 x 80 g tomato jelly (page 277)
24 wild strawberries
8 rye bread crisps (page 277)
16 semi-dried tomato strips (page 287)
small handful each fennel and basil cress
1 tsp yuzu salt (glossary), optional
2 tsp basil oil (page 281)
small handful each fresh fennel cress, basil cress and
rocket flowers

SERVES 8

TOMATO CRÈME FRAÎCHE

Reduce the tomato consommé in a small pan until it is
nearly the measurement of 2 tablespoons and has the
consistency of a glaze. Then cool completely. Put the crème
fraîche in a bowl and whisk until thickened. Fold in the
reduced consommé and season with salt and white pepper.
Put into a squeezy bottle and chill until needed.

CHERRY TOMATO HEARTS

Cut the cherry tomatoes in half and use a Parisienne scoop
to take out the hearts. Put on a plate and leave at room
temperature until needed.

SERVING

Set 80 g of tomato jelly in the bottom of a small bowl. Pipe
5 dots of the tomato crème fraîche onto each tomato jelly,
then add 2 cherry tomato hearts and 3 wild strawberries.
Break up the rye bread crisps and stand 3 pieces in the jelly.
Add 2 semi-dried tomato strips and finish with the fennel
and basil cress, a sprinkling of yuzu salt and 5 drops of the
basil oil.

Although this dish may not
help resolve the argument
about whether tomatoes
are a fruit or a vegetable,
the combination shows
how the simple can become
the extraordinary. If wild
strawberries are unavailable,
try this recipe with halved
cherries that have been
sprinkled with a little salt for
10 minutes before serving.

DENIS HEALY, ONE OF THE PIONEERS OF ORGANIC GROWING IN IRELAND, RUNS HIS FARM IN THE HEART OF THE WICKLOW COUNTRYSIDE. HE HAS A VAST ARRAY OF QUALITY FRUIT, VEGETABLES, HERBS AND LIVESTOCK. WE LOVE SEEING WHAT EACH NEW SEASON WILL BRING TO OUR PALETTE IN THE KITCHEN.

SPICED CHESTNUT SOUP *with* HAZELNUT CREAM *and* WHITE TRUFFLE

FOR THE SOUP
1 celery stick, sliced
½ leek, sliced
2 shallots, sliced
1 garlic clove, finely sliced
1 small sprig each fresh rosemary, thyme, sage and tarragon
125 g butter
50 g smoked bacon rind
1 star anise
15 fennel seeds
6 juniper berries
6 cardamom pods
2.5 litres pheasant stock (page 286)
600 g chestnuts, cooked and peeled or vacuum packed
25 ml Cabernet Sauvignon wine vinegar

FOR THE HAZELNUT CREAM
200 ml cream
60 ml hazelnut oil

TO SERVE
4 cooked peeled chestnuts, vacuum packed
½ white truffle, optional
handful dried mushroom slices (page 281)
2 tsp mushroom powder (page 281)

SERVES 8

This is one of our finest soups and a marriage of two royal autumn ingredients: chestnuts and pheasant. Folded into these flavours are star anise, fennel, juniper berries and cardamom, giving deep, complex notes. The pheasant stock gives a slightly gamier flavour and there is a zing from tarragon, sage and vinegar. The hazelnut cream and white truffle crown the flavours.

SOUP

Sweat the celery, leek, shallots, garlic and herbs with the butter and bacon rind in a large pan until softened. Crush the spices together in a pestle and mortar and add to the sweated vegetables. Pour in the stock and bring to the boil, then add the chestnuts and simmer gently for 10 minutes. Blitz in a food processor until smooth and pass through a chinois. Finish with the wine vinegar and season.

HAZELNUT CREAM

Salt and lightly whip the cream with the hazelnut oil.

SERVING

Heat the soup, being careful not to let it boil, and pour into heated serving bowls. Spoon on a little of the hazelnut cream and then use a mandolin to shave over the chestnuts and the white truffle, if using. Finish with a sprinkling each of the dried mushrooms and mushroom powder.

WARM BLACK TRUFFLE JELLY *with* SWEETCORN PURÉE

A simple, almost classic combination of warm black truffle jelly with a hot sweetcorn purée made with David Burne's sweetcorn. There is chewy sweetcorn on top from the dried kernels, some crunch from the brioche croûtons and a slick of cream giving the dish layers of richness and texture. I could eat this all day.

FOR THE TRUFFLE JELLY

250 g Paris brown mushrooms
250 g flat mushrooms
125 g onions, peeled
10 g garlic, peeled
100 g leeks
100 g carrots, peeled
100 g celery
1.5 litres water
2 black peppercorns
1 bay leaf
2 fresh thyme sprigs
50 g dried mixed wild mushrooms
50 ml Madeira
20 ml medium sherry
1 gold leaf gelatine
200 ml truffle juice (glossary)
2 g agar agar powder (glossary)

FOR THE SWEETCORN PURÉE

200 ml cream
330 g fresh sweetcorn kernels
25 g butter
150 ml milk
1 garlic clove, finely chopped
3–4 drops white truffle oil

FOR THE DRIED SWEETCORN

100 g sweetcorn kernels
1 tbsp olive oil

TO SERVE

100 ml cream, lightly whipped but still runny
6 brioche croûtons (page 277)
1/2 tsp mushroom powder (page 281)

SERVES 8

TRUFFLE JELLY

Using a food processor, mince the fresh mushrooms and vegetables. Bring the water to a simmer in a large pan with a lid and add the minced vegetables, along with the peppercorns, bay leaf and thyme. Cover and simmer for 1 hour. Remove from the heat and add the dried mushrooms and Madeira, then leave to sit at room temperature for 2 hours. Strain through a muslin into a clean pan and reduce to 400 ml. Season with salt and add the sherry. Put the gelatine into a bowl of cold water and set aside for 10 minutes. Meanwhile, heat the mushroom reduction and truffle juice until just boiling. Whisk in the agar agar, then return to the boil for 10 seconds and remove from the heat. Lift out the gelatine and squeeze out the excess water, then whisk it into the mushroom mixture to dissolve. Pass through a chinois. Weigh 35 g portions into serving bowls. Allow to set.

SWEETCORN PURÉE

Reduce the cream by half. Place the sweetcorn in a Thermomix with the reduced cream, butter, milk and garlic. Cook on full power at 90°C for 20 minutes, then pulse on the turbo setting for 2–3 minutes. Pass through a fine chinois. Season with salt and white pepper, and add the white truffle oil.

DRIED SWEETCORN

Preheat the oven to 90°C. Mix the sweetcorn and a generous pinch of sea salt with enough olive oil to lightly coat. Spread on a baking sheet and place in the oven for 1 hour until the kernels are dried out and chewy. Leave to cool.

SERVING

Heat the sweetcorn purée in a pan, being careful not to let it catch, and put it into a foam gun. Charge with 2 gas chargers and keep warm in a pan of hot water. Warm the jellies in a shallow pan of water for 5 minutes until warm to the touch. Using the foam gun, pipe a layer of sweetcorn purée roughly 2 cm thick onto each jelly. Drizzle with the whipped cream and sprinkle 10–12 dried sweetcorn kernels on each one. Gently crumble the brioche croûtons on top and sprinkle with mushroom powder.

FETA CHEESE MOUSSE *with* SALT BAKED BEETROOT, CAPER SPROUT PURÉE, *with* MARINATED RED ONION *and* PICKLED CUCUMBER

For me beetroot really embodies the flavour of mother earth. It has a beautiful velvety texture, earthy and sweet, and we've really set it off here with the orange oil. The creamy saltiness of the feta is brought back to earth by the acidity of the red onion, cucumber, and caper sprout purée. A perfectly balanced dish.

FOR THE BEETROOT AND
HORSERADISH SAUCE
800 g raw beetroot
150 g celery sticks
150 g onions, peeled
20 g creamed horseradish
10 g sherry vinegar
a little thickener (glossary)
4 small fresh tarragon sprigs

FOR THE FETA MOUSSE
375 g feta cheese
175 g cream cheese
100 ml milk
50 ml cream

FOR THE ORANGE OIL
6 oranges
300 ml sunflower oil

TO SERVE
4 tsp caper sprout purée (page 283)
3 tbsp pickled baby cucumber (page 281), finely diced
3 tbsp red onion relish (page 284)
8 roasted red beetroot discs (page 284)
16 roasted golden and candy beetroot pieces (page 284)
16 deep-fried beetroot crisps (page 277)
2 tsp beetroot powder (page 281)
handful fresh rocket flowers and micro herbs

SERVES 8

BEETROOT AND HORSERADISH SAUCE

Juice the vegetables. Warm the juice gently in a pan, adding the creamed horseradish and sherry vinegar to taste. Thicken with thickener, whisking in a pinch at a time. Pass through a sieve and season with salt, then add the tarragon and leave for 1 hour. Remove the tarragon and put the sauce into a squeezy bottle.

FETA MOUSSE

Place the feta, cream cheese and 50 ml of the milk in a blender on a medium speed until smooth. Meanwhile, place the remaining 50 ml of milk in a small pan with the cream and bring to the boil, then whisk in the hy-foamer and xanthan powder. Whisk over a medium heat for a minute or until it starts to cool and thicken, then pour into the feta mixture while still mixing at a medium speed. Continue to blend until smooth and glossy.

ORANGE OIL

Use a microplane to remove the zest from the oranges, being careful not to include any pith. Blend the oil with the orange zest in a Thermomix on full speed for 15 minutes at 50°C. Pass through a chinois and allow to settle for 30 minutes. When a layer of water separates out at the bottom, the oil can then be poured off. Transfer to a squeezy bottle and keep in the fridge.

SERVING

Put the caper sprout purée into a piping bag. Mix the pickled cucumber with the red onion relish. Put the feta mousse into a foam gun and charge with 2 gas chargers. Put 2 tablespoons of the beetroot and horseradish sauce in each serving bowl. Place a roasted beetroot disc on top, then season with salt and pepper. Pipe on 1/2 a teaspoon of caper sprout purée, followed by an equal quantity of the red onion and cucumber mixture. Using the foam gun, pipe on the feta mousse to make a smooth dome cover, then top with a couple of the golden or candy beetroot dice and the beetroot crisps. Finish with a dusting of beetroot powder on the mousse, drops of orange oil around the beetroot and horseradish sauce, some rocket flowers and micro herbs.

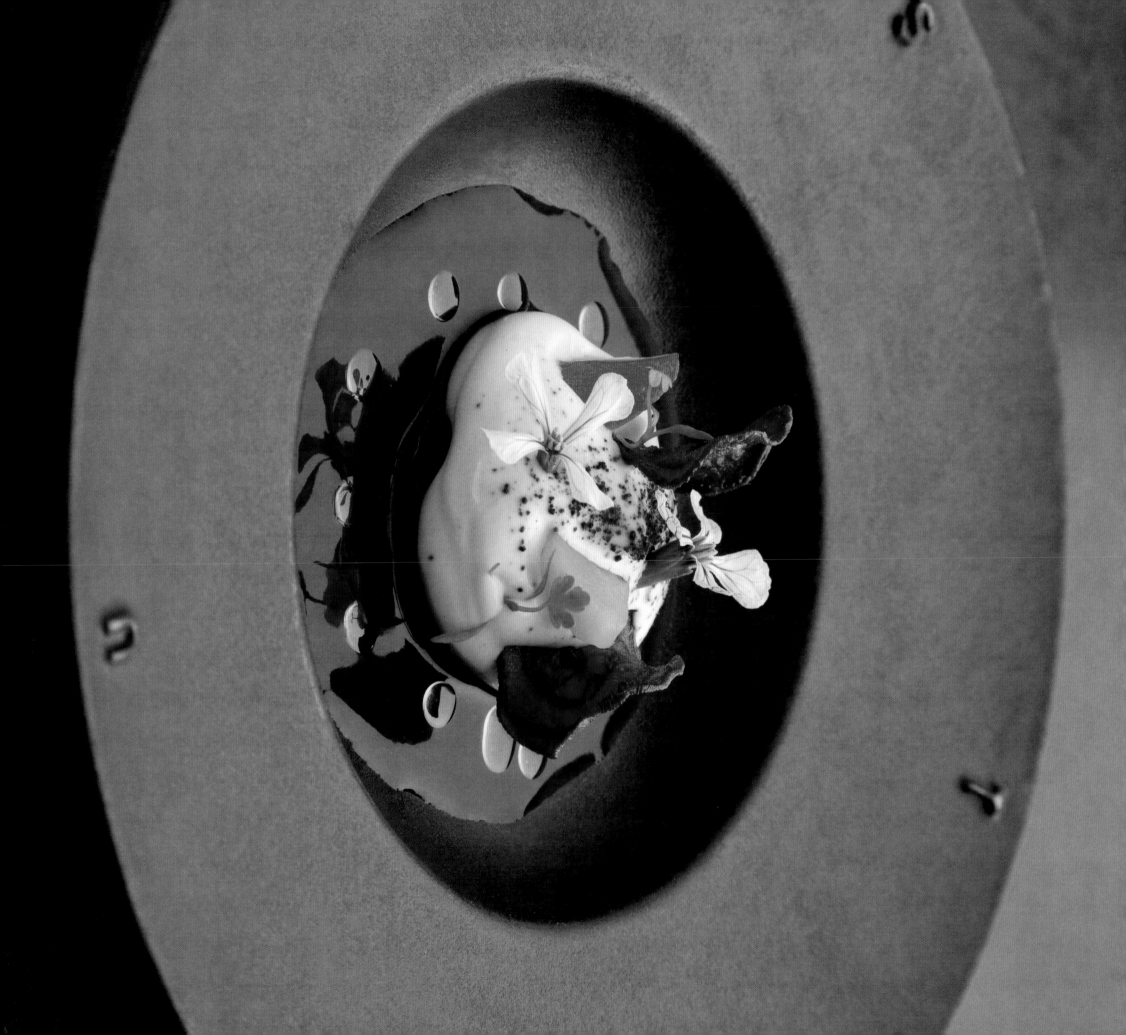

WINTER PICKLED VEGETABLE SALAD *with* MARINATED GREEN RAISINS *and* CAPER SPROUTS, BEURRE NOISETTE *and* FRESH SALTED HAZELNUTS

This is a beautiful way to start a meal. The golden raisins, caper and hazelnuts make for a play of textures and flavours. Different pickling liquids combine saltiness and acidity with the crunch of the vegetables. Fresh salted hazelnuts add further to the texture, so we've everything from sweet, sour and salty to umami. The carrot purée adds the all-important ingredient of luxury.

FOR THE MARINATED GREEN RAISINS
50 g large green raisins, 40 in total
100 ml Sauternes wine

FOR THE PICKLED CARROT
3 large carrots
handful of salt
50 ml water
50 g sugar
100 ml Llewellyn's apple balsamic cider vinegar (glossary)
2 tsp Japanese apple vinegar (glossary), optional
5 coriander seeds
1/2 star anise
1 tsp caraway seeds

FOR THE PICKLED CAULIFLOWER
1/4 cauliflower, tough core removed
4 g salt, plus a handful for the cauliflower slices
600 g rice wine vinegar
40 g sugar
5 g lemon zest

SERVES 8

FOR THE PICKLED PUMPKIN
1/4 small crown prince pumpkin
6 g salt, plus a handful for the pumpkin slices
250 ml Hondashi stock (glossary)
30 ml mirin
30 ml sake
5 g rice vinegar
30 ml dark soy sauce
350 ml pickling liquor from the pickled cauliflower

FOR THE PICKLED WHITE RADISH
1/2 white radish, scrubbed
600 g rice wine vinegar
40 g sugar
5 g lemon zest
4 g salt
pinch of ascorbic acid

FOR THE PICKLED RED RADISH
10 radishes, scrubbed
100 g Llewellyn's apple balsamic cider vinegar (glossary)
50 g sugar

FOR THE ROASTED HAZELNUTS
20 g skinned hazelnuts
25 g butter

TO SERVE
250 g carrot and brown butter purée with black cumin (page 283)
16 pickled Ballyhoura king oyster mushrooms (page 282)
handful caper sprouts (glossary)
100 ml beurre noisette (page 276)
fresh micro herbs

MARINATED GREEN RAISINS

Bring the raisins and wine to a simmer and then leave to infuse for 24 hours. Drain.

PICKLED CARROT

Slice the carrots on a mandolin. Lay on a tray, sprinkle evenly with salt and leave for 20 minutes. Rinse and pat dry. Put the water, sugar and vinegars in a pan together with the spices and bring to the boil until the sugar has dissolved. Leave to cool, then pour over the carrots and pickle for at least 2–3 hours.

PICKLED CAULIFLOWER

Slice the cauliflower on a mandolin. Lay on a tray, sprinkle with salt and leave for 20 minutes. Rinse and pat dry. Bring the vinegar to the boil with the sugar, zest and salt. When the sugar is dissolved, allow to cool. Reserve 350 ml of the pickle for the pumpkin and pour the rest over the cauliflower. Pickle for at least 2 hours.

PICKLED PUMPKIN

Peel the pumpkin and then slice on a mandolin. Lay on a tray, sprinkle with salt and leave for 20 minutes. Rinse and wring out in a clean tea towel to get rid of as much water as possible. Bring the Hondashi stock, mirin, sake, vinegar and soy to the boil with the salt. Leave to cool, then mix with the 350 ml of reserved pickle from the cauliflower recipe. Pour over the pumpkin slices and pickle for at least 2 hours.

PICKLED WHITE RADISH

Finely slice the white radish on a mandolin. Bring the vinegar to the boil with the sugar, zest and salt. When the sugar is dissolved, remove from the heat and add the ascorbic acid, then leave to cool. Pour over the radish slices and pickle for at least 2 hours.

PICKLED RED RADISH

Finely slice the red radishes on a mandolin. Bring the vinegar to the boil, then add the sugar and allow to dissolve and cool. Pour over the radish slices just before serving.

ROASTED HAZELNUTS

Heat the butter in a sauté pan until it starts to brown. Add the hazelnuts and pan-roast them, tossing frequently, until they are an even golden brown. Drain on kitchen paper and season with salt, then crack with the blade of a knife.

SERVING

Put the carrot purée into a squeezy bottle. Pipe a 4 cm line of purée onto the left-hand side of each serving plate, then use an offset palette knife to spread the purée to form a long rectangle across the middle of each serving plate. Gently warm the beurre noisette. Arrange 2 pieces of each pickled vegetable, as well as 2 pieces of pickled mushroom, on and around the purée, then add 3–4 caper sprouts and some of the marinated raisins and then dress with a little of the beurre noisette. Garnish with the fresh micro herbs.

MUSHROOM CONSOMMÉ *with* SMOKED POTATO *and* BUTTERMILK EMULSION

FOR THE MUSHROOM CONSOMMÉ

500 g Paris brown mushrooms
500 g flat mushrooms
250 g onions, peeled
20 g garlic, peeled
200 g leeks, peeled
200 g carrots, peeled
200 g celery sticks
3 litres water
8 black peppercorns
4 fresh thyme sprigs
2 bay leaves
100 g dried mixed wild mushrooms
3 tbsp Madeira
3 tbsp medium sherry

FOR THE SMOKED POTATO AND BUTTERMILK

4 garlic cloves, finely chopped
110 g beurre noisette (page 276)
150 g white onion purée (page 284)
large pinch ground Sarawak pepper (glossary)
large pinch ground mace
¼ tsp smoked paprika
40 ml milk
110 ml buttermilk
160 g smoked potato purée (page 283)
200 ml chicken stock (page 285)
30 ml tarragon vinegar reduction (page 287)
30 ml white wine shallot essence (page 278)

TO SERVE

40 chanterelle mushrooms, trimmed and halved if large
good handful caper flowers (glossary)
handful dried mushroom slices (page 281)
2 tbsp dried mushroom powder (page 281)

SERVES 8

MUSHROOM CONSOMMÉ

Using a food processor, mince the vegetables. Bring the water to a simmer in a large pan with a lid and add the minced vegetables with the peppercorns, thyme and bay leaves. Cover and simmer for 1 hour. Remove from the heat and add the dried mushrooms, then leave to sit at room temperature for 2 hours. Strain through a muslin into a clean pan and reduce to 1 litre. Season with salt and black pepper, and add the Madeira and sherry.

SMOKED POTATO AND BUTTERMILK

Sweat off the garlic in the beurre noisette in a pan with a lid, then add the white onion purée, pepper, mace, paprika, milk, buttermilk, smoked potato purée and stock, stirring to combine. Cover and simmer gently for 15 minutes. Blend in a food processor and then pass through a chinois. Season the soup with salt and black pepper, then add the tarragon vinegar reduction and shallot essence. Transfer to a foam gun and charge with 2 gas chargers.

SERVING

Heat the consommé, then add the chanterelle mushrooms and simmer for 1 minute or until just tender. Place in warmed serving bowls and top with the smoked potato and buttermilk from the gas canister. Garnish with 6–8 caper flowers per bowl and top with the dried mushrooms and mushroom powder.

This soup has an incredibly rich mouthfeel. We make it with water rather than chicken stock so that it doesn't dilute the mushroom flavour. The earthy umami of the mushrooms combined with smoked potatoes and buttermilk create a sophisticated dish from homely Irish ingredients. The caper flowers act as a counterpoint and lift the soup into aromatic richness.

MARK CRIBBIN, A GREAT MAN TO TALK ABOUT NATURE WITH, GROWS A HUGE RANGE OF
SPECIALIST MUSHROOMS AT BALLYHOURA MOUNTAIN MUSHROOMS IN COUNTY CORK.
HE IS ALSO A RENOWNED SUPPLIER OF FORAGED WILD IRISH FOODS.

RICH ONION BROTH *with* BROCCOLI RABÉ *and* ORGANIC CELERIAC BAKED *in* SALT, JERUSALEM ARTICHOKE EMULSION *and* CULTIVATED MUSHROOMS

This soup had its genesis in French onion soup but we decided to burn the onions a little, add some sugar to enhance the flavour of the onions and then finish with vinegar. We added the broccoli rabé which is quite bitter, so it is almost a French-style sweet and sour onion soup, with the bitterness and pickled mushrooms balanced by the Jerusalem artichoke emulsion. A real bowlful of great flavour and goodness.

FOR THE ONION CONSOMMÉ

125 g beurre noisette (page 276)

2 kg white Spanish onions, sliced, skins reserved

300 g leeks, sliced

175 g shallots, sliced

25 g garlic, finely sliced

25 g sugar

100 ml white wine

500 ml white wine vinegar, reduced by half

4 litres double chicken stock (page 286)

1 fresh thyme sprig

1 bay leaf

2 tbsp Worcestershire sauce

5 egg whites

FOR THE JERUSALEM ARTICHOKE EMULSION

50 g smoked bacon rind

1 fresh thyme sprig

2 shallots, finely sliced

2 tbsp olive oil

150 g Jerusalem artichokes, peeled and roughly sliced

450 ml milk

1 garlic clove, finely chopped

FOR THE BABY POTATOES

150 g very small baby potatoes

FOR THE SALT-BAKED CELERIAC AND BROCCOLI RABÉ

200 g coarse sea salt

200 g piece celeriac

200 g broccoli rabé

TO SERVE

50 g pickled velvet pioppino mushrooms (page 282), alternatively use pickled shiitake or button mushrooms

1 spring onion, very finely sliced

handful wild garlic leaves, finely julienned

2 black garlic cloves, finely sliced (glossary), optional

about 1 tsp onion powder (glossary), optional

SERVES 8

ONION CONSOMMÉ

Heat the beurre noisette in a large pan and add the onions. Cook over a low heat until the onions are dark brown and soft, then add the leeks, shallots and garlic. Continue cooking over a low heat until all the vegetables are softened and deeply caramelised, then stir in the sugar and heat until dissolved. Add the white wine, turn up to a medium heat and reduce by half. Add the reduced vinegar and reduce by half again. Add the stock, herbs and reserved onion skins, and bring to the boil. Simmer for 20 minutes, then remove from the heat. Add the Worcestershire sauce and leave the soup to infuse for another 20 minutes. Pass through a double layer of muslin into a clean pan and leave to cool. Then whisk the egg whites in and slowly bring to a very low boil. When the egg whites have solidified into a raft, pass through a double layer of muslin.

JERUSALEM ARTICHOKE EMULSION

Put the smoked bacon and thyme into a large ovenproof pan with the shallots and olive oil. Sweat until softened, without colouring the shallots. Place the artichokes in the pan with the milk and garlic, and simmer until completely cooked. Remove the bacon and thyme, then purée the emulsion in a blender until smooth and pass through a fine chinois. When ready to serve, heat the emulsion in a pan and put it into a foam gun. Charge with 2 gas chargers and keep warm.

BABY POTATOES

Boil the potatoes in salted water until cooked. Cool and cut into 2 mm slices.

SALT-BAKED CELERIAC AND BROCCOLI RABÉ

Preheat the oven to 160°C. Put the salt in a small roasting tray to a depth of 2 cm and put the vegetables on top. Bake until soft when tested with a sharp knife, then cool and cut into 4 mm dice, discarding the skin and any woody bits. Blanch the broccoli rabé in boiling salted water for 2–3 minutes, then drain and refresh in a bowl of iced water.

SERVING

Heat the consommé in a pan with the baby potato slices, mushrooms, spring onion, celeriac, broccoli rabé and wild garlic until warmed through. Divide among warmed serving bowls. Pipe artichoke emulsion on top and finish each one with 3 pieces of black garlic and a sprinkling of onion powder if using.

PEARL TAPIOCA *and* KNOCKDRINNA SHEEP'S CHEESE *with* SUMMER PEAS, BROAD BEANS *and* BLACK GARLIC

I like the surprise of this dish, tapioca normally being a dessert. It relies on the combination of different textures and a very soft, gelatinous type of creaminess from the tapioca. There is a dark molasses-like sweetness from the black garlic, which is a wonderful counterpoint to the creamy–salty sheep's cheese. It is comfort food elevated to another level with a great Irish twist.

FOR THE PEA PURÉE
25 g butter
100 g onions, sliced
½ garlic clove
250 g fresh or frozen shelled peas
1 fresh sage sprig
1 fresh tarragon sprig

FOR THE TAPIOCA
100 g shelled broad beans
100 g fresh shelled peas
1 litre chicken stock (page 285)
1 litre water
160 g tapioca
35 g Pecorino, finely grated
60 g Knockdrinna sheep's cheese, finely grated
225 g crème fraîche

TO SERVE
300 ml chicken stock (page 285) or water
4 black garlic cloves, thinly sliced (glossary)
8 fresh pea shoots

SERVES 8

PEA PURÉE

Melt the butter in a small pan. Sweat the onions and garlic over a low heat until softened. Add the peas and herbs to the onions along with a pinch of salt. Bring to the boil and simmer until the peas are just cooked, then purée in a blender. Pass through a fine chinois and cool quickly to retain the green colour.

TAPIOCA

Blanch the beans in boiling water until just cooked and then refresh in a bowl of iced water. Peel off the tough outer skins. Next blanch the peas in the same way. If they are very large, peel off their skins as well, but this is not necessary. Bring the stock and water to the boil, then add the tapioca and a pinch of salt, and reduce to a simmer. Cook the tapioca for 15 minutes or until a small white dot remains in the middle of the grain, stirring continuously. Drain in a fine chinois and rinse under warm running water until the stickiness washes away. Mix together the Pecorino, Knockdrinna and crème fraîche.

SERVING

Reheat the tapioca with the stock or water. Stir in the cheese mixture. The texture should be like a creamy risotto. Stir in the peas and beans, and season with salt and black pepper. Put 2 tablespoons (30 g) of pea purée in each warmed serving bowl, and add 100 g of the tapioca and the black garlic slices. Garnish with a sprig of fresh pea shoot.

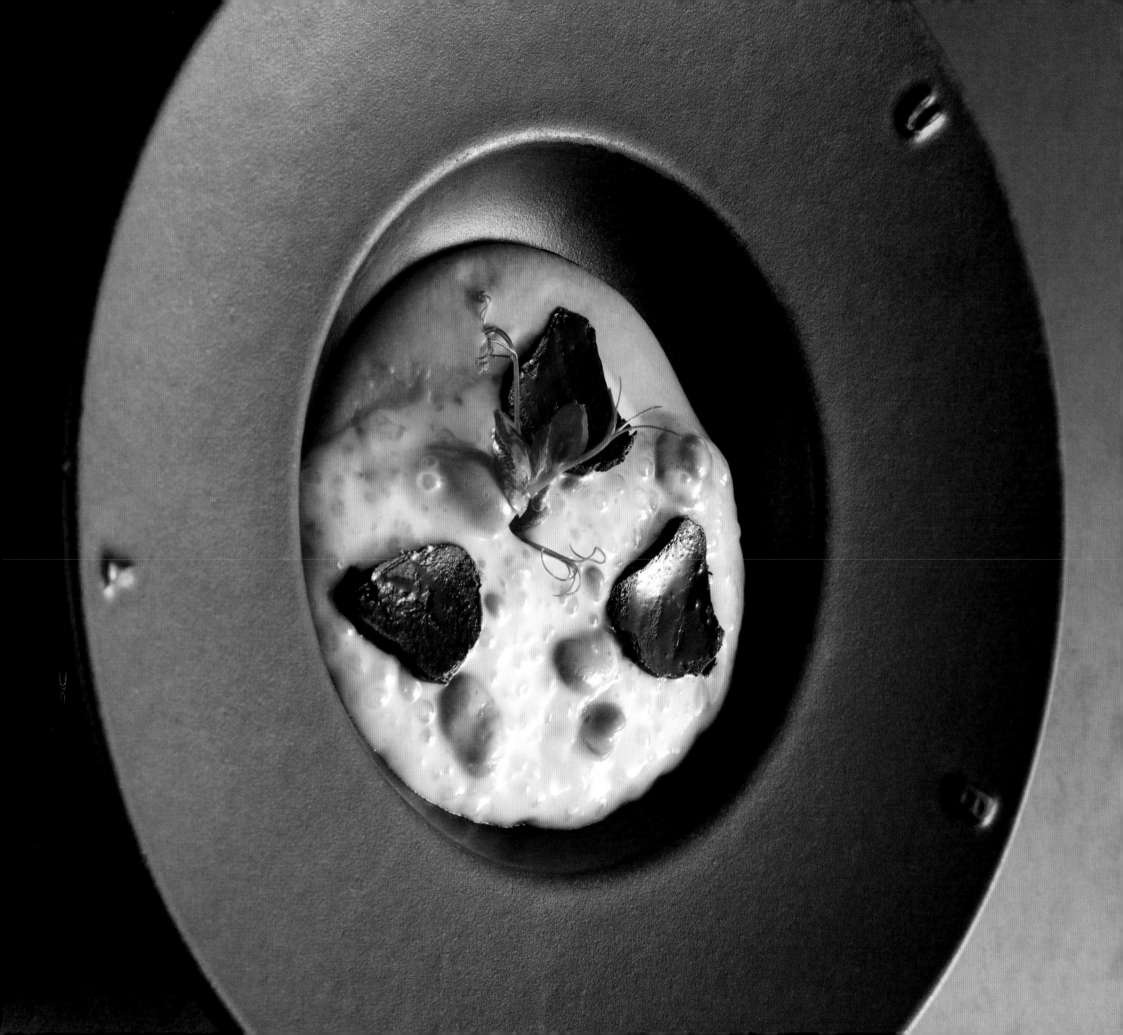

ARDSALLAGH GOAT'S CHEESE PARFAIT *with* SPRING VEGETABLES *and* APPLE BALSAMIC VINEGAR GEL

FOR THE GOAT'S CHEESE PARFAIT
4 gold leaf gelatine leaves
300 ml cream
250 g soft goat's cheese
125 g hard goat's cheese, rind removed
150 ml milk
1 g Espelette pepper (glossary)
a little groundnut oil

FOR THE BASIL CRUMB
250 g onion bread (page 264), crusts removed and
   torn into pieces
15 g fresh flat-leaf parsley
15 g fresh basil leaves

FOR THE APPLE BALSAMIC VINEGAR GEL
100 ml apple balsamic cider vinegar (glossary)
a little thickener (glossary)

FOR THE BEETROOT GEL
400 g raw beetroot
75 g celery sticks
75 g onion, peeled
2 tsp creamed horseradish (glossary)
1 tsp aged sherry vinegar
1 small fresh tarragon sprig
a little thickener (glossary)

FOR THE SHAVED ASPARAGUS
8 large asparagus spears, trimmed
juice of ½ lemon

FOR THE SPRING VEGETABLES
8 asparagus spears, trimmed
100 g fresh shelled peas
100 g shelled broad beans

FOR THE RED CHICORY
1 head red chicory

FOR THE LEMON AND OLIVE OIL DRESSING
1 tbsp lemon juice
½ tsp sugar
4 tbsp olive oil

SERVES 8

TO SERVE
24 x 2.5 cm roasted beetroot discs (page 284), 10 mm thick
a little Maldon sea salt, flakes
8 beetroot crisps (page 277)
3–4 tbsp extra virgin olive oil

GOAT'S CHEESE PARFAIT

Put the gelatine in a bowl of cold water for 10 minutes. Whip the cream to soft peaks in another bowl. Place both goat's cheeses in a blender with 5 tablespoons of the milk and blitz on a medium speed until smooth. Squeeze out the excess liquid from the gelatine. Heat the rest of the milk until just below boiling point and remove from the heat, then whisk in the soaked gelatine until dissolved. Leave to cool and then pour into the blender with the goat's cheese mix, still mixing on a medium speed. When smooth and combined, pass through a chinois into a bowl and fold in the Espelette pepper and the cream. Lightly oil a 1 litre straight-sided tin, 5 cm deep, and then line with clingfilm. Add the goat's cheese mix and chill overnight to set.

BASIL CRUMB

Put the onion bread in a blender with the herbs and blitz to a fine crumb, but don't blitz for too long or it will go brown. Pass through a tamis and chill.

In our attempt over the years to find the perfect use for some of the great Irish spring and summer goat's cheeses, we feel we've found perfect balance in this dish. The vinegar cuts through the cheese with a beautiful fruity acidity and the light parfait allows the star ingredient to really shine.

APPLE BALSAMIC VINEGAR GEL

Warm the vinegar gently in a pan and reduce to 60 ml, then whisk in the thickener, a pinch at a time, until it reaches a thick gel. Put into a squeezy bottle.

BEETROOT GEL

Juice the vegetables and then gently warm the juice in a pan with the creamed horseradish and sherry vinegar. Thicken, a pinch at a time, to a gel consistency. Pass through a fine chinois and season with salt, then add the tarragon and leave for 1 hour. Remove the tarragon and put the gel into a squeezy bottle.

SHAVED ASPARAGUS

Preheat the oven to 50°C or use a dehydrator. Using a Japanese mandolin, slice the asparagus lengthways as thinly as possible. Toss the sliced asparagus in the lemon juice and spread on a tray. Dry in the oven or dehydrator until crisp. Keep in an airtight container.

SPRING VEGETABLES

Blanch the asparagus in a pan of boiling salted water until just tender and then refresh in a bowl of iced water. Blanch the peas and the broad beans separately in a pan of boiling salted water until tender and then refresh separately in a bowl of iced water. Peel the skins off the beans and chill.

RED CHICORY

Divide the chicory into separate leaves. Use a knife to cut down either side of the white central vein so that each leaf is in 2 pieces. Drop these into a bowl of iced water for 5 minutes so that they curl up. Drain on kitchen paper and chill.

LEMON AND OLIVE OIL DRESSING

Whisk together the lemon juice and sugar with a pinch of salt until the sugar and salt have dissolved, then whisk in the oil to form an emulsion.

SERVING

Turn the goat's cheese parfait out onto a chopping board and remove the clingfilm, then use a hot knife to cut it into 4 cm squares. Put the basil crumb into a shallow dish and use it to coat the goat's cheese squares, ensuring that they are evenly coated. Repeat until you have 8 in total. Arrange on serving plates with 3 of the roasted beetroot discs and top the discs with a little of the beetroot gel. Dress the asparagus with the extra virgin olive oil, some Maldon salt, and a light grinding of pepper, then place alongside the beetroot. Pipe 4 dots of the apple balsamic vinegar gel around each plate. Coat the peas and beans in a bowl with the lemon dressing, and spoon it around the goat's cheese parfait. Finish with a red chicory curl, a piece of shaved asparagus and a beetroot crisp.

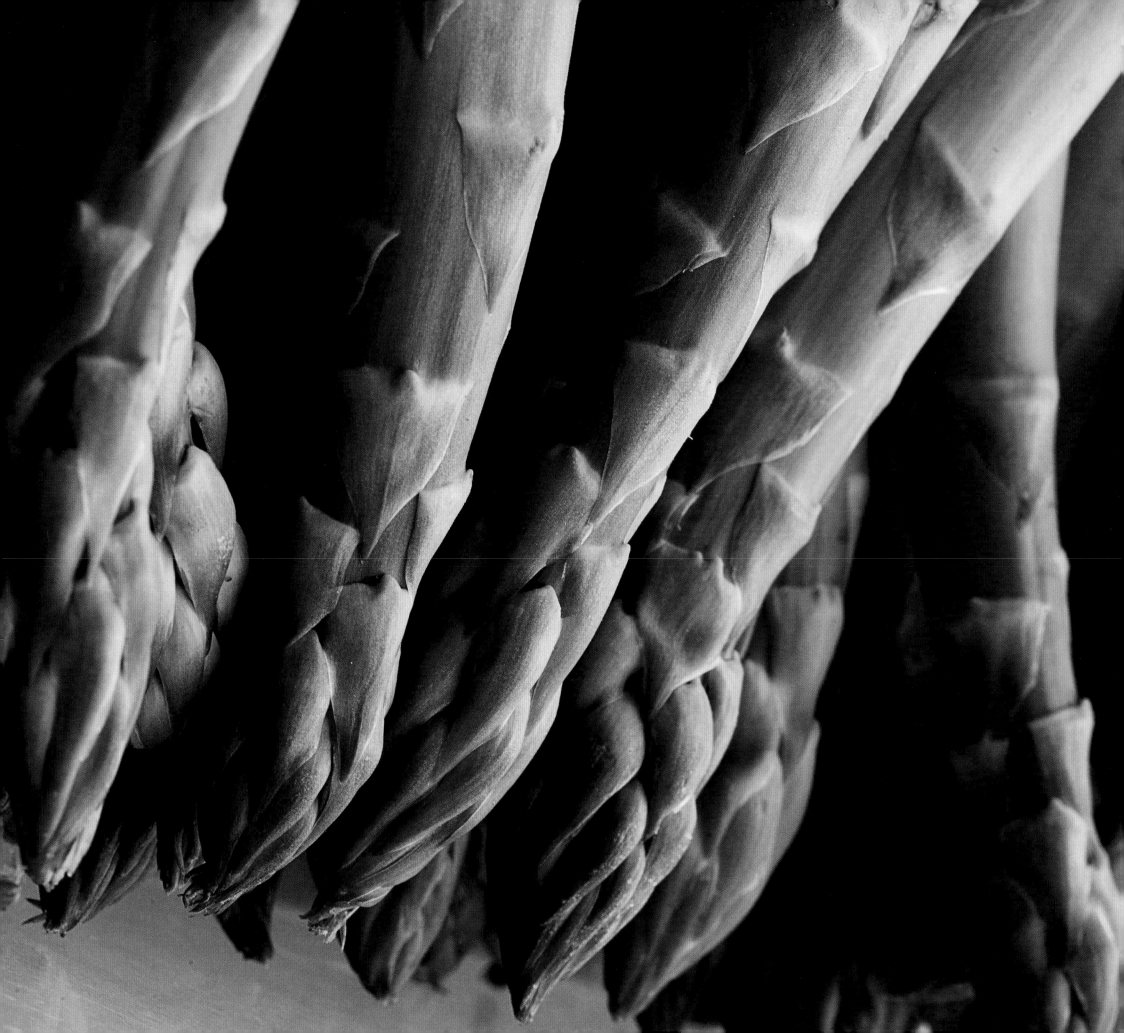

JESSICA LEWIS.

DECLAN MAXWELL, RESTAURANT MANAGER.

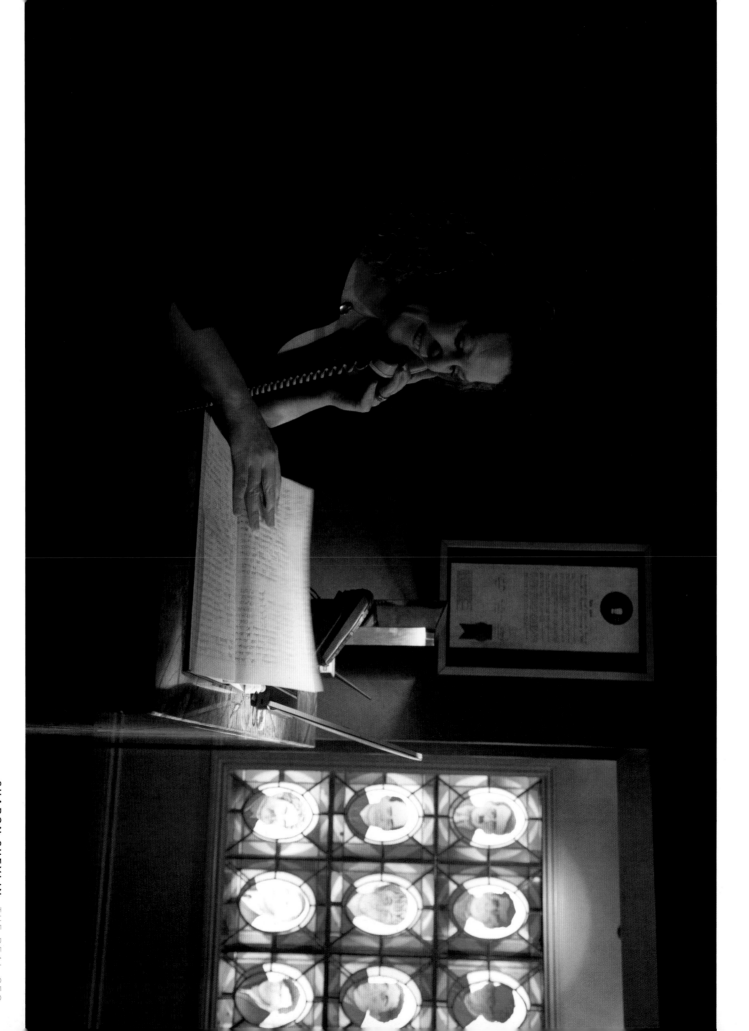

SHARON SHEVLIN. THE REAL CEO.

THE LEENANE MOUNTAINS, CONNEMARA, ON A BLUSTERY SUMMER'S DAY

SECOND COURSE

The Irish home has always been a place of conviviality, from the most humble cup of tea to the grandest offering of a traditional Irish coffee. Chapter One has worked hard and excelled at reflecting the great Irish welcome. Never feeling it was enough to simply do things correctly, we wanted people to feel comfortable in their surroundings, as if they were in their own home. In the early days of our pre-theatre menu, we encouraged people to come back after the show to have their desserts so that they wouldn't feel rushed. Our later bookings grew and grew and started to make this difficult, so to ensure a well-paced dining experience, we decided to open for pre-theatre even earlier.

Really good service has a well-tested system, which diners shouldn't even see; they should only feel welcomed. Martin Corbett, co-owner of Chapter One, is something of a front-of-house legend. He is as quick to offer a witty remark as he is to seamlessly relax those who are exploring the menu for the first time. Like an actor on stage, the trolley is his prop, where he makes and serves our traditional Irish coffees, made with Jameson Irish whiskey, naturally.

Martin is ably supported by Declan Maxwell who manages the busy ebb and flow of customers leaving and arriving like old friends. An eagle eye is kept on any flicker of attention required from a table and chats with diners are gently sprinkled or liberally spread depending on their wants. Our daily brief is not only an opportunity for the kitchen to communicate the details of the menu to front-of-house but also a chance to finesse the minutiae of service. We match feedback from the wait team with comments from customers to ensure our service and welcome are underpinned by invisible professionalism for the greatest of Irish welcomes.

I also had the opportunity to extend our great Irish welcome to Queen Elizabeth II on her first ever visit to the Republic. I created the menu for the official State dinner in Dublin Castle, ably supported by the catering company With Taste. The following section opens with the first course from that menu and each subsequent section also opens with a dish from that historic dinner.

CURED SALMON *with* BURREN SMOKED SALMON CREAM *and* LEMON BALM JELLY, HORSERADISH *and* WILD WATERCRESS, KILKENNY ORGANIC COLD PRESSED RAPESEED OIL

FOR THE CURED SALMON
1.25 litres water
200 g rock salt
400 g sugar
1 tbsp black peppercorns
10 g star anise
5 whole cloves
4 juniper berries
½ tbsp white wine vinegar
1 side fresh organic salmon, skin on and pin bones left in
1 bunch fresh coriander
1 fennel bulb, trimmed and finely sliced

FOR THE WATERCRESS PURÉE
500 g wild watercress, well picked over
300 ml cream
2 tbsp Worcestershire sauce

FOR THE WILD SMOKED SALMON CREAM
150 g piece Burren Smokehouse wild smoked salmon
400 g crème fraîche
1 tsp lemon juice
½ tsp Tabasco sauce
½ tsp smoked paprika

FOR THE LEMON BALM JELLY
200 g celery, sliced
300 g fennel, sliced
10 g root ginger, peeled and finely chopped
1 garlic clove, finely chopped
200 ml white wine
50 ml white wine vinegar
2 litres still mineral water
2 star anise
30 black peppercorns
1 tbsp lemon purée (page 289)
200 g lemon verbena (glossary)
200 g lemon balm (glossary)
8 gold leaf gelatine leaves

FOR THE HORSERADISH CREAM
200 g crème fraîche
1 tbsp creamed horseradish (glossary)
1 tbsp white wine vinegar

FOR THE PICKLED RADISH AND ONION
200 ml apple balsamic cider vinegar (glossary)
50 g sugar
2 shallots, finely sliced and separated out into 24 small rings
4 radishes, finely sliced, 24 slices in total

TO SERVE
handful each tiny rosemary flowers and fresh bronze fennel sprigs
50 ml cold pressed organic rapeseed oil (glossary), in a squeezy bottle

SERVES 8

I created this dish for the official State dinner marking the first visit of a reigning British monarch to the Irish Republic. It was served to Queen Elizabeth II, President McAleese and other dignitaries in St Patrick's Hall, Dublin Castle on 18 May 2011. This dish articulated the very best of what our rich larder has to offer in May, as well as being a celebration of our historic food culture.

CURED SALMON

Place all the marinade ingredients in a pan, except for the coriander and fennel, and bring to the boil. Remove from the heat and add the fennel and coriander, then cool. When the marinade is completely cold, pour over the salmon in a tray deep enough to keep it submerged. Cure in the fridge for 18 hours, then lift the salmon out of the cure and transfer to a drying rack. Leave to dry uncovered in the fridge for 24 hours.

WATERCRESS PURÉE

Blanch the watercress in a pan of boiling water and refresh in a bowl of iced water. Squeeze as much water out as possible using kitchen paper, then transfer to a Pacojet container and freeze overnight. Reduce the cream by half and cool. When the watercress is frozen, place in a Pacojet and blend 3 times, then transfer to a blender with the reduced cream and blend until smooth. Add the Worcestershire sauce and season with salt and black pepper. Pass through a chinois and put into a small squeezy bottle, then chill until needed.

WILD SMOKED SALMON CREAM

Remove the skin from the smoked salmon and trim down the flesh. Bring the skin, trimmings and half the crème fraîche to the boil in a pan. Cool and pass through a chinois. Place the smoked salmon in a Pacojet container with the infused crème fraîche and freeze overnight. Blend the frozen salmon mix and pass through a tamis, then fold in the rest of the crème fraîche. Add the lemon juice, Tabasco and paprika, and season with salt and black pepper. Transfer to a piping bag and chill until needed.

LEMON BALM JELLY

Put all the ingredients in a pan except for the lemon verbena, lemon balm and gelatine. Cover and simmer gently for 40 minutes. Pass through a chinois and pour onto the lemon verbena and lemon balm. Cover and leave to infuse for 2–3 hours, then pass through a double layer of muslin and measure out 1 litre. Put the gelatine in a bowl of cold water and set aside for 10 minutes. Heat 200 ml of the lemon balm liquid in a pan until just below boiling and whisk in the softened gelatine. Combine with the other 800 ml and mix well, then pass through a chinois into a jug. Pipe 25 ml of the smoked salmon cream into the bottom of each small serving bowl and cover with 100 ml of the lemon balm jelly. Chill for 3–4 hours to set.

HORSERADISH CREAM

Whisk the crème fraîche with the creamed horseradish, vinegar and a pinch of salt until just before it gets to a stiff peak. Put into a squeezy bottle and chill.

PICKLED RADISH AND ONION

Bring the vinegar, sugar and 2–3 generous pinches of salt to the boil, stirring to dissolve, then remove from the heat and allow to cool. When cold, pour over the vegetables and leave to marinate for 20–30 minutes.

SERVING

Take the skin off the cured salmon and remove the pin bones with a tweezers. Carve into 5 × 10 cm pieces from the thick end of the fillet and then cut into cubes – you'll need 24 in total. Arrange 3 cured salmon cubes on each lemon balm jelly and add 2–3 of the pickled radish slices and 2–3 of the pickled onion rings. Add 3 dots of the horseradish cream and 3 dots of the watercress purée. Finish each one with the rosemary flowers, the bronze fennel sprigs and a drizzle of the rapeseed oil.

BROWN CRAB with PICKLED RED DULSE SEAWEED, CUCUMBER

with SUMMER PEAS and CORIANDER OIL

We know summer is here when the best crab starts to arrive, matched by sweet-tasting seasonal peas. We get a wonderful crop of seaweed from Manus McGonagle in Donegal. We pickle it and combine it with cucumber jelly, so this dish is fresh, summery and salty, with a sweetness from the crab. There is a deep umami flavour from the seaweed with the sweet-popping peas and the cucumber jelly makes it a real summer favourite at the restaurant.

FOR THE CRAB
2 litres water
40 g salt
1 kg crab claws
splash of spirit vinegar
40 g egg white mayonnaise (page 280)
1 spring onion, very finely sliced
1 tbsp finely chopped fresh chives
4 drops Tabasco sauce
juice of ½ lemon
pinch of cayenne pepper or smoked sweet paprika

FOR THE CUCUMBER JELLY
1.5 gold leaf gelatine leaves
2 cucumbers
2 tsp mirin
1 tbsp light soy sauce
2 g salt

FOR THE MARINATED CUCUMBER
1 cucumber
1 tbsp mirin

FOR THE FRESH PEAS
50 g shelled fresh peas

TO SERVE
125 g pickled red dulse and sea spaghetti (page 282)
about 2 tsp coriander oil (page 281), in a small squeezy bottle
400 ml crab juice (page 279)

SERVES 8

CRAB

Put the water in a large pan with the salt and vinegar, and bring to the boil. Blanch the crab claws. For medium claws, cook for 5 minutes; if they are larger or smaller, add or subtract a minute. Lift out and transfer into iced water. When cool use the back of a heavy knife to gently crack the shells and remove the meat, picking out any bits of shell. (This amount of crab claws should yield at least 200 g of meat.) In a bowl, combine the crab with the mayonnaise, spring onion and chives. Season with the Tabasco, lemon juice, cayenne pepper or paprika and a pinch of salt.

CUCUMBER JELLY

Put the gelatine into a bowl of cold water and set aside. Juice the cucumbers, skin on, and pass the juice through a double layer of muslin. Measure out 200 ml of juice and add the mirin, soy sauce and salt, mixing well and checking the seasoning. Heat 100 ml of the mixture in a small pan until hot but not boiling and then take it off the heat. Gently squeeze the gelatine to remove excess water and whisk it into the hot cucumber juice. When dissolved combine with the rest of the mixture and whisk together. Pour into a bowl and place in the fridge to set.

MARINATED CUCUMBER

Square off the cucumber and use a mandolin to cut it into ribbons – you'll need 3 per portion. Lay the cucumber ribbons on a tray and sprinkle over a teaspoon of salt and the mirin. Leave for an hour and then freeze, covered with clingfilm. Remove from the freezer 10 minutes before serving, then drain, reserving the liquid.

PEAS

Bring a small pan of water to the boil and prepare a bowl of iced water. Blanch the peas until just cooked and refresh in the iced water, then drain.

SERVING

Spoon an eighth (about 30 g) of the crab mayonnaise mixture into the centre of each shallow serving bowl. Put 3 pieces of the marinated cucumber on top of this and then add 2–3 pieces of the pickled red dulse on the crab and 2 pieces of the sea spaghetti around the plate. Use a teaspoon to put small spoonfuls of cucumber jelly around the plate and add a few of the peas. Finish with a little of the reserved cucumber liquid, 4–5 spoonfuls of crab juice and some dots of coriander oil around the crab.

DUBLIN BAY PRAWN, SMOKED BACON *and* BASIL SPRING ROLL
with RED PEPPER ESCABÈCHE PURÉE

FOR THE RED PEPPER ESCABÈCHE

2 shallots, diced
2 garlic cloves, finely sliced
125 ml extra virgin olive oil
pinch of saffron filaments (glossary)
2–3 pinches Espelette pepper (glossary)
4 slices smoked bacon or pancetta, diced
2 plum tomatoes
200 g preserved roasted red peppers (glossary), julienned
2 fresh thyme sprigs
2 fresh basil sprigs
15 ml aged sherry vinegar

FOR THE DUBLIN BAY PRAWN MOUSSE

130 g raw Dublin Bay prawn flesh, shelled and cleaned
5 g salt
1 egg white
150 ml cream

FOR THE SPRING ROLLS

20 spring roll wrappers, thawed if frozen
400 g raw Dublin Bay prawn flesh, shelled and cleaned
12 fresh basil leaves, finely sliced into strips
5 x 1–2 mm slices yeast-cooked bacon (page 288), finely sliced
2 egg whites

TO SERVE

vegetable oil, for deep-frying
1 tsp basil oil (page 281), in a squeezy bottle
small handful tiny tat soi leaves (glossary)

SERVES 8

RED PEPPER ESCABÈCHE

Sweat the shallots and garlic in the olive oil with the saffron, Espelette pepper and smoked bacon or pancetta over a low heat until softened. Bring a small pan of water to the boil and blanch the tomatoes for 1 minute. Transfer to a bowl of iced water to cool. Drain and peel the tomatoes, remove the seeds, and finely slice. Add to the pan with the roasted red pepper and thyme. Cook over a low heat for 20–30 minutes until softened. Add the basil and vinegar, and cook for 3 minutes. Remove from the heat. Drain the excess liquid off into a clean pan and reduce to a syrup. Remove the thyme, basil and bacon. Blend the escabèche mixture, adding back some of the reduced liquid as necessary to create a purée with a dropping consistency. Pass through a fine chinois and season with salt and black pepper if necessary. Put into a squeezy bottle and keep at room temperature until needed.

DUBLIN BAY PRAWN MOUSSE

Blend all the ingredients together and pass through a drum sieve. Put into a piping bag and chill until needed.

SPRING ROLLS

Lay out one spring roll wrapper and use a knife to cut a rectangle 22 x 11 cm. For one roll, you will need around 20 g of prawn flesh. Halve the prawns lengthways and lay the pieces end to end on the spring roll wrapper, about 2.5 cm from the bottom. Put a single line of bacon pieces onto the wrapper, then pipe a fine line of prawn mousse on top and cover with the prawns. Finish each one with 4–5 basil strips. Roll up the prawns tightly in the wrapper, keeping an even pressure along the length. Seal the edge with a brush of the egg white. Keep the spring rolls on a tray lined with greaseproof paper in the fridge until needed.

SERVING

Preheat the vegetable oil to 190°C in a deep fat fryer. Deep-fry the spring rolls, in two batches if necessary, until golden brown and crispy. Drain on kitchen paper and slice off the ends of the rolls at a 45° angle, then cut each one in half. Put dots of the room temperature pepper escabèche onto each serving plate and arrange the pieces of spring roll around them. Finish with a little basil oil and garnish with the tat soi leaves.

This is one of our most popular dishes; it has complex flavours which add to the initial sweetness of the Dublin Bay prawn. A combination of preserved red peppers and Espelette pepper give this a sweet, smoky depth as the peppers are cooked over wood. I've been instructed by my daughters never to take this dish off the menu.

VINE RIPENED CHERRY TOMATO, AVOCADO *and* CLAM COCKTAIL

Razor and surf clam is much undervalued as seafood. This dish celebrates the clam's particular flavour and texture, and for a dish with no dairy, it is incredibly clean but with a very rich mouthfeel. An excellent balance of flavours with acidity, sweetness and saltiness.

FOR THE CLAMS AND CLAM VINAIGRETTE
200 ml white wine
6 shallots, sliced
2 celery sticks, finely chopped
½ leek, white part only, sliced
750 g razor clams and Irish surf palourde clams, scrubbed
a little thickener (glossary)
juice of 2 limes
100 ml olive oil
½ red chilli, seeded

FOR THE AVOCADO PURÉE
3 ripe avocados
juice of 1 lime
1 tbsp crème fraîche
pinch of smoked paprika
2 dashes Tabasco sauce

FOR THE CHERRY TOMATO HEARTS
20 cherry tomatoes

TO SERVE
800 g tomato jelly (page 277)
40 pieces confit tomato (page 287)
small handful fresh coriander cress
10 ml basil oil (page 281), in a squeezy bottle
2 tsp fennel pollen

SERVES 8

CLAMS AND CLAM VINAIGRETTE

Heat the white wine in a large pan and add the shallots, celery and leek. Tip in the clams, cover with the lid and cook for 2–3 minutes, shaking the pan once or twice. Remove from the heat and strain the liquid into a clean pan. Remove the clams from their shells and chill until needed. Throw away any that do not open. Return the clam cooking liquor to the heat and reduce by a third, then thicken, a pinch at a time, until there is a light sauce consistency. Leave to cool and add the lime juice, then whisk in the oil to emulsify. Season with salt and black pepper, then transfer to a bottle with the chilli to infuse for at least 6 hours.

AVOCADO PURÉE

Halve and peel the avocados and place in a blender with the lime juice, crème fraîche, paprika, Tabasco and a pinch of salt. Purée until smooth and season with salt and black pepper. Pass through a chinois and put into a squeezy bottle or piping bag. Chill until needed.

CHERRY TOMATO HEARTS

Cut the cherry tomatoes in half and use a Parisienne scoop to take out the hearts. Put on a plate and leave at room temperature until needed.

SERVING

Place 100 g of the tomato jelly into the bottom of each chilled serving glass and add some dots of the avocado purée. Toss the clams with 2 tablespoons of the clam vinaigrette and season with salt and black pepper, then spoon two tablespoons over each jelly. Add 5 pieces of the confit tomato with 5 of the tomato hearts. Scatter over the coriander cress, a few drops of basil oil and the fennel pollen.

CARPACCIO OF VEAL HAUNCH POACHED IN MILK *with* BLACK OLIVES *from* THASSOS ISLAND *and* PICKLED GREEN TOMATO, TUNA EMULSION *and* CAPER SPROUTS

We get three to four whole bluefin tuna every year, which are landed in West Cork. We were inspired by the Italian dish vitello tonnato and the intensely fruity black olives from the Greek island of Thassos. We've cooked the veal in milk because the acidity of the milk gives texture to the meat and we've aerated the tuna which adds to the lightness of the dish.

FOR THE VEAL
750 g cushion of milk-fed veal
2 litres milk

FOR THE TUNA EMULSION
200 g tuna
300 g light olive oil, plus extra if necessary
zest of 1 lemon
zest of 1 orange
1 garlic clove, lightly smashed
1 fresh thyme sprig
2 eggs
50 ml cream, chilled
juice of ½ lemon
pinch of smoked paprika

TO SERVE
juice of ½ lemon
50 ml extra virgin olive oil, in a small squeezy bottle
150 g green tomatoes, drained and cut in half if large
32–40 Thassos Island black olives
1 tbsp caper sprouts (glossary) or rinsed capers if unavailable
8 onion bread crisps (page 277)
about 8 tsp black olive oil (page 281)
handful fresh flat-leaf parsley leaves
8 small fresh dill sprigs

SERVES 8

VEAL

Trim the veal, removing any sinews and connective tissues. Vacuum pack with the milk and leave in the fridge overnight to tenderise the meat. Cook in a steam oven at 69°C on 100 per cent steam for 1 hour. Transfer to an ice bath until cold, then take the veal out of the milk and dry it on kitchen paper.

TUNA EMULSION

Put the tuna in a small pan and add the oil, making sure the tuna is completely submerged; if not, add some more oil. Add the lemon and orange zests, garlic and thyme, and simmer over a very low heat for about 20 minutes until the tuna is well cooked through, about 20 minutes. Allow to cool completely in the oil. Chill until needed – you'll need 200 g of the confit tuna and 100 ml of the oil for this recipe. Boil the eggs for 6 minutes, then cool and chill down. (Ensure the ingredients are all fridge-cold before beginning the emulsion.) Peel the eggs, discarding the whites. Put the yolks in a blender with the confit tuna and blend for about 3 minutes to a fine purée. If the mixture has warmed up at all, it will need to be chilled in the fridge before adding the oil. With the blender running on a medium speed, pour in the confit oil in a steady, slow stream until it is all incorporated and the mixture is smooth and glossy. Then add the cream. Season with the lemon juice, smoked paprika, salt and black pepper. Pass through a fine chinois and put into a foam gun. Charge with 2 gas chargers. Alternatively, the tuna emulsion can be put into a squeezy bottle.

SERVING

Cut the veal into thin slices – you'll need approximately 50–70 g per portion – and lay these flat on each serving plate. Season with salt, lemon juice and extra virgin olive oil. Use the foam gun to pipe on 3 large dots of the tuna emulsion. Arrange 3 green tomato pieces and 4–5 black olives around the plate. Follow this with the caper sprouts or capers and some dots of black olive oil, then break each onion bread crisp into 3 and put the pieces on top. Finish with the parsley leaves, dill sprigs and a little more extra virgin olive oil.

MARIO FONTANA OF AL DI LA IS A FOOD-TREASURE HUNTER WITH A GLINT IN HIS EYE. A PASSIONATE, WELL-TRAVELLED ITALIAN WHOSE FIRST LOVE IS FOOD, HE IMPORTS THE FINEST FRESH AND PRESERVED FOODS FROM THE SOUTH OF ITALY.

PICKLED MACKEREL with PEAR and HORSERADISH RELISH, SMOKED POTATO and CRÈME FRAÎCHE

In the autumn mackerel in Ireland is lovely and plump with a really good fat content. Herring works well with this dish too. It is ideal with pears, grated onion and mustard notes. The smokiness of the potatoes and the creaminess from the crème fraîche frame the flavours from the preserving liquids. Irish people love mackerel and everyone looks forward to this dish, which is fresh tasting but autumnal too.

FOR THE FIRST MARINADE

1.5 kg whole mackerel
2 litres water
650 ml white wine vinegar
60 g salt
60 g sugar
14 bay leaves
20 juniper berries
20 allspice berries

FOR THE SECOND MARINADE

2 litres water
650 ml spirit vinegar
10 bay leaves
60 g salt
400 g sugar
25 g fresh dill sprigs
10 juniper berries
35 allspice berries
50 black peppercorns
8 garlic cloves, peeled
5 small white onions, thinly sliced
5 carrots, pared into ribbons

FOR THE PEAR AND HORSERADISH RELISH

50 g pear, peeled and finely grated
15 g onion, finely grated
8 g root ginger, peeled and finely grated
½ garlic clove, finely grated
50 ml dark soy sauce
25 ml rice vinegar
2 tsp sesame oil
1 tbsp wholegrain mustard
1½ tbsp creamed horseradish (glossary)
1½ tsp mirin or sake

TO SERVE

25 g butter
50 ml water
200 g cooked smoked potato slices (page 287)
50 g crème fraîche
1 small pear, cut into julienne
fresh coriander cress

SERVES 8

FIRST MARINADE

Fillet and trim down the mackerel, leaving the and the pin bones intact. Place on a tray. Brin vinegar, salt, sugar, bay leaves and spices to th leave to cool. Pour over the mackerel, ensurin fillets are submerged and do not stick togethe surface with greaseproof paper and wrap with Chill for 48 hours.

SECOND MARINADE

Make this at the same time as the first marina the water, spirit vinegar, bay leaves, salt and s pan with all of the dill and spices, and bring to Add the vegetables and continue to simmer u are just cooked through. Leave to cool and inf fridge for 48 hours. Then transfer the mackere 1st marinade to the 2nd marinade and store in The fish will be ready to use in 24 hours, altho keep in the marinade for up to 2 weeks. To se transparent outer membrane off the skin, kee skin intact. Cut the fillet lengthways on either pin bone, then cut these two pieces in half, dis the pin bones. You need 5 pieces per portion. vegetables from the marinade to use as a garn

PEAR AND HORSERADISH REL

Whisk all the ingredients in a bowl and check seasoning. Chill until needed.

SERVING

Heat the butter in a small sauté pan and add t make an emulsion, using this to heat the smo slices. Then drain and season with salt and bla and keep warm. Lightly season the crème fra and pepper, then put into a small squeezy bot Lay a piece of mackerel on each serving plate. 2 teaspoons of the pear and horseradish relish each plate and garnish with the reserved carro from the marinade, smoked potato slices, cre pear julienne and coriander cress.

CHARCUTERIE TROLLEY: PIG'S TROTTER BOUDIN with RAISINS and MADEIRA JUS; RABBIT and HAM JELLY with CELERIAC REMOULADE; AIR DRIED CURED PORK LOIN; CURED PORK JOWL with PICCALILLI; CURED PRESSED FOIE GRAS and MEAT JELLY SERVED with WATERCRESS, APPLE and HAZELNUT SALAD, and TOASTED SOURDOUGH

An innovation of the first few years of the restaurant and part of our desire to provide some theatre for the customers, this dish is something that became a mainstay of the restaurant. We use an Irish walnut trolley to serve and cut charcuterie at the table. This offering is really a chef's dream, a carnivore's delight and a meal in itself.

SERVES 8

FOR THE PIG'S TROTTER
750 ml red wine
100 ml olive oil
1 onion, sliced
2 carrots, sliced
3 celery sticks, sliced
4 garlic cloves, peeled and lightly smashed
1 bay leaf
1 each fresh thyme and rosemary sprig
4 pig's trotters
750 ml chicken stock (page 285) or water
750 ml red wine

FOR THE TROTTER BOUDIN
50 g shallots, finely diced
1 tbsp each fresh tarragon and sage, finely chopped
2 tbsp fresh flat-leaf parsley, finely chopped
30 g butter
50 g chicken mousse (page 280)
50 g sausage meat (glossary)

FOR THE SAUTERNES RAISINS
40 g large yellow raisins
100 ml Sauternes or sweet white wine
30 ml water

FOR THE POTTED RABBIT AND SMOKED HAM HOCK JELLY
1–1.5 kg rabbit
1 smoked ham hock, pulled from the bone and chopped finely
1 litre each water and chicken stock (page 285)
300 ml white wine, Pinot Gris is best but any dry wine like Chablis will do
2 tbsp vegetable oil
2 garlic cloves, crushed
2 carrots, finely diced
2 celery sticks, finely diced
1 onion, finely diced
2 fresh bay leaves
1 fresh rosemary sprig
3 fresh sage leaves
100 g shallot, finely chopped
2 tbsp extra virgin olive oil, light and fruity if possible
2 tbsp fresh mixed herbs (tarragon, flat-leaf parsley and chervil), finely chopped
4 drops Tabasco
pinch each of ground mace and dry English mustard powder
3 tbsp wholegrain mustard
5 gold leaf gelatine leaves

FOR THE CELERIAC REMOULADE
200 g celeriac
1 Granny Smith apple
150 g crème fraîche
75 g mayonnaise (page 280)
1 tsp Dijon mustard
2 tsp wholegrain mustard
juice of ½ lemon

FOR THE MEAT JELLY
1 ham hock
1 oxtail, chopped or in 5–6 pieces
1 chicken leg
2 carrots, sliced
4 shallots, sliced
10 black peppercorns
2 fresh bay leaves
3 fresh thyme sprigs
2.5 litres water
300 g green grapes
125 ml white wine, Pinot Gris or Riesling
125 ml cream
7 gold leaf gelatine leaves

FOR THE PICCALILLI
1 head of cauliflower, broken into small florets
5 small carrots, channelled and cut into 2 mm slices
40 small silver-skinned onions, peeled
1 tbsp mustard seeds
2 tbsp olive oil
1 tbsp English dry mustard powder
2 tsp ground turmeric
1 bay leaf
1½ tsp ground ginger
500 ml white wine vinegar
200 g sugar
3 tbsp cornflour, slaked with water
12 g ginger gel (glossary), optional
2 tbsp mango chutney
pinch of freshly grated nutmeg
6 drops Tabasco

FOR THE WATERCRESS, APPLE AND HAZELNUT SALAD
1 Granny Smith apple
1 shallot, cut into rings
1 large bunch fresh watercress, well picked over
30 roasted salted hazelnuts
4 tbsp hazelnut dressing (page 278)

TO SERVE
2 tbsp olive oil
100 ml Madeira jus (page 279)
8 slices air dried cured pork loin (glossary)
8 slices cured pork jowl (glossary)
400 g cured pressed foie gras terrine (page 288)
16 slices sourdough toast (page 266)
8 viola flowers

PIG'S TROTTER

Marinate the pig's trotters in the red wine for 24 hours. Preheat the oven to 120°C. Heat the olive oil in a pan and cook the vegetables and herbs over a medium to high heat, stirring frequently, until well browned. Add the trotters and wine, and cover with the chicken stock or water and wine. Bring to a simmer, then cover and place in the oven. Cook for 2 hours, then remove the lid and cook uncovered for another 1 hour. Allow to cool in the liquor.

TROTTER BOUDIN

Lift the trotters out of the cooking liquid and take all the skin, fat and meat off the bones, and then chop finely. Heat a large non-stick sauté pan over a high heat and sauté the trotter meat in batches until mildly caramelised. Sweat the chopped shallots in the butter, then allow to cool. As you take the meat off the heat, fold in the chopped herbs and sweated shallots. Allow to cool, then add the chicken mousse and sausage meat, mixing well. While still warm, form into a sausage and roll in 2–3 layers of clingfilm to a thickness of about 4 cm, securely twisting the ends. Chill overnight.

SAUTERNES RAISINS

Put all the ingredients in a small pan and bring to a simmer for 3–5 minutes until the raisins are plump and completely soft. Allow to cool in the liquid. These will keep in the fridge for 2–3 weeks.

CELERIAC REMOULADE

Peel the celeriac and use a Japanese mandolin or meat slicer to cut thin slices, then slice as finely as possible into a julienne with a sharp knife. Repeat with the apple and then combine with the celeriac. Mix the crème fraîche, mayonnaise and mustards, and fold into the celeriac, a tablespoon at a time, until the remoulade is creamy to taste. Then add a pinch of salt, lemon juice and, if you prefer a creamier remoulade, a little more crème fraîche and mayonnaise. Chill until needed.

POTTED RABBIT AND SMOKED HAM HOCK JELLY

Preheat the oven to 130°C. Remove any insides from the rabbit and then place the rabbit in a casserole dish with the ham hock, water, chicken stock and white wine. Heat the vegetable oil in a separate pan and sweat the garlic, onions, carrots and celery, without colouring, until soft. Then add to the casserole dish along with the bay leaves, rosemary and sage. Cover the casserole dish and cook for 70 minutes, then remove the rabbit, increase the oven temperature to 160°C and leave the ham to cook for another hour or until soft. Leave the rabbit to cool, then take the meat off the bones and shred, chopping any large pieces into 1 cm dice. Once the ham is cooked, strain the liquid through a fine chinois and bring to the boil, setting aside the ham to cool. Reduce the liquid by a third or until you have a nice aromatic flavoured stock – you will need 1 litre in total. Pass through a muslin and then cool. Once the ham is cold, shred the meat, chopping any large pieces into 1 cm dice and discarding the fat. Sweat the shallots in the olive oil until soft, then cool. Place the shredded rabbit in a large bowl with the ham, herbs, Tabasco, mace, mustard powder and wholegrain mustard. Check the seasoning and season with a pinch of white pepper and a little salt if necessary. (Bear in mind the jelly is usually salty anyway.) Transfer the rabbit and ham mix to a small oval casserole dish. Soak the gelatine in a bowl of cold water for 10 minutes, then drain and squeeze out the excess liquid. Heat a little of the reserved cooking liquid in a small pan and whisk in the gelatine until dissolved, then stir back into the rest of the reserved cooking liquid. Then pour over the rabbit and ham mix until the meat is just covered. Chill overnight to set.

MEAT JELLY

Place all the ingredients, except for the cream and gelatine, in a covered pan and simmer for 40 minutes to 1 hour. Strain through a fine chinois, bring the liquid back to the boil and reduce by half, then strain through double muslin. Soak the gelatine in a bowl of cold water for 10 minutes. Take 200 ml of the stock and add the gelatine, then simmer until the gelatine is melted and pour back into the stock. Stir in the cream and bring to a brisk simmer, then take off the heat, and season with salt and freshly ground white pepper. Pour into a rectangular terrine mould that has been lined with clingfilm to a 15 mm depth. (We use a Le Creuset no. 32 terrine mould 8 × 6 × 29 cm that is 5 cm deep.) Allow to set in the fridge.

PICCALILLI

Lightly salt all the vegetables on a tray overnight. The next day sauté the mustard seeds in the olive oil, then add the mustard powder, turmeric, bay leaf and ginger, and continue to cook for 2–3 minutes. Add the vinegar and sugar, and bring to a simmer, then add the cornflour and simmer until it begins to thicken. When it is thick, add in the vegetables and continue to cook for 10 minutes. Remove from the heat and add the ginger gel if using, along with the mango chutney, nutmeg and Tabasco. Season with a pinch of white pepper.

WATERCRESS, APPLE AND HAZELNUT SALAD

Using a Japanese mandolin, cut the apple into fine julienne and place in a bowl with the shallot, watercress and hazelnuts. Pour over enough of the dressing to just barely coat the salad. Season with salt and freshly ground black pepper.

SERVING

Preheat the grill to medium. Slice the pig's trotter boudin into 8 × 15 mm thick pieces. Season before shallow frying in a little hot olive oil over medium heat for 2 minutes each side, then transfer to the grill for another 3 minutes. Heat the Madeira jus in a small pan. Drain the Sauternes raisins. Arrange a slice of the warm pig's trotter boudin on each serving plate and drizzle over a little of the Madeira jus, then add a small pile of the Sauternes raisins to each one. Scoop out a large spoonful of the potted rabbit and smoked ham hock jelly, each one about 40 g, and put one on each plate with a tablespoonful of the celeriac remoulade. Add a slice each of the air dried cured pork loin and cured pork jowl, and then put a spoonful of the piccalilli alongside. Cut 8 × 50 g slices from the cured pressed foie gras and cover with the same amount of the meat jelly that has been cut into slices, and place them on the plates. Finish with the apple and hazelnut salad, 2 slices of sourdough toast and a viola flower.

CHAPTER ONE WHITE PUDDING *with* PARSNIP, BRAMLEY APPLE *and* HORSERADISH COMPÔTE

We worked on perfecting this white pudding over three years and as a result it is one of our most popular dishes. It eats extremely well and I feel it is a major part of our menu. It is a dish that we do best at Chapter One, a real expression of our work ethos and our food loves.

FOR THE PARSNIP PURÉE

500 g parsnips, finely diced
50 g butter
100 ml milk, plus extra if necessary

FOR THE APPLE AND HORSERADISH COMPÔTE

5 large Bramley apples, peeled and diced
40 g butter
100 g sugar
zest and juice of 1 orange and 1 lemon
5 Granny Smith apples, peeled, cored and grated
2 tbsp creamed horseradish (glossary)

FOR THE SALT BAKED PARSNIPS AND CRISPS

300 g rock salt
4 medium parsnips
vegetable oil, for deep-frying

TO SERVE

720 g white pudding (page 288), chilled
1 tbsp light olive oil
100 ml Madeira jus (page 279)
fresh beetroot leaves

SERVES 8

PARSNIP PURÉE

Preheat the steam oven to 80°C. Vacuum pack the parsnip with the butter, milk and a pinch of salt and black pepper. Cook on 100 per cent steam for 30 minutes until completely soft. Strain the parsnip, reserving the liquid. Purée the parsnip in a blender with as much of the strained liquid as necessary to make a smooth thick purée. If the purée is still too stiff, add a little extra warm milk. Season with salt and black pepper, then chill.

APPLE AND HORSERADISH COMPÔTE

Sweat the Bramley apples in a pan with the butter until softened. Add the sugar, orange and lemon zests and juices, and continue to cook until the apples are soft and broken down. Stir in the Granny Smith apples and cook for another 10 minutes, stirring occasionally to ensure the mix does not stick to the bottom of the pan. Purée in a blender with the creamed horseradish until completely smooth. Pass through a chinois, then cool and put the mixture into a squeezy bottle.

SALT BAKED PARSNIPS AND CRISPS

Preheat the oven to 160°C. Put the salt in a small ovenproof tray to a depth of 2 cm and put the parsnips on top. Bake for 40 minutes or until soft when tested with a sharp knife, then leave to cool. Peel the parsnip skins in one whole piece, reserving the skins to deep-fry. Cut 2 slices from the wide ends of each of the parsnips and then use an apple corer to cut out long cylinders from the rest of the parsnip – cut 2 pieces per portion. Chill until needed. Deep-fry the reserved parsnip skins in the vegetable oil at 160°C until golden brown and crisp. Drain on kitchen paper and set aside for up to 1 hour.

SERVING

Preheat the oven to 160°C. Cut 8 × 90 g slices from the chilled white pudding. Heat the oil in an ovenproof frying pan and add the white pudding slices. Cook until browned on one side, then transfer to the oven for 5 minutes or until warmed through. Place the salt baked parsnip discs and cylinders on a separate tray, then place in the same oven as the white pudding slices for 3–4 minutes to heat through. Warm the parsnip purée in a small pan and put into a squeezy bottle. Pipe a tablespoon onto each warmed serving plate and swipe with an offset palette knife. Put the white pudding on this, with a disc of salt baked parsnip on top, and top with a blob of apple and horseradish compôte. Arrange a cylinder of parsnip and a parsnip crisp alongside, and finish by pouring over a little Madeira jus. Garnish with fresh beetroot leaves.

CURED *and* SMOKED IRISH RED DEER VENISON *with* FOIE GRAS, MADEIRA JELLY, ICEWINE VERJUS *and* GRILLED ONION BREAD

FOR THE MADEIRA JELLY
200 ml Madeira
4 gold leaf gelatine sheets
600 ml duck neck consommé (page 286)

FOR THE ICEWINE VERJUS
300 ml icewine verjus (glossary)
a little thickener (glossary)

TO SERVE
500 g piece smoked venison
320 g cured pressed foie gras terrine (page 288)
8 onion bread crisps (page 277)
handful fresh kohlrabi

SERVES 8

MADEIRA JELLY

Reduce the Madeira by half in a pan. Soak the gelatine in a bowl of cold water for 10 minutes, then squeeze out the excess liquid. Add the stock to the Madeira reduction and bring up to the boil, then whisk in the gelatine. Pour into a rectangular terrine mould. (We use a Le Creuset no. 32 terrine mould 8 × 6 × 29 cm that is 5 cm deep.) Allow to set in the fridge.

ICEWINE VERJUS

Gently heat the icewine verjus in a small pan. Whisk in the thickener, a pinch at a time, until it has a gel consistency. (The mixture will thicken further as it cools so allow for this.) Put into a small squeezy bottle.

SERVING

Slice 4 thin slices of smoked venison per portion and place on each of the serving plates. Fill a tall flask or jar with very hot water and use this to heat your knife. Turn the jelly out onto a board, and using the hot knife, slice 3 thin slices and arrange on each plate. Again using the hot knife, cut thin slices of the foie gras terrine, 3–4 per plate depending on size (30–40 g), and place these on the venison and the jelly. Dot the icewine verjus on and around the foie gras, add the onion bread crisps and finish with the kohlrabi.

This venison is cured and then it is smoked, which gives it a beautifully rounded smoky flavour, almost a fermented taste. The interplay between this, the foie gras and the sweet acidity of the verjus is what this dish hinges on.

GAME TERRINE of SNIPE and WOOD PIGEON with MUSTARD QUINCE PURÉE and SMOKED PEAR

When I think of this dish, I imagine a pear has fallen from a tree beside all the game, so it feels like a very natural combination. We caramelise the meats and flavour them with winter spices. The quince, mustard and smoked pear finish the dish with some creamy sweet and high notes.

FOR THE STUFFING

35 g duck liver, cut into 5 mm dice
1 tbsp Calvados
1 tbsp port
15 g pistachio, raw, roughly chopped
35 g cured pressed foie gras terrine, cut into 5 mm dice (page 288)
35 g duck or venison meat, cut into 5 mm dice
1 tsp olive oil
25 g spring onion, finely sliced
85 g firm ripe pears, peeled, cored and cut into 5 mm dice

FOR THE FARCE

50 g white bread, crusts removed
35 g cream
1 g juniper berries
4 g ground cinnamon
75 g duck meat, cut into 2 cm dice
75 g venison leg meat, cut into 2 cm dice
150 g pork belly, cut into 2 cm dice
70 g duck liver, cut into 2 cm dice
50 ml olive oil
25 ml Cognac

TO MAKE THE TERRINE

vegetable oil, to oil the mould
300 g piece lardo di colonnata (glossary), frozen
4 wood pigeon breasts
8 snipe breasts

FOR THE MUSTARD AND QUINCE PURÉE

400 g quinces
50 g butter
200 ml water, plus a little extra if necessary
100 g sugar
1–2 drops mustard essence

FOR THE SMOKED PEAR

3 pears

TO SERVE

16 fresh watercress sprigs
extra virgin olive oil, to drizzle

SERVES 12

STUFFING

Marinate the duck liver in the Calvados and port overnight. Combine with the other ingredients in a large bowl.

FARCE

Soak the bread in the cream. In a spice grinder, finely grind the juniper berries with the ground cinnamon. In a hot heavy-based frying pan, season, and then caramelise each meat in a little olive oil, making sure the inside is still rare. Cook in small batches, with a splash of Cognac, and season well with the spice mixture, salt and black pepper. When cool, finely mince with the bread and cream using a mincer attachment on a KitchenAid. Fold into the stuffing and season to taste.

TERRINE

Oil the inside of a terrine mould that is about 700 ml in volume and line with a triple layer of clingfilm, leaving a large overlap. Using a meat slicer, thinly slice the lardo and use it to line the mould, overlapping the strips and leaving a long overlap to cover the top of the terrine. Slice more strips of lardo to wrap the snipe and pigeon. Put half the stuffing and farce mix into the mould, making sure there are no air pockets. Arrange the wrapped snipe and pigeon in the mixture, and then add the rest of the mix, again firming down to make sure there are no gaps. Fold the rest of the lardo over the top and cut more slices to cover any gaps if necessary, then cover tightly with the clingfilm. Preheat a steam oven to 80°C and cook the terrine on 100 per cent steam for 90 minutes or until the centre is 64°C. To cook through to well done, cook to a core temperature of 73°C for 2–3 minutes. Cool quickly in a blast chiller or by setting the mould into a tray of ice.

MUSTARD AND QUINCE PURÉE

Peel, core and thinly slice the quinces. Melt the butter in a pan and add the quinces and sugar, and sweat for 10 minutes without colouring. Add the water and simmer for 30 minutes or until tender, adding a little more water if the pan gets too dry. Strain off excess liquid and reserve. Blend the quinces until smooth, adding enough of the reserved liquid back into the purée if it is too dry. Then pass through a fine chinois and chill. Add the mustard essence to taste. Mix well and put into a squeezy bottle to use.

SMOKED PEAR

Preheat a steam oven to 100°C. Peel the pears, being careful to keep a smooth shape. Steam the pears on 100 per cent steam for 5 minutes, then place in a smoker for 5 minutes. Allow to cool. When ready to serve, cut the pears lengthways into 3 pieces and remove the cores with a small knife.

SERVING

On the right-hand side of each serving plate, pipe the quince purée and put a piece of the smoked pear on top. Using a hot knife, cut 5 mm slices of the terrine and place on the other side of the plate. Garnish with the watercress sprigs and a drizzle of extra virgin olive oil.

MICK HEALY OF WILD IRISH GAME IS THE OWNER OF ONE OF THE LONGEST-ESTABLISHED GAME PROCESSING COMPANIES IN IRELAND. GAME IS ONE OF THE MOST IMPORTANT ELEMENTS OF CHAPTER ONE'S WINTER LARDER.

GOOSE *and* OATMEAL SAUSAGE *with* PICKLED CHERRIES, SHAVED PEAR *and* CELERIAC PURÉE

FOR THE PICKLED CHERRIES AND GEL

250 ml white wine vinegar
250 g light brown sugar
200 ml water
7 g salt
¼ tsp ground mace
1 tsp dried rose petals
3 star anise
15 coriander seeds
15 peppercorns
25 g fresh root ginger, peeled and sliced
500 g cherries
a little thickener (glossary)

FOR THE SAUSAGE

120 g chicken liver, trimmed and roughly chopped, organic or
 free range
120 g fresh foie gras
50 g port
50 g brandy
a little vegetable oil
100 g shallots, finely diced
2 slices white bread
180 ml cream
900 g goose meat, roughly chopped
270 g lardo di colonnata (glossary)
12 g salt
2 eggs
60 g oatmeal
40 g pinhead oats
2 g Lucky Duck spice mix (glossary)
75 mm sausage skins

FOR THE PEAR SLICES

100 g sugar
100 ml water
juice of 1 lime
zest of ½ lemon
pinch of ascorbic acid
2 firm ripe pears

FOR THE CELERIAC CRISPS

½ head celeriac
1 tsp salt
vegetable oil, for deep-frying

TO SERVE

200 ml celeriac purée (page 283)
16 fresh watercress sprigs
100 ml Madeira jus (page 279)

SERVES 8

You know it is Christmas
when the goose and oatmeal
sausage appears on our
menu. We pickle the cherries
in July especially for this dish
and they combine beautifully
with the sweetness of the
autumn pears. The spices,
oatmeal, lardo di colonnata,
foie gras, liver and port
make this an indulgent,
seasonal favourite. The
goose in this recipe can also
be substituted for duck if
desired.

PICKLED CHERRIES AND GEL

Bring the vinegar, sugar, water, salt, rose petals and spices to the boil, stirring to dissolve the sugar. Add the cherries, remove from the heat and then allow to cool in the liquid. Leave to pickle in the fridge for up to 6 months. Strain the cherries through a chinois, reserving the pickling liquor. Remove the stones with a cherry stoner and cut each cherry in half. To make the gel, measure out 400 ml of the pickling liquor into a pan and reduce it by half. Then whisk in the thickener, a pinch at a time, until it reaches a gel consistency and put into a squeezy bottle.

SAUSAGE

Soak the chicken livers and foie gras in the port and brandy overnight. Soak the bread in the cream. Drain the livers, reserving the liquid, and caramelise the chicken livers in a hot pan in a little oil. Reduce the marinating alcohol to a glaze in a pan with the shallots. Using a mincer, mince all the ingredients, then add the bread and cream mixture and reduced alcohol, and season with salt and black pepper. Mix well. In a hot pan, fry off a patty of sausage mix to check the seasoning. Using a sausage maker, fill the skins and tie off tightly. Preheat a steam oven to 85°C and cook on 100 per cent steam for 45 minutes or until 73°C in the centre for 3 minutes. Cool quickly in a blast chiller or ice bath.

PEAR SLICES

Bring the sugar, water and lime juice to the boil. Remove from the heat and add the lemon zest and ascorbic acid. Leave to cool and then pass through a fine chinois. When ready to serve, slice the pears on a mandolin and add them to the syrup.

CELERIAC CRISPS

Peel the celeriac and shave into thin slices, approximately 1 mm thick, on a meat slicer or mandolin. Lay the slices on a tray, sprinkle evenly with the salt and leave for 20 minutes. Squeeze well, without rinsing, and then deep-fry in the oil at 165°C until a light golden brown colour. Drain on kitchen paper.

TO FINISH THE SAUSAGE

Preheat the oven to 160°C. Peel the skin off the sausages and cut 4 × 10 cm long pieces. Cut each of these in half lengthways to make 8 portions. Heat a little oil in a large frying pan and caramelise the cut side of the sausage pieces, then place on a tray in the oven for 5–7 minutes until warmed through.

SERVING

Pipe a line of celeriac purée onto each warmed serving plate. Using a small offset palette knife, evenly spread the purée to make a rough square shape. Place a piece of the hot goose sausage on the purée and top with the drained pear slices. Place 3 pickled cherry halves on and around the sausage and top with a little of the cherry gel. Add a celeriac crisp and the watercress sprigs, then pour a little of the warmed Madeira jus over the sausage to finish.

BRAISED PRIME HEREFORD OXTAIL *with* MACARONI *and* ROOT VEGETABLES COOKED *in* ROCK SALT

This oxtail dish is the hallmark of my cooking and what I love about it is the slow cooking of the meats with the juices, herbs, alcohol and spices and their resulting complex flavours. This is a classic example of where we've used that principle to the maximum.

FOR THE OXTAIL

2 kg whole oxtail, cut into pieces across the joints
500 ml red wine
3 litres chicken stock (page 285)
3 garlic cloves, lightly crushed
1 onion, quartered
1 leek, roughly chopped
4 celery sticks, chopped
2 carrots, roughly chopped
200 g button mushrooms
bunch each fresh rosemary and thyme
50 ml olive oil

FOR OXTAIL SOUP

2 shallots, diced
2 carrots, diced
1 celery stick, chopped
a little olive oil
2 garlic cloves, finely sliced
100 g smoked bacon, finely chopped
2 bay leaves
2 fresh thyme sprigs
300 ml passata
100 ml white wine
300 ml double chicken stock (page 286)
a little cornflour, salted with water

FOR THE DICED VEGETABLES

200 g piece celeriac
200 g large carrots
1 leek, cut into 4 mm dice
300 g rock salt

TO SERVE

generous knob of butter
100 g dried macaroni pasta
150 ml celeriac purée (page 283)
3–4 tbsp water
350 g Parmesan cream (page 277)

SERVES 8

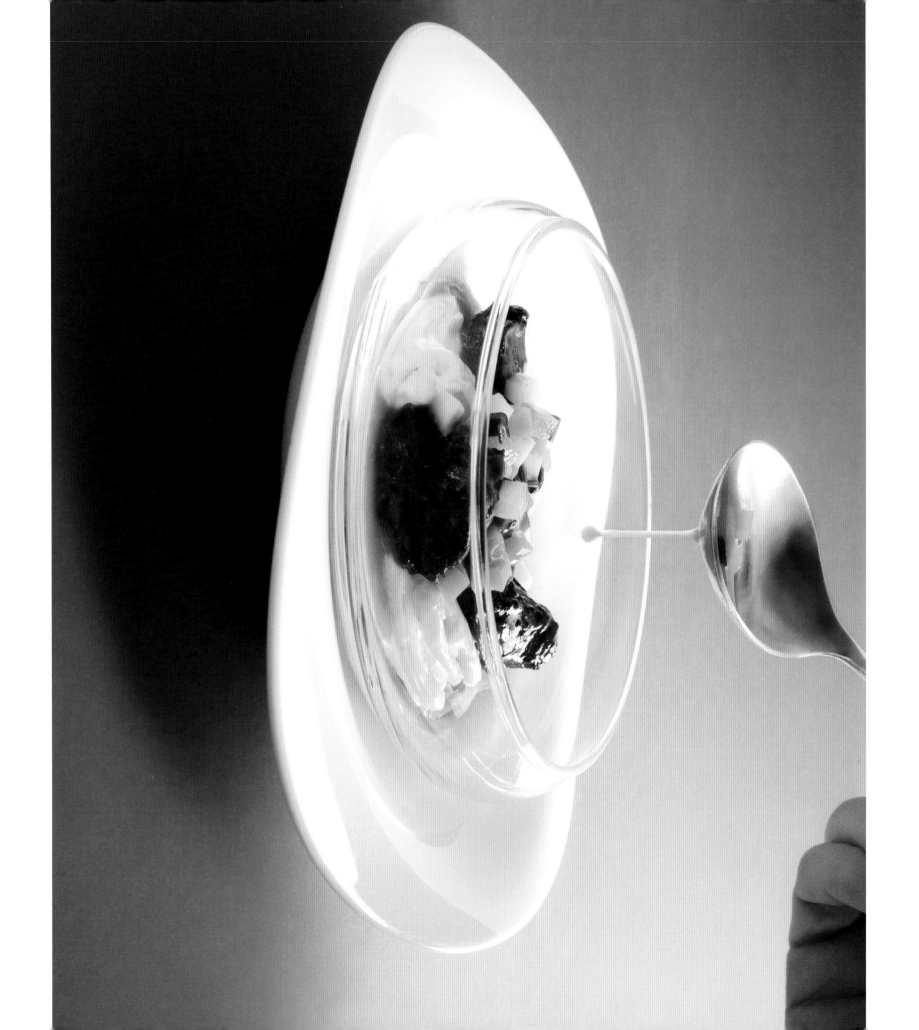

OXTAIL

Cut the oxtail into pieces across the joints and put in a deep tray with the wine, stock, vegetables and herbs. Cover and marinate for 24 hours. Drain the marinade liquor into a clean pan and bring to the boil. Boil for 2–3 minutes to solidify any impurities from the meat, then remove from the heat and pass through a fine chinois. Preheat an oven to 150°C. Heat a large, heavy sauté pan and add 30 ml of the oil. Dry the pieces of oxtail on kitchen paper and brown evenly on all sides in the oil, being careful not to burn it. Heat the rest of the oil in an ovenproof pan and add the marinated vegetables. Cook over a high heat, stirring occasionally, until well browned. Add the browned oxtail with the reserved liquor. Bring to the boil and skim off any fat that collects on the surface. Cover with a double layer of foil, then place in the oven and cook for 3 ¹/₂–4 hours or until the oxtail is falling off the bone. Cool to room temperature, then take the meat off the bones, being careful to keep the pieces as large as possible. Pass the stock through a fine chinois and reserve.

OXTAIL SOUP

Sweat the shallots, carrots and celery in olive oil until soft and starting to colour. Add the garlic, bacon and herbs, and cook for another 5 minutes, then add the wine and simmer to reduce by half. Add the passata, chicken stock and 700 ml of the reserved oxtail stock, and simmer for 20 minutes, then pass through muslin and season to taste. Reduce by about 30 per cent or until you have a nice aromatic flavour, then thicken slightly with cornflour.

DICED VEGETABLES

Preheat the oven to 160°C. Put the rock salt in a small tray to a depth of 2 cm and put the celeriac and carrots on top. Bake for 30 minutes or until soft when tested with a sharp knife, then cool and cut into 4 mm dice. Blanch the leek in a pan of salted water until just cooked and quickly refresh in iced water. Keep cold.

TO FINISH THE DISH

Reduce the leftover oxtail stock by half or until sticky, then mount with the butter. Use this to heat up 200 g of the oxtail meat. Cook the macaroni pasta in boiling salted water for 10–12 minutes or until cooked. Meanwhile, heat 200 ml of the oxtail soup in a small pan, add the diced vegetables and allow to warm through. Warm the celeriac purée and put into a squeezy bottle. Warm the macaroni in a pan with the water and a generous amount of the Parmesan cream. Allow to warm through until the Parmesan cream thickly coats the macaroni. Season with salt and white pepper.

SERVING

Arrange 3 tablespoon piles of macaroni in a circle in each wide serving bowl. Between these, put three similar-sized pieces of the oxtail. Pipe about a tablespoon of the celeriac purée into the middle of these. Serve the diced vegetables and oxtail soup in a sauceboat on the side.

PIG'S TAIL STUFFED *with* FINGAL FERGUSON'S BACON *and* RAZOR CLAMS, BASIL PURÉE *with* LAND CRESS *and* MUSTARD LIME FRUIT

FOR THE PIG'S TAIL STUFFING

2 onions, finely diced
20 g duck fat
50 g pata negra ham
50 g smoked bacon
50 g lardo di colonnata (glossary)
50 g Morteau sausage (glossary)
50 g razor clam flesh, cut into 5 mm slices
200 g chicken mousse (page 280)

FOR THE PIG'S TAIL

8 good-sized pigs' tails, trimmed
30 ml vegetable oil
1 large onion, sliced
2 large carrots, chopped
½ head of celery, chopped
1 fresh thyme sprig
1 fresh rosemary sprig
2 bay leaves
3 garlic cloves, smashed
50 g black treacle
200 ml Madeira
3 litres chicken stock (page 285)

TO SERVE

1 tbsp fresh lemon juice
4 tbsp olive oil
½ tsp sugar
pinch of salt
½ Granny smith apple, core removed
50 g slice celeriac, peeled
100 g fresh land cress, well picked over
8 tbsp basil purée (page 282)
50 g mustard fruits (glossary), cut into 4 mm dice

SERVES 8

If I were to nominate a dish to tell the story of Chapter One, this would be it. This is my cooking at its most heartfelt: making use of the tail of the pig. There is nothing to beat the flavour of pork and pork fat. There is almost a sweet flavour to it so we added a very rich, smoked bacon farce from Fingal Ferguson's smoked bacon, along with razor clams. There is a balance from the basil, candied lime, apple and celeriac in an acidic vinaigrette to cut through the richness of the pig's tail. A simple, earthy, sweet dish yet it represents what our kitchen is all about.

STUFFING

Simmer the onion and duck fat in a pan over a low heat for 20 minutes until the onion is soft, caramelised and sweet. Weigh out 50 g of the confit onion for this recipe and pass through a mincer twice with the pata negra ham, smoked bacon, lardo and Morteau sausage to ensure a very fine result. Fold in this mince along with the razor clam flesh and the chicken mousse.

PIG'S TAIL

Preheat an oven to 140°C. Scorch the pigs' tails with a blow torch to remove any hairs and then put them into a large pan with water. Bring to the boil and boil for 2 minutes. Drain and rinse well, then put them into a large, deep roasting tray. Heat the oil in a large pan and add the vegetables and herbs, then cook over a medium to high heat until well browned. Add the treacle and Madeira, and cook to reduce the alcohol by half. Add the stock and bring to the boil, then pour over the pigs' tails. Cover the tray with a double layer of foil and put it in the oven for 3 hours. Leave until cool enough to handle, then lift out the pigs' tails and strain the liquid into a clean wide pan. Reduce to a glaze over a high heat. Place a pig's tail on a chopping board and use a knife to cut lengthways to expose the bone. Using your fingers, gently remove the bone, being careful not to break the skin. Fill the tail with the bacon and razor clam stuffing, and roll in clingfilm, tying the ends tightly to create a sausage shape. Repeat with the other tails and then poach in a pan of simmering water for 10 minutes. Then plunge in an ice bath and chill. This can be done a day in advance.

TO FINISH THE DISH

Preheat the oven to 180°C. Heat 200 ml of the reduced glaze in a sauté pan, add the pigs' tails and warm through, turning frequently and basting the tails with the glaze. Finish in the oven for 5–8 minutes until heated through.

SERVING

Whisk together the lemon juice and olive oil to make a dressing, then add the sugar and salt. Cut the apple and celeriac into fine batons and dress with the land cress in a little of the dressing, reserving some land cress for garnish. In the centre of each large, shallow bowl, spread a line of basil purée just longer than the pig's tail. Put a glazed pig's tail on top of each one, then some of the apple and celeriac and the mustard fruit dice. Finish with the land cress.

POACHED CHILLED ROCK OYSTERS *with a* SMOKED RED DULSE JELLY, OYSTER CREAM *and* WILTED BABY GEM LETTUCE *with* SMOKED BACON CRACKERS

The key to the success of this dish is that the oysters are poached in the shell under vacuum at 65°C and then chilled down. The result is a really creamy, briny flavour with earthy umami from the smoked seaweed. I love that we've two traditional Irish seaweeds in this: kelp and red dulse, also known as riseach. Obviously there are some Japanese undertones to this but it is in essence a native creation.

FOR THE BACON CRACKERS
130 g smoked bacon, well chilled
175 g Madeira jus (page 279)
175 g water
300 g tapioca flour
12 g salt
vegetable oil, for deep-frying

FOR THE SMOKED RED DULSE JELLY
15 g red dulse
1 kg pork ribs
125 g leeks, finely sliced
125 g onions, finely sliced
100 g fresh watercress stalks
5 g sugar
5 egg whites
3 g bonito powder (glossary)
2 tsp dark soy sauce
25 ml mirin
2 g agar agar powder (glossary)
1.5 g gold leaf gelatine leaves

FOR THE OYSTER CREAM
5 g spring onions
5 g leek
5 g fennel
5 g celery
15 ml olive oil
250 ml milk
3 raw shelled oysters
a little thickener (glossary)

FOR THE PICKLED KELP
600 ml rice vinegar
7 g salt
75 g sugar
5 g lemon zest
150 g kelp seaweed

FOR THE BLANCHED LETTUCE
2 baby gem lettuces

FOR THE OYSTERS
24 oysters, in their shells
a little bonito rice wine vinegar (glossary), optional, or fresh lemon juice

TO SERVE
16 pieces pickled white radish (page 282)

SERVES 8

This is best begun the day before you need it. Preheat a steam oven to 100°C. Chill the food bowl of a blender in the freezer for 30 minutes. Use the blender to purée the chilled bacon and then pass through a tamis into a bowl. Rub together with the tapioca flour and salt, then transfer the mixture to a KitchenAid fitted with a paddle and add the Madeira jus and water, mixing well. Transfer to a bowl and wrap with clingfilm into black pudding-sized rolls, then steam in the oven for 1 hour at 100 per cent steam. Leave to cool, then wrap in fresh clingfilm and chill in the fridge, preferably overnight. It will keep for 2–3 days like this or it can be frozen for up to a month. When cold, slice 1 mm thick strips on a meat slicer – you need 3 per portion. Place on a tray in a dehydrater and dry for 20 minutes at 70°C until the crisps have the texture of semi-dried pasta. To serve, deep-fry at 190°C until puffed up and golden. Season with salt and drain on kitchen paper.

SMOKED RED DULSE JELLY

Smoke the red dulse in a smoker for 15 minutes until reasonably heavily smoked. When cool, crumble finely. Put the pork ribs in a pan and cover with water. Bring to the boil, then drain and rinse under running water. Put the ribs back into a clean pan with the leeks, onions, watercress stalks and sugar. Simmer for 2 hours, then pass through a fine chinois and chill down. To clarify the stock, whisk the egg whites with the bonito powder, smoked red dulse, soy sauce and mirin, then add this to a large pan with the cold pork stock. Whisk together. Slowly bring the stock up to a very low simmer until the egg solidifies on the surface of the stock. Remove from the heat and strain through a double layer of muslin. To set the jelly, measure out 500 ml of stock. Put the gelatine in cold water and set aside for 10 minutes, then squeeze out the excess water. Bring the stock up to the boil, whisk in the agar agar and simmer for 2 minutes. Allow to cool slightly, then whisk in the gelatine. Pass the mixture through a fine chinois and pour into the serving bowls – we use a 25 g portion.

OYSTER CREAM

Sweat the vegetables in olive oil for 5 minutes, then add the milk and simmer until the vegetables are soft. Season with salt and pepper, and add the oysters. Allow to cool, then purée in a blender and pass through a fine chinois. Thicken to a cream consistency with thickener, adding a pinch at a time, then put into a squeezy bottle and chill.

PICKLED KELP

Bring all the ingredients, except the kelp, to the boil until the sugar has dissolved. Add the kelp and simmer for 2–3 minutes, then cool and chill.

BLANCHED LETTUCE

Separate the lettuces into leaves, discarding the outer ones – you'll need 3 per person. Rinse well. Blanch the lettuce in a pan of boiling water for 30 seconds or until wilted. Refresh in a bowl of iced water and drain when cold.

OYSTERS

Vacuum pack the oysters and cook in a water bath for 1 hour at 63°C. Prepare an ice bath with 50 per cent water and 50 per cent ice, then cool the oysters completely in this. Remove the shells and chill for up to 2 hours before serving. If using, season with the bonito rice wine vinegar or lemon juice.

SERVING

Remove the smoked seaweed jellies from the fridge and bring to room temperature. Arrange 3 of the cooked oysters on each one. Dress 3 pieces of blanched lettuce in a bowl with a little pickled seaweed liquor, season with salt and black pepper, and then place on each jelly with the oysters. Pipe 3 dots of oyster cream around the plate and add some pieces of drained kelp. Finish with 2 pieces of pickled white radish and 3 bacon crisps.

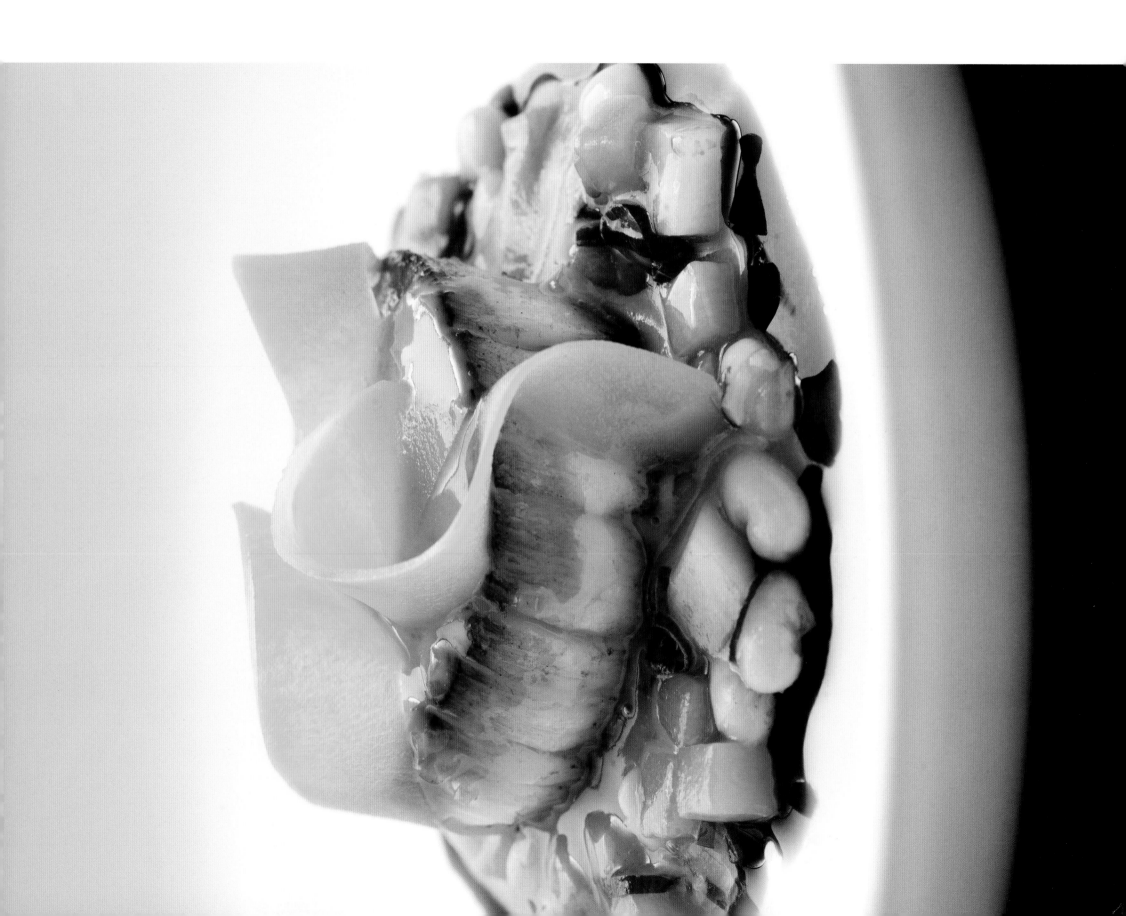

SCALLOP *with a* WHITE BEAN *and* RAZOR CLAM STEW, PUMPKIN PURÉE FLAVOURED *with* SMOKED BACON CREAM, BASIL OIL *and* PICKLED CROWN PRINCE PUMPKIN

FOR THE PUMPKIN PURÉE
125 g beurre noisette (page 276)
400 g Muscat pumpkin, peeled, seeded and diced

FOR THE SMOKED BACON CREAM
125 ml cream
75 g smoked bacon rind, roughly chopped

FOR THE RAZOR CLAM STEW
35 ml olive oil
150 g piece pumpkin, peeled, seeded and cut into 1 cm dice
200 ml clam stock (page 287)
a little thickener (glossary)
a little yuzu salt (glossary)
160 g cooked white beans cassoulet (page 276)
8–10 fresh razor clams, cut into 5 mm slices
1 spring onion, green part only, very finely sliced
50 g pickled courgettes (glossary), drained and cut into 1 cm dice

TO SERVE
8 × 60 g large scallops, preferably hand-dived, brought to room
  temperature
a little light olive oil
4 tsp basil oil (page 281)
240–250 g lemon purée butter sauce (page 285)
8 pieces pickled crown prince pumpkin (page 282)

SERVES 8

PUMPKIN PURÉE

Heat the beurre noisette in a pan and add the pumpkin. Cover with a tightly fitting lid and cook over a low heat, stirring occasionally, until the pumpkin is completely soft. Purée the pumpkin in a blender with all the liquid from the pan and pass through a fine chinois into a bowl. Season with salt and pepper.

SMOKED BACON CREAM

Put the bacon in a bowl with the cream and refrigerate overnight. When ready to use, strain through a fine chinois into a bowl and whisk to soft peaks.

RAZOR CLAM STEW

Heat a sauté pan and add 15 ml of the olive oil. Gently sauté the pumpkin, without colouring, until just cooked and then drain in a colander. Weigh out 100 g of the pumpkin dice. When ready to serve, warm the pumpkin purée in a small pan. Take it off the heat and whisk in 2 generous tablespoons of the smoked bacon cream. Bring the clam stock to a simmer and whisk in the thickener, a pinch at a time, until slightly thickened. Continue to heat and add the rest of the olive oil, simmering until emulsified. Season with yuzu salt to taste. Add the beans to the stock and heat for 30 seconds, then add the pumpkin dice with the razor clam slices, spring onion and pickled courgette. Heat for another 30 seconds.

SERVING

Heat a sauté pan until hot, season the scallops and fry in the olive oil for about 2 minutes on each side until just cooked through. Divide the bean and pumpkin mixture among warmed serving bowls and top each with about 1 teaspoon of pumpkin purée. Dot a line of basil oil around the outer edges of the beans and place a scallop in the centre of each plate. Spoon over 2 tablespoons of the lemon purée butter sauce and finish with a piece of pickled pumpkin.

This dish uses my favourite types of shellfish, regal looking and exuberant scallops. There are quite a few flavours playing in this dish but they have great harmony. It speaks of winter in Ireland and it is a great example of the bountiful fish and shellfish to be found in the Irish larder.

CARPACCIO of SPICED BEEF with CREAMED SHALLOTS and HORSERADISH, MATURE WEST CORK GOUDA and SHAVED BABY VEGETABLES, PICKLED KING OYSTER MUSHROOMS and APPLE BALSAMIC CREAM

This dish brings together some great food artisans: Tom Durcan and his spiced beef from the Cork market, Kitty Colchester and her organic cold pressed rapeseed oil and Dick Willems and his Gouda. All the flavours are perfectly aligned and work beautifully together. If ever a dish symbolised the work I do with artisans, this would be it.

FOR THE CREAMED SHALLOTS

25 ml olive oil
250 g shallots, finely diced
250 ml white wine
125 g crème fraîche
1 tbsp Dijon mustard
35 g creamed horseradish (glossary)
2 g salt
1 drop mustard essence

FOR THE APPLE BALSAMIC CREAM

100 ml cream
10 g apple balsamic cider vinegar (glossary)

TO SERVE

100 g baby root vegetables (beetroot, carrot, parsnip, radish and turnip), scrubbed
500 g piece spiced beef, frozen
50 g piece Dick Willems' Mature Gouda
100 g pickled king oyster mushrooms, sliced if very large (page 282)
handful fresh watercress leaves
juice of 1/2 lemon
100 ml cold pressed rapeseed oil

SERVES 8

CREAMED SHALLOTS

Heat the oil in a pan and add the shallots. Stir and sweat the shallots for 4 minutes, without browning, then stir in the wine. Turn up the heat and reduce until the liquid is almost gone. Lower the heat and reduce until the crème fraîche. Simmer until the mixture thickens. Remove from the heat, then mix in the Dijon, creamed horseradish and a pinch of salt. Check seasoning, adding more salt and some pepper if needed, then add the mustard essence. Mix well and chill.

APPLE BALSAMIC CREAM

Set a metal bowl into a larger bowl filled with ice. Pour the cream into the metal bowl and add a pinch of salt, then whisk until it forms soft peaks. Add the vinegar, a little at a time, to taste. Continue beating until stiff but be very careful not to overbeat. Chill. (This needs to be made just before serving.)

SERVING

Finely chop the beetroot stalks and reserve, then slice all the vegetables on a mandolin and only use the perfect slices – you will need about 10 per portion. Use a meat slicer to cut thin slices of the beef and lay on a piece of greaseproof paper, allowing 5–6 slices or around 50 g per portion. Spread a heaped teaspoon of creamed shallots in a circle in the centre of each plate and lay the slices of beef on top, overlapping to form a circle. Using a microplane, cover the beef with an even layer of grated Gouda. Toss the shaved baby vegetables and pickled king oyster mushrooms with the watercress leaves, dress with some of the oil from the mushrooms and a little lemon juice, and season with salt. Scatter on top of the beef. Using a teaspoon dipped in hot water, put a quenelle of apple balsamic cream in the centre of the beef. Finish with some of the rapeseed oil and the reserved beetroot stalks.

TOM DURCAN IS A CRAFT
BUTCHER AND AN OLD
SCHOOL FRIEND. HE IS
KNOWN AS THE MASTER
OF SPICED BEEF. THIS
UNIQUELY CORK
PRODUCT MAKES
REGULAR APPEARANCES
ON OUR MENU

CONSOMMÉ *of* DUCK *and* SPRING VEGETABLES *with* DUMPLINGS *of* FOIE GRAS *and* SESAME, SMOKED DUCK FAT

FOR THE SESAME AND FOIE GRAS DUMPLINGS
500 g piece foie gras
32 wonton wrappers, thawed if frozen
a little white sesame paste or good quality sesame oil
pinch of smoked salt

FOR THE SPRING VEGETABLES
100 g shelled peas
80 g shelled broad beans
8 baby leeks, trimmed
8 small purple sprouting broccoli florets
8 asparagus spears, cut into 5 mm slices

TO SERVE
400 ml duck neck consommé (page 286)
8 tsp smoked duck fat (page 287)
a little aged sherry vinegar

SERVES 8

SESAME AND FOIE GRAS DUMPLINGS

Slice the foie gras into 5 mm slices and then carefully cut into 15 g pieces. Place each one in the centre of a wonton skin and brush with a little white sesame paste or oil, then season with smoked salt. Dampen the edges and fold over to seal shut.

SPRING VEGETABLES

Blanch the baby vegetables separately in a pan of boiling salted water until just tender, then peel the broad beans and the outer leaves off the baby leeks.

SERVING

Heat the consommé in a pan with the vegetables and then pour into warmed serving bowls. Poach the dumplings in a pan of boiling salted water for 1 minute until just cooked and then transfer to the serving bowls. Warm the smoked duck fat and put into a small squeezy bottle. Finish the bowls with a drop of sherry vinegar and a few drops of the smoked duck fat.

This consommé is made of duck neck which has a very dense, aromatic, almost sweet duck flavour. There is a lovely crunch provided by the spring vegetables. Everybody loves looking into a consommé as it gives such a sense of elegant comfort.

CITRUS DRESSED SMOKED HADDOCK *with* ROPE MUSSELS *and* PICKLED CARROT, CELERIAC CREAM *and* SEAWEED

When we think of smoked haddock we think of winter, but this is a very light treatment of the fish. We use Irish seaweeds flavour-folded into other textures, including the skin of the haddock. There is some richness from the celeriac but dominating this dish are light, briny, sea flavours and smoky flavours, drawn from the change of winter to spring.

FOR THE SMOKED HADDOCK

2 large fillets of undyed natural smoked haddock, skin on
a little cold pressed rapeseed oil

FOR THE LEMON PURÉE DRESSING

juice of 1 lemon
juice of 1 lime
50 g lemon purée (page 289)
20 g sugar
150 ml cold pressed rapeseed oil

FOR THE MUSSELS

250 g mussels, cleaned

TO SERVE

100 g pickled sea spaghetti (page 282)
100 ml celeriac purée (page 283)
2–3 tbsp whipped cream
squeeze of lemon juice
16 pieces pickled carrot strips (page 281)
handful each celery leaves and coriander cress

SERVES 8

SMOKED HADDOCK

Lay a haddock fillet on a board, flesh side up, and score along both edges down to the skin. Turn the fish over and carefully pull the skin off the flesh, starting at the head end. Repeat with the other fillet. Trim the fish and set aside. Preheat the oven to 160°C. Descale the skin with an old knife or fish scaler, then wash under cold running water. Dry with kitchen paper, then spread the skin out on a baking sheet lined with greaseproof paper and brush with rapeseed oil. Cover with a sheet of greaseproof and another tray on top, and place in the oven for 15 minutes – the skin is ready when it is crispy and lightly coloured. Allow to cool and break up into 5 cm square pieces.

LEMON PURÉE DRESSING

Combine the lemon juice, lime juice, lemon purée, sugar and a teaspoon of salt in a bowl, then whisk in the oil to emulsify.

MUSSELS

Bring 300 ml of salted water to the boil in a pan. Add the mussels and cover, then cook for 2 minutes or until opened, shaking the pan occasionally. Discard any mussels that have not opened, then drain in a colander. When cool enough to handle, take the mussels out of the shells and chill until needed.

SERVING

With a sharp knife, cut the smoked haddock into 5 mm slices – you'll need 3 each or around 80 g per portion. Arrange the slices on a small tray and dress with 2 tablespoons of the lemon dressing. Leave to marinate for 2 minutes. Warm the celeriac purée in a small pan and then fold in the cream. Add a pinch of salt and lemon juice to taste, then put into a small squeezy bottle. Pipe about a teaspoon of the celeriac purée onto to the side of each serving plate and swipe with a spoon. Place the haddock slices in the middle of the plate and scatter the mussels on and around the fish, then roll up 2 of the pickled carrot strips and put them on either side of the fish. Arrange the pickled sea spaghetti on the plate and then spoon over some of the dressing. Finish with the crispy haddock skin, celery leaves and coriander cress.

CHARGRILLED GREEN ASPARAGUS *with* RAVIOLI *of* 36 MONTH OLD PARMESAN *and* GARLIC LEAF

FOR THE PARMESAN GEL

40 g butter
40 g plain flour
500 ml milk
250 g cream
8 g piece Parmesan, 36 month old
8 g maltodextrin powder (glossary)
3 g ground Sarawak pepper (glossary)

FOR THE PASTA

120 ml water
10 saffron filaments or small pinch of saffron powder
500 g T55 flour (glossary), plus extra to dust
3 g salt
125 g egg yolks

FOR THE ASPARAGUS PURÉE

50 g butter or 3 tbsp extra virgin olive oil
1 shallot, finely sliced
1 garlic clove, finely chopped
2 each fresh tarragon and mint sprigs
300 g asparagus, trimmed and chopped into small pieces

FOR THE LEMON BUTTER EMULSION

50 ml lemon juice
50 ml water
1 garlic clove, lightly smashed
small pinch of saffron powder, optional
75 g butter, diced

FOR THE ASPARAGUS

500 ml water
28 large asparagus spears, trimmed to an equal length
2 tbsp extra virgin olive oil

TO SERVE

1 handful wild garlic leaves

SERVES 8

PARMESAN GEL

Melt the butter over a medium heat. Stir in the flour, then gradually whisk in 100 ml of the milk. Once this is incorporated, add another 100 ml, continuing until all the milk is used up and the sauce is smooth and glossy. Cook over a very low heat for another 5–10 minutes until thickened. Reduce the cream by half in a pan. Grate the Parmesan in a food processor. Remove the white sauce from the heat and stir in the Parmesan and reduced cream. Cool to room temperature and then blend in a blender with the maltodextrin. Pass through a chinois and stir in the Sarawak pepper. Put into a piping bag and chill until needed.

PASTA

Warm the water and saffron together, and allow to infuse for 10 minutes. Combine the flour, salt and egg yolks in a food processor, and pour in the saffron water. Blend the mixture until it comes together in a ball, then transfer to a lightly floured work surface and knead until smooth. Wrap and rest in the fridge for a couple of hours or overnight, which is best for rolling. To make the ravioli, use a pasta machine to roll out the pasta to the thinnest setting. Pipe the Parmesan gel onto the pasta at intervals and cover with another sheet. Use a cutter to cut out the ravioli – you will need 24 pieces in total.

ASPARAGUS PURÉE

Sauté the shallot and garlic in the butter or oil over a low heat until soft. Cook the asparagus in a pan of boiling salted water until tender, then drain and add to the shallot and garlic mixture, then add the herbs and cook for another 4 minutes. Blend to a purée, discarding the herbs, and season with salt and black pepper. Chill until needed.

This is a straight combination of the smoky, charred, sweet asparagus flavour and warm molten liquid of 36 month old Parmesan ravioli. Very simple and beautiful to look at. It took us an age to get the ravioli just right but it was worth it.

LEMON BUTTER EMULSION

Reduce the lemon juice by half in a pan with the water, garlic and saffron if using. Remove the garlic and whisk in the butter, a little at a time, until incorporated. Season with salt and white pepper, and pass through a fine chinois. Keep warm.

ASPARAGUS

Light a charcoal grill. Bring the water to the boil in a pan with half a teaspoon of salt. Blanch the asparagus until tender, then refresh in a bowl of iced water. When ready to serve, toss 24 of the asparagus spears in the oil. Chargrill until evenly marked all over. Season with salt and black pepper, and keep warm. Use a Japanese mandolin to thinly shave the remaining 4 asparagus to use as a garnish.

SERVING

Bring a large pan of salted water to a rolling boil. Add the ravioli and cook for 2 minutes. Toss the warm chargrilled asparagus in tablespoons of lemon butter emulsion. Warm the asparagus purée in a small pan and put into a squeezy bottle. Pipe a tablespoon into the centre of each large, warmed serving plate and set 3 of the dressed chargrilled asparagus on top of each one. Drain the cooked ravioli and toss in two tablespoons of lemon butter emulsion, then arrange on each plate. Quickly wilt the wild garlic leaves and shaved asparagus in a little more lemon butter emulsion and arrange on top. Finish with black pepper.

KITTY COLCHESTER IS A SECOND GENERATION ORGANIC FARMER WHO HAS TURNED OIL PRODUCTION INTO AN ART FORM.
SECOND NATURE EXTRA VIRGIN RAPESEED OIL IS GROWN ON DRUMEEN FARM, NEAR URLINGFORD, COUNTY KILKENNY.

OX TONGUE *with* SAUTÉED SPRING LAMB SWEETBREADS, BURREN WILD MUSTARD *and* WATERCRESS PURÉE *with* PICKLED *and* DEEP-FRIED SHALLOT

Sweetbreads are a much underused food item. It excites me when spring lamb sweetbreads come along, almost more so than spring lamb itself. When combined with the almost creamy texture of cured ox tongue with some mustard, fresh radish and cured onions, this puts a real smile on my face.

FOR THE OX TONGUE
1 pickled Angus ox tongue
6 bay leaves
40 black peppercorns
250 ml white wine vinegar

FOR THE WATERCRESS PURÉE
500 g fresh watercress, well picked over
2 tbsp Worcestershire sauce
300 ml cream

FOR THE DEEP-FRIED SHALLOTS
vegetable oil, for deep-frying
25 rings of shallot
100 ml milk
50 g seasoned flour (page 287)

FOR THE SWEETBREADS
1 litre court bouillon (page 277)
200 g lamb sweetbreads
50 g seasoned flour (page 287)
3 tbsp light olive oil
50 g butter, softened

TO SERVE
6 tbsp extra virgin olive oil, peppery
3 tbsp Burren wild mustard (glossary) or similar large grain mustard such as Dalkey
25 pickled shallot rings (page 282)
28 baby radishes, scrubbed, with tops
1 tsp smoked salt (glossary) or plain is ok

SERVES 8

OX TONGUE

Put the tongue in a pan with the bay leaves, peppercorns and white wine vinegar. Pour over enough water to cover, then cover and simmer for 1½–2 hours. Cool the tongue and then peel it. Chill overnight.

WATERCRESS PURÉE

Blanch the watercress in boiling water and refresh in a bowl of iced water. Squeeze as much water out as possible using a paper towel, then transfer to a Pacojet container and freeze overnight. When frozen, spin three times in the Pacojet, then transfer to a blender. Reduce the cream by half and cool, then add to the blender with the watercress. Blend until smooth and season with the Worcestershire

sauce, a pinch of salt and freshly ground black pepper. Pass through a fine chinois and put into a small squeezy bottle. Chill until needed.

DEEP-FRIED SHALLOTS

Heat the oil in a deep-fat fryer to 180°C. Dredge the shallot rings in milk, then dust in the seasoned flour and deep-fry until crispy. Drain on kitchen paper.

SWEETBREADS

Bring the court bouillon to the boil. Blanch the sweetbreads in the court bouillon, mix for 1 minute and then transfer to a bowl of iced water. When the sweetbreads are cold, peel off the outer membrane and discard. You will need 24–32 in total. Chill until needed. When ready to serve, dust the sweetbreads in the seasoned flour. Heat a non-stick frying pan, then add the light olive oil, and when hot, sauté the seasoned sweetbreads in batches, then add a generous knob of the butter. When the butter foams, use this to baste the sweetbreads and caramelise them to a nice golden brown colour. Drain on kitchen paper. Keep warm while you finish cooking the remainder.

SERVING

Thinly slice the ox tongue lengthways on a meat slicer and place the slices on a sheet of greaseproof paper, slightly overlapping, as if to form a large rectangle. From this cut large rectangular pieces to suit the size of each serving plate. Transfer to the plates. Add 3–4 lamb sweetbreads to each plate. Mix 3 tablespoons of the extra virgin olive oil with the mustard and spoon lightly over the tongue. Finish with 4–5 dots of the watercress purée and 3–4 each of the pickled and deep-fried shallot rings. Cut 4 of the radishes into thin slices on a Japanese mandolin. Dress the radishes with the remaining extra virgin olive oil and smoked salt, and put sliced and whole ones on each plate. Finally, season the tongue with a pinch of rock salt.

WARM SMOKED CURED CLARE ISLAND SALMON with CURED PORK JOWL and BRAISED SQUID with FRESH PEAS

FOR THE SMOKED CURED SALMON
2.25 litres water
400 g rock salt
800 g sugar
30 g black peppercorns
20 g star anise
10 whole cloves
8 juniper berries
1 tbsp white wine vinegar
2 bunches fresh coriander
2 fennel bulbs, finely sliced
1 kg piece Clare Island organic salmon fillet, cut from the thick end and pin boned

FOR THE PEA PURÉE
50 g white onions, sliced
25 g butter
250 g fresh or frozen peas
3 fresh sage leaves, chopped
20 fresh tarragon leaves, chopped
pinch of sugar
3 tbsp extra virgin olive oil

FOR THE PEA STOCK
200–300 g fresh pea pods
a little thickener (glossary)

FOR THE BRAISED SQUID
200 g squid and tentacles, membrane removed and cleaned
100 ml garlic oil (page 281)

FOR THE SQUID INK SAUCE
2 tsp liquid squid ink (glossary)
100 ml fish stock (page 286)
1 tbsp cream

FOR THE PEAS
400 g pea pods

FOR THE DRESSING FOR THE SALMON
pinch of sugar
1 tbsp lemon juice
3 tbsp extra virgin olive oil

TO SERVE
24 very thin slices cured pork jowl, guanciale by Fingal Ferguson (glossary)
16 fresh pea shoots
8 borage flowers (glossary)

SERVES 8

The teaming up of two great Irish products: Clare Island salmon, as close to wild as you can get, and Fingal Ferguson's cured pork jowl called guanciale. There is a lovely salty, meaty flavour from the very thinly sliced guanciale draped over the smoked salmon, which is matched by the sweetness of the peas and the squid.

SMOKED CURED SALMON

Bring all the ingredients, except the salmon and fennel, to the boil until the sugar has dissolved. Remove from the heat and add the fennel, then leave to cool and infuse. Chill in a shallow tray deep enough to keep the salmon submerged. Add the salmon to the cure and leave for 18 hours. Drain the salmon and leave uncovered for another 24 hours in the fridge. This will give it a nice close texture. Take the salmon out of the fridge and remove the skin. Cut into 8 × 80 g pieces, approximately 11 cm length × 2 cm wide × 2 cm high. Cover and chill until needed.

PEA PURÉE

Sweat the onions in the butter over a low heat until soft. Blanch the peas in boiling salted water for 1½ minutes. Drain and tip into the softened onions, then add the herbs, sugar and olive oil with a pinch of salt. Continue to cook for 1 minute, then transfer to a blender and blend to a smooth purée. Pass through a fine chinois and chill down quickly over a bowl of ice. Check for seasoning and add salt and freshly ground black pepper if it needs it.

PEA STOCK

Blanch the pea pods, then refresh in a bowl of iced water. Use a juicer to extract the juice, then place the juice in the bottom of a shallow tray lined with clingfilm and freeze overnight. The next day, take out the tray and remove the clingfilm. Place the frozen pea juice on top of a layer of muslin on a perforated tray. Leave to defrost in the fridge overnight collecting the clear pea juice. Thicken this with the thickener, adding a pinch at a time, and season with salt and freshly ground white pepper. Alternately you can use a thickened, clear crab stock.

BRAISED SQUID

Heat a water bath to 60°C. Put the squid and tentacles in a vacuum pack bag with the garlic oil and cook for 3 hours. Chill down quickly in a bowl of iced water and then chill until needed.

SQUID INK SAUCE

Simmer all the ingredients in a shallow pan for 2–3 minutes, then immediately remove from heat. This should be thick, but if not, then thicken to the consistency of oil, and put into a small squeezy bottle. Chill until needed.

PEAS

Blanch the peas in a pan of boiling salted water, then refresh in a bowl of iced water. Remove the shells and discard. Reserve the peas. Chill until needed.

DRESSING FOR THE SALMON

Dissolve the sugar and a pinch of salt in the lemon juice, then whisk in the olive oil. Set aside until needed.

SERVING

Preheat the grill to medium. To smoke the salmon, place the cured salmon pieces in a smoker over applewood (but any wood of your choice can be used) and smoke over a mild heat for 8 minutes. Heat the pea purée in a small pan. Place the warm smoked salmon at the top of each serving plate and place a spoon of the warmed pea purée to the right of it. Place 3 slices of pork jowl over the salmon. Then warm the shelled peas in the pea stock and season with salt and freshly ground black pepper. Place 2 spoonfuls together opposite the pea purée and place 6–8 drops of the squid ink sauce on top of this. Warm the squid under the grill, then cut the body into pieces and arrange 3–4 pieces on and around each piece of salmon with 1 tentacle. Dress the salmon with the dressing and garnish each plate with 2 pea shoots and 1 borage flower.

SEAMUS MULLIGAN OF CUINNEOG, BALLA, COUNTY MAYO HAS BEEN USING CHURNING TECHNIQUES PASSED DOWN THROUGH THE GENERATIONS, TRADITIONS THAT STRETCH BACK ALMOST 2,000 YEARS, WHICH CREATE A BUTTER WITH AN ALMOST FERMENTED FLAVOUR.

BUTTER POACHED ATLANTIC LOBSTER *with a* LIGHT POTATO EMULSION *and* MALTED VINEGAR SAUCE, BROAD BEANS *and* SUMMER CABBAGE

There is nothing that surpasses the sweet saline flavour of lobster flesh, especially when poached in salted Cuinneog butter. This dish is a rich combination of old fashioned flavours delivered in a new way with light potato emulsion, summer cabbage and a malt vinegar sauce which gives it a lovely twist at the end.

FOR THE LOBSTER
4 litres salted water (page 277)
2 x 600 g live lobsters
60 g Cuinneog butter

FOR THE MALTED VINEGAR SAUCE
600 ml lobster stock (page 287)
2 tbsp Chardonnay vinegar
50 ml Hondashi stock (glossary)
100 ml liquid barley malt extract (glossary)
a little thickener (glossary)

FOR THE POTATO EMULSION
150 g potato purée (page 283)
250 ml lobster stock (page 287) or milk
2 pinches of sweet smoked paprika

FOR THE CABBAGE AND BROAD BEANS
4 summer cabbage leaves
60–80 shelled broad beans
250 ml lobster sauce (page 287)

FOR THE POTATO CRISPS
olive oil, for deep-frying
1 large Rooster potato, peeled
pinch of smoked salt (glossary) or plain salt

SERVES 8

LOBSTER

Bring the salted water to a rolling boil, then kill the lobsters and immerse in the boiling water. After approximately 1 ½ minutes, remove the lobsters from the water, pulling off both tails, and immerse immediately in a large bowl of iced water. Place the lobster claws back into the boiling water and cook for another 3–4 minutes. Remove the claws and immediately submerge in the bowl of iced water. When cold, crack and pull the meat from the claw. Then crack the tails and take the meat from the shell – if you like, you can push a wooden skewer down the length of the tails to keep them straight. Place each tail and the meat from both claws with half the butter in a vacuum pack bag and seal.

MALTED VINEGAR SAUCE

Reduce the lobster stock to 200 ml until you have achieved a glaze consistency. Add all the remaining ingredients, except for the thickener, and allow to heat through. Add the thickener, a pinch at a time, until it reaches a sauce consistency.

POTATO EMULSION

Warm the lobster stock or milk and stir in the potato purée with the paprika, then season with salt and freshly ground white pepper. The final consistency should be one of thick soup. Place the liquid in a gas canister and charge with 2 gas chargers. Keep the emulsion warm in a water bath at 60°C or in a pan of hot water.

CABBAGE AND BROAD BEANS

Blanch the cabbage leaves and broad beans in separate pans of boiling salted water for 2–3 minutes. Refresh in a bowl of iced water and then drain. Peel the skin off each broad bean and cut the cabbage leaves into small thumb-sized pieces. Chill everything separately until needed.

POTATO CRISPS

Heat the olive oil in a deep fat fryer to 160°C. Slice the potato into 2.5 cm thick slices. Then cut out with a small ring mould 1 ½–2 cm in diameter – you will need 24 in total. On a Japanese mandolin, slice into wafer thin slices and deep-fry until pale golden and crisp. Drain on a paper towel and season with the smoked salt.

SERVING

Heat a water bath to 52°C and cook the lobster for 10 minutes. Remove the lobster from the vacuum pack bag and drain off the tails. Cut in half lengthways along the tails and cut each half tail into 3–4 pieces. Cut the claw meat in half. Season with salt and freshly ground black pepper. Alternatively, you could finish the tails and claws under the grill, brushed with melted butter. Warm the broad beans and cabbage in the lobster sauce, and season with salt and pepper. Place 8–10 broad beans with some of the lobster sauce around the middle of each warmed serving plate. Then squeeze some potato emulsion from the gas canister into a small bowl and spoon 4 half tablespoons at odd places around the broad beans. Pipe 3–4 large dots of malted vinegar sauce in between the potato emulsion, broad bean and lobster sauce, forming a mosaic look. Then place the warmed ½ claw and 2 pieces of tail on top, and decorate with 2–3 pieces of the warmed cabbage and 3 of the potato crisps.

BETTY DOWD, THE REAL BOSS.

WAYNE KENNY SOUS CHEF.

MANUS McGONAGLE'S KNOWLEDGE OF THE HARVEST OF OUR SEAS IS AS DEEP AS THE OCEAN HE FARMS. HE IS THE FOUNDER OF QUALITY SEA VEG COMPANY BASED IN BURTONPORT, COUNTY DONEGAL. WHERE HE HAND-GATHERS SEA VEGETABLES FROM THE ROCKY SEASHORE OF DONEGAL.

MAIN COURSE

ROSS LEWIS AND MYRTLE ALLEN.

UNFOLDING CHAPTERS

Successful restaurants are as much a result of time, place and product as anything else. In many ways we had a lot stacked against us, located in a basement, deep in the Northside of the city. But we had plenty in our favour too. We've worked hard to make our basement feel anything but that. By using Irish and international craftspeople, we've transformed part of what was the former home of George Jameson, the whiskey maker, into a uniquely Irish dining space.

Over the years there have been moments that are still a matter of great pride to me. When I was younger, I never thought my work would end up on our national stamps, but in 2005 a collection of stamps celebrating Irish cuisine featured dishes from our kitchen. While I can take time out to thank the hardworking staff, the thank-you represented by the many awards we've received has given us the momentum and energy to continue to innovate. In 2007 we got the news that we had been awarded a Michelin star. Although it brought heavy responsibilities, it fulfilled a lifetime's ambition and was a serious endorsement for everybody's hard work.

On 17 May 2011 Queen Elizabeth II visited Ireland for the first time. It was also the first visit to Ireland by a reigning British monarch since the foundation of the State. The three-day visit was filled with moments of great historical importance and poignancy for both countries. Yet, even the great and the good have to eat, and I found myself in charge of the State dinner in Dublin Castle. It was a unique opportunity to really celebrate our culinary treasure trove. The three courses are reproduced throughout the book, sitting on State crockery with the golden harp. These dishes still give me great pride. All the more satisfying that our regal guest cleared her plate.

For all its flaky lustre the Celtic Tiger brought about a massive shift in how people engage with food. The people of Ireland became a restaurant-going nation, primarily starting in 1996 through to 2008. We are in leaner times now, and although the dining landscape has changed, we believe we've always stuck to first principles, always tried to preserve our great food traditions and always shared our culinary skills. This is why I remain an active member of Euro-toques, Europe's living archive of culinary traditions. Many may know the organisation was founded by Paul Bocuse but that is only half the story; it was co-founded by our own Myrtle Allen, who stands at the pinnacle of the great Irish food renaissance. Without her years of commitment to food integrity, the expanding repertoire of artisan produce I choose from would be a much narrower one. Nearly every season I am approached by a new artisan, and so our menu changes and grows, and new food chapters unfold.

RIB *of* SLANEY VALLEY BEEF, OX CHEEK *and* TONGUE *with* SMOKED CHAMP POTATO *and* FRIED SPRING CABBAGE, NEW SEASON BROAD BEANS *and* CARROTS *with* PICKLED GARLIC *and* WILD GARLIC LEAF

As is fitting for a dish made especially for a State occasion, the first visit of Queen Elizabeth II to the Republic, this dish is a celebration of everything that Ireland has to offer. We've put the ingredients together in a playful way, though all of them honour our landscape and tell the story of our native artisans.

FOR THE BEEF CHEEKS
4 beef cheeks
1 litre wine
8 shallots, sliced
2 tbsp Cabernet Sauvignon wine vinegar
8 garlic cloves, lightly crushed
100 g celery, sliced
200 g carrots, sliced
handful each fresh rosemary, thyme and sage
8 bay leaves
50 ml vegetable oil
1 tsp each rock salt, crushed black peppercorns and crushed coriander seeds
500 ml chicken stock (page 285)

FOR THE OX TONGUE
1 Angus ox tongue
6 bay leaves
40 black peppercorns
250 ml white wine vinegar

FOR THE RIB OF BEEF
2 garlic cloves
1 kg rolled Angus beef rib, thin end of the eye and 32 days hung
1 each fresh rosemary and thyme sprigs
1 tsp crushed coriander seeds
2 tbsp light olive oil

FOR THE PICKLED GARLIC JUS
50 ml vegetable oil
1 short rib, cut into pieces
400 g shallots, sliced
4 garlic cloves, lightly crushed
100 g carrots, sliced
100 g celery, sliced
50 g button mushrooms, sliced
½ bunch fresh thyme
2 litres chicken stock (page 285)
60 g pickled garlic, chopped (glossary)
40 ml pickled garlic juice (glossary)

FOR THE VEGETABLES IN APPLE VINEGAR BUTTER EMULSION
24 baby carrots, scrubbed
200 g broad beans
50 ml apple balsamic cider vinegar (glossary)
30 ml water
200 g butter, diced
20 ml white wine shallot essence (page 278)

FOR THE SMOKED CHAMP
1.5 kg even-sized Rooster potatoes, scrubbed
300 ml milk
8 spring onions, finely sliced
120 g butter, chilled and diced

TO SERVE
1 York cabbage
50 g foie gras butter (page 276)
5 g wild garlic leaves
8 roasted baby carrots (page 284)

SERVES 8

BEEF CHEEKS

Place all the beef in a deep tray with the wine, shallots, vinegar, vegetables and herbs, ensuring the meat is completely submerged. Cover and marinate in the fridge for 24 hours. Preheat the oven to 90°C. Drain the meat in a colander set over a clean pan and bring the marinade liquid to the boil for 2–3 minutes to solidify any impurities. Pass through a fine chinois. Dry the beef with kitchen paper and heat half the oil in a frying pan. Season the beef with the salt, pepper and coriander, then fry until well caramelised all over, being careful not to burn it. Meanwhile, heat the rest of the oil in a pan large enough to hold everything. Add the marinated vegetables and herbs, and cook over a medium to high heat until well browned, stirring frequently. Add the beef and pour over the reserved liquid and stock. Cover with greaseproof paper and wrap with two layers of tin foil. Put in the oven for 12 hours, then cool to room temperature. Lift the beef cheeks out, press between 2 trays with a heavy weight on top and leave until cold. Pass the cooking liquid through a fine chinois into a clean pan and reserve. When cold, carve the beef cheeks into 3 cm slices and then cut into 1.5 × 6 cm strips. Cover with clingfilm and chill until needed.

OX TONGUE

Put the tongue in a pan with the bay leaves, peppercorns and vinegar. Cover with water and simmer for 1 ½ hours until completely tender, then cool. Peel and cut into 5 mm slices, then cut into 1.5 × 6 cm pieces. Cover and chill.

RIB OF BEEF

Preheat a water bath to 70°C or preheat the oven to 180°C. Purée the garlic cloves and a pinch of salt with the blade of a knife. Rub the beef with the garlic purée. Vacuum pack with the herbs and stock, and cook in the water bath for 20 minutes, or caramelise in a hot pan in the oil and roast in the oven for 15 minutes until pink in the centre (56°C in the centre). Then rest and blast chill.

PICKLED GARLIC JUS

Heat the oil in a pan and heavily caramelise the rib pieces, then add the vegetables and brown thoroughly. Add the thyme and stock, and simmer for 30 minutes. Drain through a colander into a clean pan, pressing the vegetables and beef heavily to collect all the juices. Boil to reduce by half and then pass through a double layer of muslin into a bowl. Add the pickled garlic and pickled garlic juice, and then chill.

VEGETABLES IN APPLE VINEGAR BUTTER EMULSION

Blanch the carrots and broad beans separately in a pan of boiling salted water until tender. Refresh in a bowl of iced water and then peel the beans. Boil the vinegar and water in a pan, then gradually whisk in the butter cubes to create an emulsion. Add the white wine shallot essence and keep warm until needed.

SMOKED CHAMP

Boil the potatoes in a pan of salted water until tender. When cool enough to handle, peel and smoke over a medium heat for 10 minutes. Pass through a mouli and then a fine sieve. Warm the milk and spring onions in a small pan. Leave to infuse for 1 ½ minutes and then add the warm sieved potatoes. Using a plastic spatula, beat in the cubes of butter to make a smooth purée. Season with salt and white pepper. Keep warm. This is best made to order.

TO FINISH THE RIB OF BEEF

Season the cold rib of beef generously with salt, black pepper and the crushed coriander seeds. Heat the oil in a heavy-based frying pan and caramelise the meat on all sides, turning regularly. Leave to rest for 20 minutes and then slice into 8 × 70 g portions, discarding the ends. Keep warm.

SERVING

Remove and discard the outer leaves of the cabbage and choose 8 of the middle leaves, then blanch in a pan of boiling salted water until tender. Refresh in a bowl of iced water and cut into circles that are about 14 cm in diameter. Heat the foie gras butter in a frying pan and fry the cabbage circles in batches until caramelised and crispy, then drain on kitchen paper. Season the vegetables in the apple vinegar butter emulsion and stir in the garlic leaves. Warm the pickled garlic jus in a small pan. In a grill or oven warm the ox tongue and beef cheek slices, then place onto half of the fried cabbage circles, pipe on the warm smoked champ and fold over. Arrange on warmed serving plates with the rested, warm rib of beef slices. Spoon over the vegetables in the emulsion, add the roasted carrots and break with the pickled garlic jus.

Dinnéar Stáit
á óstáil ag
Uachtarán na hÉireann Máire Mhic Ghiolla Íosa
an Dr. Máirtín Mac Giolla Íosa
agus
Soilse Banríon Eilís II
agus
a Mhórgacht Ríoga Diúc Dhún Éideann
Dé Céadaoin 18 Bealtaine 2011

State Dinner
offered by
The President of Ireland Mary McAleese
and
Dr. Martin McAleese
in honour of
Her Majesty Queen Elizabeth II
and
His Royal Highness The Duke of Edinburgh

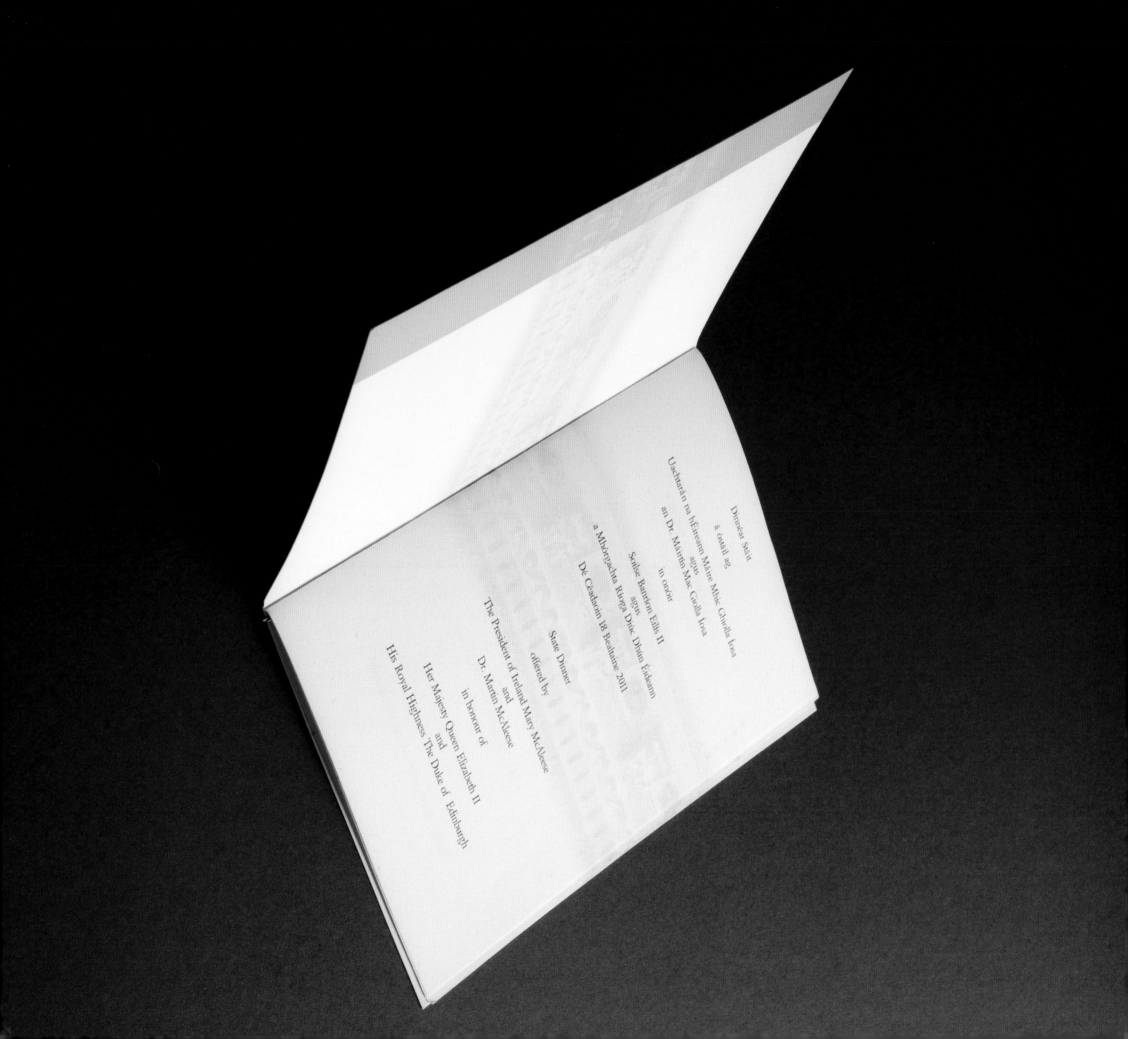

CHARGRILLED JOHN DORY *with* LOBSTER *and* SORREL, VEGETABLES COOKED *in* PARCHMENT

There is no substitute for fish cooked on the bone, but we've taken this one step further and chargrilled it on the bone. Both the lobster and the stock are wonderfully sweet and briny, and this is offset by the bitterness of the sorrel. Sunshine on a plate.

FOR THE VEGETABLES IN PARCHMENT

100 g salsify roots (glossary)
a little lemon juice
1 small celeriac
100 g carrots
2 tbsp hazelnut oil
65 ml extra virgin olive oil
110 ml white wine

FOR THE JOHN DORY

2 x 1–1.2 kg whole John Dory
2 tbsp light olive oil

FOR THE VEGETABLES

2 litres water
10 asparagus spears, woody stalks removed
400 g potatoes, Rooster
50 g broad beans
50 g fresh peas
100 g cabbage leaves, sliced into 3 cm pieces, thick stems discarded
handful Monk's beard, optional, or you could substitute with samphire (glossary)

TO SERVE

300 ml ice filtered lobster stock (page 287)
a little thickener (glossary)
4 tbsp extra virgin olive oil, fruity
400 g cooked lobster meat (page 277), cut into 3 cm pieces
100 ml lemon purée butter sauce (page 285)
5 g fresh sorrel leaves, finely sliced

SERVES 8

VEGETABLES IN PARCHMENT

Preheat the oven to 160°C. Scrub the salsify roots under cold running water, peel with a sharp knife and place in a bowl of water with the lemon juice. Peel the carrots and leave whole. Then peel the celeriac and slice into 1.5 cm square pieces – you'll need 100 g in total. Add to the salsify and lemon juice mixture to prevent them discolouring, and once all the vegetables are ready, drain and pat dry on kitchen paper. Mix the oils and white wine in a large bowl. Put each vegetable in a separate tin foil envelope. Ladle over the oil and wine mix, and season generously with salt and black pepper. Seal up the parcels, put on baking sheets and cook in the oven until tender when tested with a sharp knife. Check the celeriac after 25 minutes; the salsify and carrots will take about an hour. Cool the vegetables in their bags, then slice into 3 mm rounds. Chill until needed.

JOHN DORY

Light a charcoal grill – we use a Grill Dome barbecue. Remove the head, fins and tail from each fish, and rinse the cavities well, removing any roe. Pat dry with kitchen paper. Rub with the olive oil and season with black pepper. Grill the fish for 2 minutes, then lift and turn them to a 90 degree angle, and grill for another 2 minutes on the same side. Repeat on the other side. When the fish is just cooked through, remove from the heat and take off the bone, keeping the skin on the fillets. Keep warm.

VEGETABLES

Bring the water to the boil with ½ a teaspoon of salt. Blanch the asparagus until tender, then refresh in a bowl of iced water. Drain and cut into 2 cm pieces. Use an oliviette tool or Parisienne scoop to cut small 15 mm rounds out of the potatoes – you need approximately 200 g in cooked weight. Blanch the prepared potatoes, broad beans, peas, cabbage and Monk's beard all separately in a pan of boiling salted water until just cooked and then refresh separately in a bowl of iced water. Peel the broad beans, then cover and chill until needed.

SERVING

Bring the lobster stock to a simmer in a large sauté pan and whisk in the thickener, a pinch at a time, until it reaches a sauce consistency. Continue to heat and add the extra virgin olive oil, simmering until emulsified. Season with salt and black pepper. Add all the prepared vegetables, and Monk's beard if using, and then add the lobster pieces. Simmer briefly to warm through and then remove from the heat. Warm the lemon purée butter sauce in a pan. Spoon the lobster and vegetables onto warmed serving plates, and place a 150–160 g portion of John Dory on each one. Drizzle over the warm lemon purée butter sauce and scatter the sorrel on top.

ACHILL ISLAND BLACK FACED LAMB PLATE

Achill Island black faced lamb are half the weight of normal lamb. They are not grain fed or fattened before slaughter and come straight from the mountains, where they feed on a diet of mountain grass and herbs. They have the sweetest, most aromatic meat I've ever tasted.

FOR THE LAMB BELLY

1 small lamb belly
100 g tapenade (page 287)

FOR THE LAMB

100 g hay
400 g lamb loin, well trimmed
1 litre garlic oil (page 281)
1 small leg of lamb
1 lamb shoulder, well trimmed
100 g white truffle honey
65 g Dijon mustard

FOR THE LAMB OFFAL

1 litre court bouillon (page 277)
4 lamb tongues
200 g lamb sweetbreads
50 g cornflour
50 g plain flour
pinch each of freshly ground nutmeg and cayenne pepper
large pinch of ground black pepper
1 tsp ground coriander
½ tsp ground black cumin

FOR THE STUFFED CARROTS WITH GREMOLATA CRUMB

30 g flat-leaf parsley leaves
zest of 1 orange and 1 lemon
1 garlic clove, finely chopped
100 g fresh white bread, roughly torn, crusts removed
30 g butter, diced, at room temperature
8 large carrots, tops removed, each about 20 cm
100 ml freshly squeezed orange juice
1 each small fresh tarragon and dill sprig
½ tsp sugar
60 g unsalted butter
150 ml béarnaise sauce (page 284)

SERVES 8

FOR THE WHITE BEAN STEW

300 g shelled coco de paimpol beans (glossary) or dried white beans
1 small carrot, halved lengthways
½ celery stick
3 garlic cloves, lightly crushed
1 bay leaf
100 ml chicken stock (page 285)
150 g swede, cut into 5 mm dice
150 g celeriac, cut into 5 mm dice
200 ml lamb sauce (page 285)
2 lamb kidneys, trimmed and cut into 5 mm dice
50 ml garlic oil (page 281)
4 tbsp aged sherry vinegar

TO SERVE

160 g carrot and brown butter purée with black cumin (page 283)
30 ml fresh bay leaf juice (page 279), in a small squeezy bottle
a little vegetable oil
150 g butter, diced
8 deep-fried parsley roots (page 277)

LAMB BELLY

Preheat the oven to 140°C. Evenly spread the lamb belly with the tapenade, roll tightly and tie with butcher's string. Wrap tightly in 2 layers of tin foil, place in a tray and roast for 2½ hours. Allow to cool, preferably overnight, then carve into 8 × 4 mm slices, removing the string.

LAMB

Smoke the hay over oakwood chips on a medium heat for 10 minutes. When cold, vacuum pack a third of it with the lamb loin and 300 ml of the garlic oil. Break down the leg into muscle joints. Vacuum pack with 400 ml of the garlic oil and another third of the smoked hay. Cook both in a water bath at 55°C for 2 hours, then cool in an ice bath. When cold, trim the loin down into 8 square portions, each about 75 g. Slice the leg into 8 equal-sized pieces. Vacuum pack the shoulder with the remaining 300 ml of garlic oil and the remaining third of the hay. Cook in a water bath at 85°C for 2½ hours. While still warm, remove from the bag and put in between 2 sheets of greaseproof paper, then press between two trays with a weight on top. When cool, slice the shoulder into 8 portions. Whisk together the honey and mustard in a small bowl, and put into a squeezy bottle.

LAMB OFFAL

Bring the court bouillon to the boil. Blanch the sweetbreads for 1 minute, then transfer to iced water, reserving the court bouillon. When the sweetbreads are cold, peel off the outer membrane and discard. Chill until needed. Return the court bouillon to the boil. Add the tongues and simmer for 3 hours, topping up with water as necessary. When cool enough to handle, peel and put in a bowl. Pass the cooking liquid through a fine chinois and pour enough over the tongues to cover, then chill. To make the seasoned flour, combine the cornflour, flour and spices with a good pinch of salt in a dish.

STUFFED CARROTS WITH GREMOLATA CRUMB

Blitz the parsley in a food processor with the orange zest, lemon zest and garlic until coarsely chopped. Add the bread and pulse to a fine crumb, then gradually add the room temperature butter and pulse to mix. Roll out between 2 sheets of greaseproof paper to a 2 mm thickness and chill. Then cut 8 × 1.5 × 12 cm rectangles and chill again until needed. Preheat a steam oven to 100°C. Vacuum pack the carrots tightly in a single layer with the orange juice, tarragon, dill, sugar, 2 pinches of salt and the unsalted butter. Cook for 45 minutes at 100 per cent steam or until the carrots are tender when pierced with a knife. When cool enough to handle, pour off the liquid and reserve. Trim the carrots to a uniform 15 cm and use an apple corer to remove a cylinder along the length of the carrot, then finely chop and mix with the béarnaise to make the stuffing that goes back into the carrots. Keep in a warm place.

WHITE BEAN STEW

Put the beans in a pan with the carrot, celery, garlic and bay leaf. Add the stock and enough water to comfortably cover the beans. Simmer on a low heat until the beans are completely soft with no resistance at all. Remove the vegetables and bay leaf, and season with salt. Cool and chill until needed. Cook the swede and celeriac separately in boiling salted water until tender. Refresh in a bowl of iced water, then chill until needed. To finish, heat the lamb sauce with 8 tablespoons of the white beans and 4 tablespoons of the vegetable dice. Add the kidneys and cook for 1 minute, then whisk in the garlic oil and aged sherry vinegar, and season with salt and black pepper. Keep warm.

SERVING

Preheat the oven to 150°C and preheat the grill. Heat the carrots in the reserved liquid, adding extra warm water if necessary, until warmed through. Fill with the warm stuffing and top with the gremolata crumb. Toast under the grill until the crumb is hot and the butter is starting to foam. Heat a little oil in a large frying pan and sear the loin, leg and shoulder, fat side down, in batches until caramelised. Brush the loin with the honey mustard glaze. Put everything in a tray and warm through in the oven for 4 minutes. Place the belly on a tray and heat under the grill. Heat a knob of butter in a frying pan. Cut each tongue in half lengthways, and once the butter begins to foam, fry the pieces of tongue until well caramelised and warmed through. Warm the carrot purée and put into a squeezy bottle. Pipe a teaspoon of the purée onto each warmed serving plate at 12 o'clock and swipe with the back of a spoon, then put a stuffed carrot on top. Spoon 2 tablespoons of the bean stew onto the left-hand side of each plate. Heat a frying pan with a good knob of butter, coat the sweetbreads in the seasoned flour and add to the pan once the butter is foaming. Fry until golden brown on all sides and then drain on kitchen paper. Arrange the loin, leg, shoulder, belly, sweetbreads and tongue on the plates. Finish with some more honey mustard glaze, dots of the

EDWARD JOHNSTON IS AN ACHILL ISLAND FARMER'S SON TURNED CORPORATE SOLICITOR. HE HAS BEEN INSTRUMENTAL IN SUPPORTING THE BLACKFACE MOUNTAIN LAMB INITIATIVE ON ACHILL ISLAND AND THE NEIGHBOURING CURRAUN PENINSULA IN MAYO THROUGH CAORACLA LTD.

LOIN *of* RABBIT STUFFED *with a* LIGHT PATA NEGRA FARCE, CARROT *and* BROWN BUTTER PURÉE *with* BLACK CUMIN, TOASTED SEEDS *with* BEE POLLEN *and* RABBIT SAUCE BROKEN *with* CARROT OIL

Rabbit and carrot: a straightforward dish which almost has a hint of humour about it. The purée has brown butter and black cumin which give a smoky flavour to the carrot. Pata negra and spice in the farce help bring out the flavour of the rabbit, and the carrot oil breaks the sauce, creating a lovely, delicate dish.

FOR THE STUFFED RABBIT

4 rabbits, livers intact
250 g pata negra farce (page 278)
50 g melted butter, for brushing the tin foil
500 g piece pancetta, frozen
200 g piece lardo di colonnata (glossary), frozen
1 tsp Lucky Duck spice mix (glossary), optional
40 ml light olive oil

FOR THE ROASTED CARROT OIL

750 g carrots, roughly chopped
375 ml light olive oil

FOR THE BEE POLLEN AND FLAX SEED GRANOLA

30 g butter
50 g red quinoa
50 g white quinoa
35 g flax seeds
25 g bee pollen (glossary), optional

FOR THE CARROT CRISPS AND DEEP-FRIED CARROT TOPS

vegetable oil, for deep-frying
2 medium carrots, scrubbed

TO SERVE

50 g butter
200 g carrot and brown butter purée with black cumin (page 283)
200 ml rabbit jus (page 280)
16 roasted carrots (page 284)
2–3 tbsp aged sherry vinegar

SERVES 8

STUFFED RABBIT

Preheat the oven to 180°C. Take the two loins off each rabbit carcass and trim the bellies to an even length. Reserve the carcasses to make the jus and the livers to use as a garnish. Spread a thin even strip of the farce on the side of each belly nearest the loin and roll up from the loin side of the belly, until the belly nearly overlaps itself. Trim off any excess. Cut 8 × 50 × 50 cm tin foil squares and brush with butter. Cut thin slices of pancetta and lay 4–5 side by side, slightly overlapping in the middle of each piece of buttered foil, then cut a slice of lardo and lay it across the ends of the pancetta. Dust with a little Lucky Duck spice mix if using. Put a loin on top and roll up, securely twisting the ends.

ROASTED CARROT OIL

Place the carrots in a pan with the olive oil and simmer gently for 3–4 hours until the carrots are dehydrated. This can also be done in a low oven overnight. Leave to cool. Blend in a blender and pass through a fine chinois.

BEE POLLEN AND FLAX SEED GRANOLA

Heat the butter in a sauté pan, add the red and white quinoa, and sauté, stirring continually until golden brown. Add the flax seeds to the pan and cook for another 3 minutes. At this stage add half the pollen if using and season with salt. Drain the granola on kitchen paper. When cool, add the remainder of the pollen if using and mix well.

CARROT CRISPS AND DEEP-FRIED CARROT TOPS

Preheat a deep fat fryer to 140°C with oil. Cut the tops off the carrots and reserve. Peel the carrots and slice finely on a mandolin. Deep-fry until crisp. Drain on kitchen paper and season with salt. Deep-fry the carrot tops for a few seconds until crispy and season with salt.

TO FINISH THE STUFFED RABBIT

Preheat the oven to 180°C. Heat half the oil in a sauté pan and add the wrapped rabbit loins. Transfer to the oven for 8–10 minutes. Allow to rest for 8–10 minutes, then unwrap and dry well with kitchen paper. Return a clean sauté pan to the heat with the rest of the oil and add the unwrapped roasted rabbit loins. Sauté until the bacon turns brown, turning frequently. Leave to rest for a few minutes, then trim off the ends and cut each one into 3 equal-sized pieces.

SERVING

Slice the reserved rabbit livers in half and trim down. Heat a large sauté pan, add the butter and heat until foaming. Season the rabbit livers, then sauté in the hot pan for 1 minute on each side. Drain on kitchen paper. Warm the carrot purée and put into a squeezy bottle. Warm the rabbit jus, add 40 ml of the roasted carrot oil and 2–3 tablespoons of the aged sherry vinegar. Pipe a line of purée on the left side of each warmed serving plate and use an offset palette knife to spread across the plate. Sprinkle a fine line of granola along one side of the purée. Place the slices of stuffed rabbit loin on the plate to one side of the purée with the carrots, then add the rabbit livers and crisps. Pour over the rabbit jus and break this with the roasted carrot oil.

RARE BREED PORK PLATE: POACHED FILLET *in a* BACON CRUMB, SLOW COOKED PORK BELLY, CHEEK COOKED *in* APPLE SUGAR *with a* SMOKED AÏOLI, BARLEY *and* PARSLEY PURÉE, *and* PORK SAUCE *with* PICKLED THISTLE

If you are looking for Ireland on a plate, this is it. From O'Doherty's slow cooked pork and Highbank Farm's apple sugar syrup to Jack McCarthy's eponymous black pudding and Fingal Ferguson's smoked bacon, this dish combines the best of the best of Irish pork with the classic accompaniments of cabbage and barley. A real celebration of native flavours and textures.

FOR THE SLOW COOKED PORK BELLY
1 kg piece pork belly, well trimmed and skinned
150 g tapenade (page 287)
1 tbsp chopped fresh sage

FOR THE PORK CHEEKS AND THISTLE SAUCE
2 carrots, finely chopped
1 onion, sliced
1 celery stick, finely chopped
½ leek, finely chopped
4 garlic cloves, lightly crushed
3 fresh thyme sprigs
1 bay leaf
500 ml white wine
8 medium pork cheeks, well trimmed
2 tbsp olive oil
60 g Highbank Farm apple sugar syrup (glossary)
60 ml Llewellyn's apple balsamic cider vinegar (glossary)
500 ml chicken stock (page 285)
a little thickener (glossary)
50 g pickled thistle (glossary), thinly sliced
25 g butter, diced

FOR THE PORK FILLET
300 g pork fillet, trimmed
2–3 fresh thyme sprigs
4–5 fresh sage leaves
4 tbsp vegetable oil
150 g Fingal Ferguson's smoked streaky bacon
1 litre chicken stock (page 285)

FOR THE SMOKED AÏOLI
2 garlic cloves, peeled
2 cooked egg yolks
2 raw egg yolks
25 ml Chardonnay vinegar
pinch each of smoked salt, smoked paprika and saffron powder (glossary)
100 g cooked smoked potatoes (page 287) or ordinary potatoes
½ red chilli, seeded
200 ml light olive oil

SERVES 8

FOR THE PEARL BARLEY
250 g pearl barley
2 litres chicken stock (page 285)
100 g butter
75 g shallots, very finely diced
1 garlic clove, finely chopped

FOR THE SAVOY CABBAGE
8 Savoy cabbage leaves, even-sized
50 g butter
30 ml hot water

TO SERVE
a little hot water
2 small roasted carrots (page 284), finely sliced into rounds
60 g crème fraîche
60 g parsley purée (page 282)
½ lemon
200 g Jack McCarthy's black pudding
30 g butter
½ tsp smoked salt (glossary)

PORK BELLY

Preheat the oven to 140°C. Spread the tapenade over the meat side of the pork belly, then season with salt and pepper, and sprinkle with the sage. Roll tightly and tie with butcher's string. Wrap tightly in a double layer of tin foil and cook in the oven for 2½ hours. Cool, preferably overnight, and then slice into 4 mm rounds, discarding the ends and string.

PORK CHEEKS AND THISTLE SAUCE

Put the vegetables, herbs and wine in a deep tray with the pork cheeks and leave to marinate for 24 hours. The next day, preheat the oven to 160°C. Drain the pork cheeks in a colander. Bring the marinade up to the boil and boil for 2–3 minutes to solidify any impurities from the meat, then remove from the heat and pass through a fine chinois. , Heat a large sauté pan and fry the pork cheeks in batches in a little of the olive oil until well browned. Deglaze with a little of the marinade. In an ovenproof dish brown the drained vegetables over a medium heat in the rest of the oil. Add the pork cheeks with the pan juices, 50 g of the apple sugar syrup and 50 ml of the apple balsamic. Pour over the marinade liquid and the stock, and wrap with a double layer of tin foil. Cook for 1½–2 hours or until the cheeks are soft. Cool, then drain and pass the cooking liquid through a double layer of muslin into a clean pan.

Put the cheeks on a tray and chill until needed. Reserve a little of the cooking liquid to use to reheat the pork cheeks. Bring the remainder to the boil and then reduce by half, skimming off the fat. Thicken, a pinch at a time. To finish, put 250 ml of the sauce in a pan with the remaining 10 g of apple sugar syrup and the remaining 10 ml of the apple balsamic vinegar. Season with salt and pepper, then stir in the thistle. Chill until needed.

PORK FILLET

Preheat a water bath to 75°C. Roll the fillet tightly in clingfilm with the thyme and sage, and tie the ends, then vacuum pack and put into the water bath for 2 hours. Cool in an ice bath, then unwrap and cut into 8 even-sized pieces. Chill until needed. To make the bacon crumb, sauté the bacon over a medium heat in the vegetable oil until completely crisp. Put on a tray and dry in a dehydrator or low oven (40°C) until dried out, then put into the blender and blitz to a crumb.

SMOKED AÏOLI

Put the garlic, all the egg yolks, vinegar, salt, paprika, saffron, potatoes and chilli in a blender. Blend briefly, and then with the blender on a medium speed, pour in the oil in a slow, steady stream until it is all incorporated. Season with salt and black pepper. If it is too stiff, add a little warm water – the aïoli should be like a thick mayonnaise. Pass through a fine chinois and put into a small squeezy bottle.

PEARL BARLEY

Rinse the barley twice in cold water and drain. Heat the stock. In a separate pan heat the butter, then add the shallots and garlic, and sauté gently, without colouring, until soft. Add the barley, a pinch of salt and a ladleful of the hot stock, and stir. Turn the pan up to a gentle simmer, adding the stock a ladle at a time until it has all been absorbed and the barley is cooked. Cool and chill until needed – you'll need 250 g.

SAVOY CABBAGE

Remove the tough ribs from the cabbage leaves and then blanch in a pan of boiling salted water until cooked. Refresh in a bowl of iced water. Drain and cut into 24 even-sized pieces. Chill until needed.

TO FINISH THE PORK

Preheat the oven to 180°C and preheat the grill. Place the chicken stock in a pan and simmer the pork fillet portions for 5 minutes until warmed through. Dry lightly, season with salt and pepper, and then roll in the bacon crumb. Keep warm. Arrange the pieces of pork belly on a tray and place under the grill until hot and crispy. Heat up the reserved pork cheek cooking liquor in a pan and whisk in the 25 g diced butter. Add the pork cheeks and transfer to the oven for 5 minutes or until hot. Turn the cheeks in the liquor until nicely glazed.

SERVING

Heat the thistle sauce in a small pan. Heat the barley in a separate pan, adding a little hot water as necessary. Add the sliced carrots and crème fraîche, then the parsley purée, and season with salt, black pepper and a little lemon juice. Slice the black pudding into 8 pieces and heat on a small baking tray under the grill. Heat 50 g of butter with 30 ml of hot water in a medium sauté pan and use this to heat the cabbage through. Drain, then season with salt and black pepper. Place a piece of crispy pork belly on top of the black pudding and place down the centre of the plate, with the fillet rolled in bacon crumb and the glazed pork cheeks. Heat the thistle sauce and whisk in 30 g butter. Add a heaped tablespoon of the pearl barley on either side of the plate and add the Savoy cabbage, then pipe some aïoli onto the cheeks and sprinkle with the smoked salt. Spoon over the thistle sauce to finish.

JACK McCARTHY OF KANTURK, COUNTY CORK, IS A LEGENDARY STORYTELLER AND A FIFTH-GENERATION BUTCHER FAMED FOR HIS SUPERIOR BLACK PUDDING. THE CELEBRATED BOUDIN NOIR USES FRESH BLOOD FROM FREE RANGE PIGS.

CHARGRILLED BLACK SOLE *with* CASTLETOWNBERE SHRIMP, CHASSELAS GRAPES *and* CAULIFLOWER *with* CHANTERELLE MUSHROOMS *and* LEEKS

There is a magic combination here of smokiness from the chargrilled black sole with fresh, pink, sweet shrimps, mildly aromatic grapes and cauliflower flavours. The whole dish is underpinned by a sauce inspired by sauce Veronique but with a smoked bacon edge.

FOR THE SMOKED BACON SAUCE

2 litres chicken stock (page 285)
1 litre clam stock (page 287)
6 shallots, chopped
4 celery sticks, chopped
a little vegetable oil
300 g smoked bacon or bacon rind, roughly diced
100 ml dry white wine
1 tbsp Dijon mustard
3 tbsp tarragon vinegar reduction (page 287), more to taste
a little thickener (glossary)
40–48 raw small brown shrimps
100 g Chasselas grapes (glossary)
20g butter, diced and chilled, or 20 ml fruity virgin olive oil
100 g chanterelle mushrooms, trimmed and halved if large

FOR THE CAULIFLOWER AND LEEKS

1 small cauliflower head
3 medium leeks
100 ml water
50 g butter

FOR THE BLACK SOLE

8 x 160 g double black sole fillets
a little olive oil

TO SERVE

120 g cauliflower purée (page 283)

SERVES 8

SMOKED BACON SAUCE

Put the chicken and clam stock in a pan, and reduce over a high heat to 1.5 litres. Meanwhile, sweat the shallots, celery and smoked bacon in a little oil over a medium heat for about 10 minutes until lightly browned and softened. Deglaze with the wine and then add the reduced down stock. Simmer for 20 minutes, skimming regularly, and then pass through a double layer of muslin into a clean pan. Add the vinegar and check the seasoning, adding the mustard and more vinegar if necessary. Thicken, a pinch at a time, and pass through the muslin again – you will need 200 ml in total. Blanch the shrimps for 1 minute in boiling salted water and refresh in cold water, then peel and set aside. Peel the outer skin from the grapes, cut them in half and remove the seeds. Chill.

CAULIFLOWER AND LEEKS

Cut the cauliflower into quarters and discard the core. Using a mandolin, cut into 2 mm slices – you will need 40 pieces in total. Blanch in a pan of boiling salted until just cooked, then refresh in a bowl of iced water. Drain and place on a tray lined with kitchen paper. Cut 40 × 5 mm slices 5 mm from the bottom half of the leeks. Cook as per the cauliflower. When ready to serve, whisk the water and butter in a sauté pan to create an emulsion. Add the cauliflower and leeks, and allow to just warm through, being careful not to break them up. Drain and season with salt and black pepper.

BLACK SOLE

Light a barbecue or charcoal grill – we use a Grill Dome barbecue. Preheat the grill. Brush the sole fillets with the olive oil and then season with salt and pepper. Cook for 3 minutes in the barbecue or on a charcoal grill, then carefully turn over and cook for another 3 minutes or until cooked through.

SERVING

Heat the reserved bacon sauce and whisk in the diced butter or olive oil. Add the prepared shrimps, halved grapes and chanterelle mushrooms, and heat through. Warm the cauliflower purée and spread a generous tablespoon in the centre of each warmed serving plate, just longer than the fish. Put a sole fillet on top of each one, followed by the cauliflower and leeks. Spoon the sauce over the fish to finish.

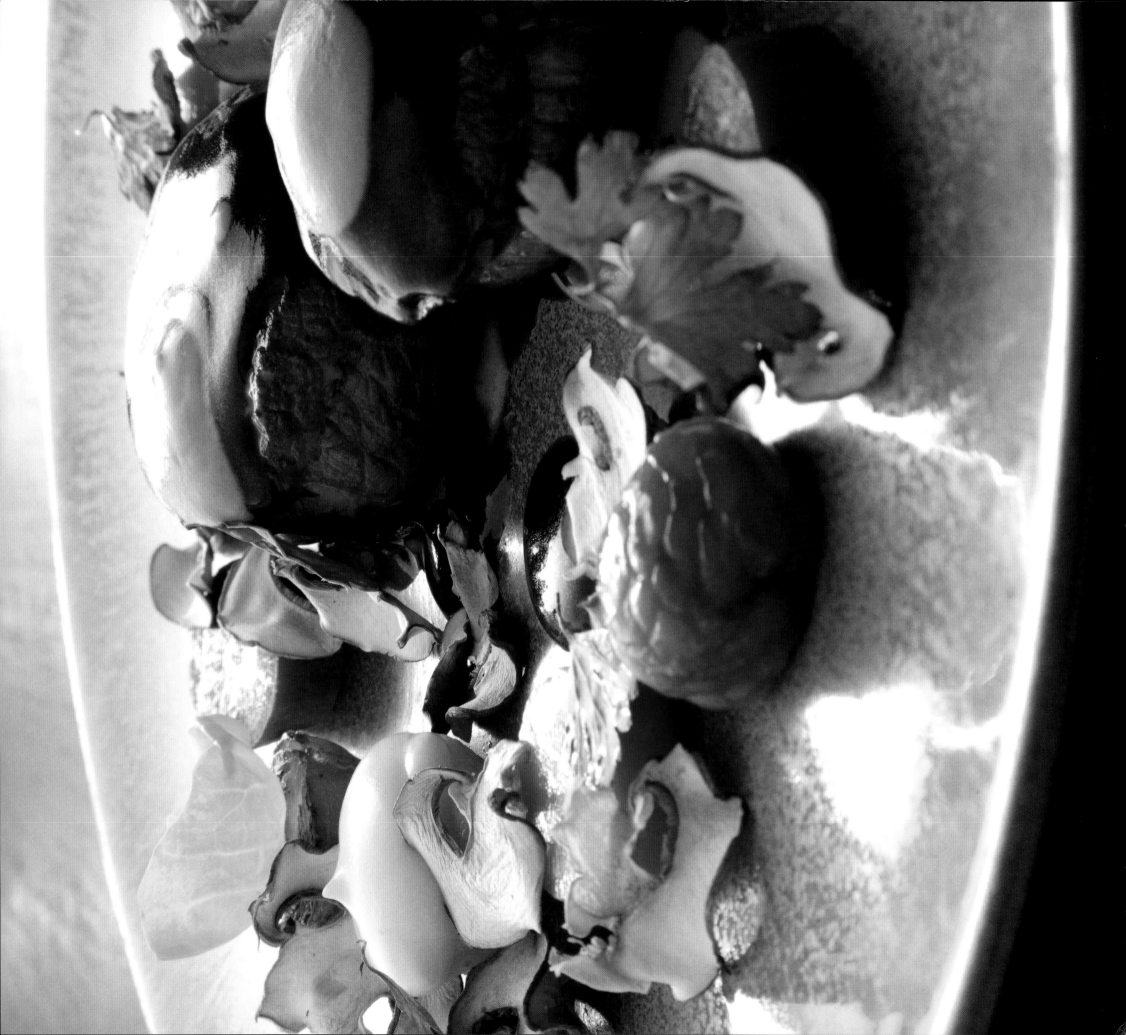

PEPPERED SIKA VENISON LOIN with CEP PURÉE and ROOT VEGETABLES, CONFIT SPROUTS and CHESTNUTS with PARSNIP PURÉE and a RICH GAME SAUCE

Sika deer is a little bit smaller than native red deer, but it has a marbling through the meat that gives it a moistness and a better flavour than other venison. The cep purée is mildly sweet, and the brandy, port and garlic give this dish a robust flavour, while the venison sauce is slightly enriched with chocolate. To me this dish looks like a palette of autumn forest colours. A rich, fulfilling hearty combination of all our wonderful Irish ingredients.

FOR THE DRIED MUSHROOMS
300 g field mushrooms

FOR THE CHOCOLATE BUTTER
50 g plain chocolate, at least 73% cocoa solids, broken into squares
200 g butter, at room temperature

FOR THE CONFIT CHESTNUTS
10 fresh chestnuts
vegetable oil, for deep-frying
2 g salt
2 g sugar
150 g duck fat

FOR THE CONFIT BRUSSELS SPROUTS
16 large Brussels sprouts
200 g duck fat

FOR THE CEP CREAM
2 shallots, finely sliced
2 garlic cloves, finely chopped
1 tbsp olive oil
300 g cep mushrooms, trimmed and finely sliced
160 ml Madeira
100 ml port
100 ml cream

FOR THE PARSNIP PURÉE
500 g parsnip, finely diced
100 g butter
100 ml milk, plus extra if necessary

FOR THE ROOT VEGETABLES
150 ml hazelnut oil
250 ml extra virgin olive oil
200 ml white wine
250 g carrots, peeled, tops removed
250 g parsnips, peeled, tops removed
250 g long beetroot, peeled, tops removed
250 g celeriac, sliced into 3 cm square lengths

FOR THE VENISON
1.2 kg venison loin, trimmed
2 tsp Sarawak pepper (glossary), roughly ground
50 ml vegetable oil
25 g butter
1 fresh thyme sprig
1 garlic clove, crushed

TO SERVE
a little icing sugar
300 ml venison sauce (page 285)
3-4 tbsp butter emulsion (page 278)
fried flat-leaf parsley leaves, to garnish (page 279)

SERVES 8

DRIED MUSHROOMS

Slice the mushrooms using a mandolin. Spread out on dehydrator trays and dry for 6 hours at 165°C until completely dried out. Store at room temperature.

CHOCOLATE BUTTER

Melt the chocolate over a pan of simmering water. Allow to cool slightly. Place the melted chocolate in a blender and, on a low speed, gradually add the butter. When blended together, roll in clingfilm or greaseproof paper, and securely twisting the ends, and chill. This can then be kept in the fridge and sliced as needed – you will need 50 g in total for this recipe. It can also be frozen.

CONFIT CHESTNUTS

Preheat a steam oven to 85°C. With a sharp knife, make a small cut in the chestnuts. Drop the chestnuts into a deep fat fryer filled with vegetable oil heated to 350°F, cover with a lid for 1 minute or until they pop, lift out of the oil and allow to cool. When cool enough to handle, peel off both the outer shell and the membrane, then seal in a vacuum bag with the salt, sugar and duck fat. Cook in the oven at 100 per cent steam for 45 minutes or until soft. Leave to cool in the vacuum bag and chill until needed. Alternatively, cook the chestnuts in a preheated oven at 140°C in a deep tray covered with the duck fat, salt and sugar until tender.

CONFIT BRUSSELS SPROUTS

Preheat a steam oven to 85°C. Using a sharp knife, trim the sprouts and remove any less than perfect outer leaves. Take off 24 perfect leaves, being careful not to break them, then blanch in boiling water and reserve for garnish. Vacuum pack the Brussels sprouts with the duck fat and a pinch of salt, and cook at 100 per cent steam for 45 minutes. The sprouts are ready when they are still al dente. Leave to cool in the vacuum bag and chill until needed. Alternatively, cook the Brussels sprouts in a preheated oven for 140°C in a deep tray covered with the duck fat and a pinch of salt until tender.

CEP CREAM

Sweat the shallots and garlic in the oil until soft. Lightly season the ceps and sauté for 3–4 minutes, then add the Madeira and port, and cook until reduced to a syrup. Stir in the cream and simmer until the cream starts to thicken, then blend until smooth and pass through a fine chinois. Season with salt and black pepper if needed.

PARSNIP PURÉE

Preheat a steam oven to 85°C. Vacuum pack the parsnips with the butter, milk, a pinch of salt and pepper. Cook on 100 per cent steam for 30 minutes or until soft. Strain the parsnips, reserving the liquid. Blitz in a blender with as much of the liquid as needed to make a smooth purée. If it is still too stiff, add a little more milk, and season.

ROOT VEGETABLES

Preheat the oven to 160°C. Mix the oils and wine in a large bowl. Make 4 tin foil envelopes and put each vegetable into a separate one. Divide the cooking liquid among them and add a pinch of salt and pepper to each one. Seal the parcels and cook in the oven until tender when tested with a sharp knife – check the celeriac and parsnips after 25 minutes; the beetroot and carrots will take around an hour. Leave the vegetables to cool in their bags, then slice across the carrots, celeriac, parsnips and beetroots in 5 mm rounds. Reserve 2 large slices of each vegetable per portion. Reserve the cooking liquor for heating up the vegetables. When ready to serve, warm 2 ladles in 2 separate small pans. In one, heat 16 pieces each of carrot, celeriac and parsnip. In the other, warm the beetroot. Drain on kitchen paper, keeping them separate. Keep warm.

VENISON

Cut the venison into 16 × 70 g medallions and season heavily with the Sarawak pepper. Heat a heavy sauté pan until very hot. Add the oil, then add the venison medallions and cook for 2–3 minutes on each side. Add the butter, garlic and thyme to the pan, and baste the meat with the hot pan juices, then continue to cook for another 2–3 minutes. Leave to rest for 5 minutes in a warm place before serving.

SERVING

Heat a sauté pan and cut the confit Brussels sprouts in half lengthways. Dust the cut sides with icing sugar and season with salt. Place cut side down in the hot pan until caramelised and warmed through. Warm the cep cream and parsnip purée, and put them into separate squeezy bottles. Warm the venison sauce in a small pan and whisk in 50 g of the chocolate butter. Warm the sprout leaves in the butter emulsion. Put 2 circles of the cep cream on each warmed serving plate and place the rested venison on top. Arrange the warm vegetables, chestnuts and caramelised Brussels sprouts, cut side up, around the outside of the plate. Pipe a little of the parsnip purée on top of the parsnip and put one of the sprout leaves on top of each Brussels sprout. Scatter dried mushrooms over the vegetables and pour the chocolate sauce over the venison. Finish the venison with a little more cep cream on top and scatter around the fried flat-leaf parsley leaves.

ED HICK OF HICKS TRADITIONAL IRISH BUTCHERS IN DÚN LAOGHAIRE IS ONE OF SEVERAL GENERATIONS OF BUTCHERS, AND THERE'S NO BETTER MAN AROUND TO TALK FOOD WITH.

POACHED GUINEA HEN *with a* SET SWEETCORN CREAM *and* SAGE JUICES, WHITE PUDDING *and* ROASTED VEAL SWEETBREADS

I look forward to September and October when David Burne arrives in through the back door of the kitchen with his sweetcorn – it is so fresh and so sweet. This is one of my favourite dishes using the sweetcorn. It blends beautifully with the light, white meat and I love the union with the aromatic Pinot Gris. The resulting flavour you get from the guinea fowl, along with the sweetcorn, and the textural combination from the crispy skin and sage is just wonderful. The caramelised sweetbreads and white pudding add further richness.

FOR THE GUINEA HEN

8 guinea hen breasts
80 g butter
240 ml Pinot Gris
4 rindless smoked streaky bacon rashers, cut in half
8 small fresh thyme sprigs
400 ml chicken stock, optional (page 285)
5 g smoked salt (glossary) or plain salt
3 tbsp olive oil

FOR THE VEAL SWEETBREADS

200 g veal sweetbreads
1½ litre court bouillon (page 277)
50 g seasoned flour (page 287)
3 tbsp vegetable oil
3 tbsp softened butter

FOR THE SWEETCORN PURÉE

135 ml cream
220 g sweetcorn kernels
20 g butter
100 ml milk
½ tsp crushed garlic
5–6 drops white truffle oil

FOR THE SET SWEETCORN CREAM

250 g sweetcorn purée (see above)
85 g milk
10 g cornflour, slated with water
60 g egg yolks

TO SERVE

225 ml cream
squeeze of lemon juice
160 g white pudding (page 288)
1 tbsp vegetable oil
8 roasted grelot onions (page 279)
8 deep-fried sage leaves (page 278)
25 g dried sweetcorn (page 278)
10 ml sage juices (page 279)

SERVES 8

GUINEA HEN

Preheat a water bath to 65°C. Remove the skins from the guinea hen breasts and set aside. Place each guinea hen breast in a vacuum pack bag with 10 g of butter, 30 ml of Pinot Gris, a thyme sprig and a piece of smoked bacon. Cook for 18 minutes. Alternatively, preheat the oven to 140°C and place the guinea hen breasts in a shallow roasting tray with those same ingredients, along with the chicken stock. Cover with clingfilm and tin foil, and poach in the oven for 15 minutes until just cooked through and tender. Keep warm. Season the skins with smoked or normal salt by rubbing into the skin. Leave for 1 hour and then preheat the oven to 160°C. Place the salted skins in a cold non-stick pan with the olive oil. Slowly bring up the heat, then transfer to the oven and cook for approximately 15–20 minutes or until brown and crispy.

VEAL SWEETBREADS

Blanch the sweetbreads in the court bouillon for 1 minute and then transfer to a bowl of iced water. When the sweetbreads are cold, peel off the outer membrane and discard. Pat them dry and dredge in seasoned flour. Then, in a hot sauté pan, fry the sweetbreads in batches in a little vegetable oil with a tablespoon of butter until golden brown. Keep warm.

SWEETCORN PURÉE

Reduce the cream to 70 ml and blanch the sweetcorn. Place in a Thermomix with the rest of the ingredients, except for the white truffle oil, at 90°C for 20 minutes. Then pulse on turbo for 2–3 minutes. Pass through a fine chinois or tamis. Season with salt and white pepper, and add the white truffle oil. Retain 8 tablespoons of the purée for the garnish; the remainder is to be used for the set sweetcorn cream.

SET SWEETCORN CREAM

Preheat the oven to 100°C. Warm the remaining sweetcorn purée and milk together, then add in the cornflour. Remove from the heat and allow to cool. Then whisk in the egg yolks and season with salt and white pepper. Cook the mixture in 8 × 60 g circular-moulded or oval-moulded rubber mats or in moulds. Cook in the oven for 20 minutes or until set. Keep warm.

SERVING

Preheat the oven to low or preheat the grill. To make the Pinot Gris sauce, remove the guinea hen breast from the vacuum pack bag or roasting tin and strain off the cooking liquid through a fine chinois into a pan. Keep the breasts warm in the oven or under the grill and add the cream to the cooking liquid. Season to taste and add the lemon juice, then reheat gently and lighten with a hand blender. Cut the white pudding into 8 × 1 cm thick rounds and sauté in a frying pan in the vegetable oil for 2 minutes each side. Keep warm under the grill or in the oven. Place a guinea hen breast in the centre of each warmed serving plate and place one of the warm set sweetcorn creams beside it. Put the warm sautéed sweetbreads on top of the sautéed white pudding to the other side and then garnish with a roasted grelot onion. Pour 1 tablespoon of the reserved sweetcorn purée over the set sweetcorn cream and garnish with deep-fried sage leaf and dried sweetcorn kernels. Dot around the sage juices, spoon the Pinot Gris sauce over the guinea hen breasts and finish with the pieces of crispy skin.

FINGAL FERGUSON OF THE AWARD-WINNING GUBBEEN SMOKEHOUSE PRODUCES HIGH-QUALITY SMOKED BACON AND OTHER CURED MEATS FROM WHEY-FED PIGS ON THE FERGUSONS' FARM IN SCHULL, WEST CORK.

BRAISED TOP RIB *of* PRIME HEREFORD BEEF *and* SKERRIES NATIVE POTATOES *with* BUTTERMILK *and* SAVOY CABBAGE, RICH RED WINE *and* SHALLOT SAUCE

FOR THE BRAISED BEEF
3 kg top rib of beef on the bone
3 onions, sliced
4 large carrots, roughly chopped
2 celery sticks, roughly chopped
2 garlic bulbs, sliced in half
3 bay leaves
large handful each fresh thyme and rosemary sprigs
2 litres red wine
50 ml vegetable oil
2 litres chicken stock (page 285)

FOR THE SAVOY CABBAGE
1 Savoy cabbage, tough core removed

FOR THE BUTTERMILK POTATO PURÉE
AND CRISPY POTATOES
1.5 kg Skerries native potatoes, scrubbed
150 ml milk
40 g spring onions, finely sliced
1 tbsp thickener (glossary)
200 g unsalted butter, chilled and diced
150 ml buttermilk

FOR THE BEEF SAUCE
250 ml red wine sauce (page 285)
50 ml cream
50–60 small Paris brown mushrooms, stems removed
50 g butter
50 g shallots, finely chopped
30 ml tarragon vinegar reduction (page 287)
50 ml red wine shallot essence (page 278)

TO SERVE
40 g butter, diced
4 tsp butter emulsion (page 278)

SERVES 8

This is really the very best that our grass-based agricultural economy has to offer. From the richly textured and somewhat fatty top rib of beef cooked on the bone to the very floury Skerries native potatoes. The twist here is the addition of the buttermilk to the potato purée, giving it a slightly acidulated flavour, and this combined with the crispy potato skin and small pieces of baked potato make it the complete picture.

BRAISED BEEF

Place the beef in a deep tray with the vegetables, herbs and wine, ensuring the meat is completely submerged. Chill for 24 hours. Preheat the oven to 90°C. Drain the meat in a colander over a clean pan, bring the liquid to the boil for 2–3 minutes to solidify any impurities and then pass through a fine chinois. Dry the beef with kitchen paper and heat half the vegetable oil in a pan. Sauté the beef in batches until well caramelised all over, being careful not to burn it. Meanwhile, heat the rest of the oil in a pan large enough to hold the meat, vegetables and liquid. Add the vegetables and cook over a medium to high heat, stirring frequently, until well browned. Add the browned meat and pour over the reserved liquid and the stock. Cover the surface with greaseproof paper and wrap in 2 layers of foil, then cook in the oven for 9–10 hours until the beef is completely tender and the ribs can easily be pulled out. Cool to room temperature and then lift out the beef. Take out the ribs and remove the connective tissue. Press the remaining meat lightly between 2 trays with a weight on top and leave until cold. When cold, slice the beef into 8 × 150 g portions. Bring the reserved cooking liquid to the boil and reduce to 1 litre. Chill until needed.

SAVOY CABBAGE

Remove the central ribs from the cabbage leaves and blanch in a pan of boiling salted water until just cooked. Refresh in a bowl of iced water, pat dry with kitchen paper and then cut into ribbons. Cover and chill until needed.

BUTTERMILK POTATO PURÉE AND CRISPY POTATOES

Preheat a steam oven to 140°C on 50 per cent steam. Bake the potatoes for 30 minutes or until completely cooked through. Alternatively, boil in salted water until tender. Combine the milk and spring onions in a small pan, and warm through, being careful not to boil, then remove from the heat and add the onion powder if using. Leave to infuse. While the potatoes are still warm, reserve 2, then peel the rest, reserving the skins, and put the flesh through a mouli to make 600 g of milled potato. Pass the spring onion infusion through a chinois and whisk in the thickener, a pinch at a time, until thickened. Pour onto the milled potato and transfer to a blender. Add the butter and buttermilk, a little at a time, then pass through a drum sieve. Keep warm. Meanwhile, preheat the oven to 150°C. Cut the reserved potatoes in half and scoop out the flesh onto a tray, then break into pieces. Add the potato skins and season with salt, then bake in the oven for 10 minutes until the potato pieces are golden brown and the skins are crispy. Break the potato skins into similar-sized pieces. Keep warm. These are all best made before serving.

BEEF SAUCE

Put 200 ml of the reserved cooking liquid in a pan with the red wine sauce and bring to the boil, then stir in the cream and pass through a fine chinois into a clean pan. Sauté the mushrooms in the butter over a medium to high heat until cooked through. Reduce the shallots with the tarragon vinegar until the vinegar has evaporated. Add to the sauce with the mushrooms, then whisk in the red wine shallot essence. Keep warm.

SERVING

Preheat the oven to 140°C. Heat the remaining 800 ml of the beef cooking liquid in a sauté pan and whisk in the butter, then add the slices of beef. Transfer to the oven for 10 minutes to warm through, turning once. Heat the cabbage ribbons in the butter emulsion. Put a large spoonful of the buttermilk purée in the centre of each warmed serving plate and tap the underside to spread it. Turn the beef again in the glaze and then place it in the centre of the purée. Stick pieces of the crispy potatoes, skins and cabbage ribbons into the surface of the purée, then spoon the beef sauce over the meat.

ROASTED WOODCOCK *with* RED CABBAGE, SMOKED POTATO *and* WILD MUSHROOM GRATIN *with* SMOKED BACON COOKED *in* YEAST

FOR THE RED CABBAGE

30 g unsalted butter
1 onion, thinly sliced
100 g smoked bacon rind
75 ml Cabernet Sauvignon vinegar
400 g red cabbage, core removed and very thinly sliced
1 cooking apple, peeled, cored and coarsely grated
200 ml red wine
125 ml port
25 g demerara sugar
2 tsp red cabbage spice (glossary)
1 bay leaf
juice of 1 orange
zest of ½ orange
a little thickener (glossary)

FOR THE CEP GRATIN

15 g duck fat
60 g smoked bacon, cut into lardons
2 shallots, finely diced
10 cm piece leek, finely diced
½ stick celery, finely diced
2 garlic cloves, finely chopped
250 g cep mushrooms, trimmed and finely sliced
25 ml olive oil
300 ml Madeira
600 ml double chicken stock (page 286)

FOR THE ROASTED WOODCOCK

8 whole woodcock, plucked
8 thin slices lardo di colonnata (glossary)
24 thin slices yeast-cooked bacon (page 288)
2 tbsp vegetable oil
400 g unsalted butter, diced
8 rye bread croûtons (page 277)

FOR THE SMOKED POTATO FOAM

200 ml milk, plus extra if needed
700 g smoked potato purée (page 283) or normal potato
 purée is fine (page 283)
30 g Parmesan, freshly grated
3 egg yolks
few drops white truffle oil

TO SERVE

100 g chanterelle and/or girolle mushrooms, trimmed and
 halved if large, optional
a little vegetable oil, optional
400 ml Madeira jus (page 279)
4 tbsp pata negra fat (glossary)
1 tbsp aged sherry vinegar

SERVES 8

Woodcock is just about
perfect in November.
It migrates back from
Scandinavia to us and at
this stage you have a very
muscular bird, so it is better
if it has been here a couple
of weeks to fatten up. We
cook it with the entrails and
the liver which give it a rich
gamey flavour. A real hearty
dish.

RED CABBAGE

Preheat the oven to 140°C. Melt the butter in a flameproof casserole dish and sweat the onion and bacon rind over a low heat until soft. Add the vinegar and reduce by half. Add the other ingredients, except for the thickener, mix well and bring to a simmer. Cover the surface with a greaseproof paper cartouche and transfer to the oven for 40 minutes or until the cabbage is softened. Strain the cabbage in a colander, reserving the liquid. Put the liquid in a clean pan and bring to a simmer. Whisk in the thickener, a pinch at a time, until the liquid becomes a syrup, then fold back into the cabbage. Season with salt and black pepper. Chill until needed – ideally this should be made the day before.

CEP GRATIN

Heat the duck fat in a pan over a medium heat and add the lardons, shallots, leek, celery and garlic, then sweat until softened. Sauté the ceps in the oil in a frying pan and add to the vegetables. Turn up the heat, add 250 ml of the Madeira and cook until the liquid is reduced to a syrup. Add the stock, a little at a time, continuously reducing until the liquid reaches a jus consistency. Add the rest of the Madeira and season with salt and pepper to taste.

ROASTED WOODCOCK

Preheat the oven to 180°C. Wrap the breast of each bird first with 1 slice of lardo and then with 3 slices of the yeast-cooked bacon. Truss the birds with butcher's string. Heat a little oil in 2 large ovenproof pans and sear the birds on all sides until nicely coloured. Add the butter – around 50 g per bird. Allow to foam and baste the birds with the pan juices. Transfer to the oven and roast for 6 minutes. Baste again and transfer to a cooling rack to rest for 5 minutes.

SMOKED POTATO FOAM

Bring the milk up to the boil in a pan. Then use a large whisk to mix in the smoked potato purée, followed by the Parmesan. When cool, whisk in the egg yolks – the mixture should be a smooth, runny purée, but if it is too stiff, add a little more warm milk. Add a few drops of truffle oil to taste and make sure everything is thoroughly mixed, then pass through a chinois and put into a foam gun. Charge with 2 gas chargers and keep warm in a pan of hot water.

TO FINISH THE WOODCOCK

Lift the bacon off the woodcocks and reserve. Remove the head of each bird and split lengthways along the beak. Carve off the breasts and the legs. Remove the liver from the cavities of the birds, roughly chop and season with salt and pepper, then spoon onto the warmed rye bread croûton. Keep warm.

SERVING

Warm the cep casserole in a pan. If using the mushrooms, heat a sauté pan with the oil and use to sauté the mushrooms over a high heat until soft. Then mix the sautéed mushrooms into the cep casserole, place 2 tablespoons onto each warmed serving plate and pipe potato foam to cover. Put each plate under a hot grill until the potato is browned. Heat the Madeira jus with the pata negra fat and aged sherry vinegar. Warm the red cabbage in a pan and add 2 spoonfuls to each plate. Top with the woodcock breasts. Arrange the legs and one half of the head on each plate with the chopped liver and rye bread croûton. Finish with the reserved pieces of the bacon and the warmed Madeira jus.

BRAISED STUFFED HARE *with a* RICH RED WINE SAUCE *and*
GRATINATED CAULIFLOWER *with* TRUFFLE

Cauliflower and hare are two of the most wonderful products from the winter larder. One is very common and the other is now very rare. They come together here to make a decadently rich feast. Cauliflower with truffle is a magnificent combination which adds extra richness to the hare.

FOR THE HARE
2.5 kg hare
2 onions, sliced
2 carrots, chopped
4 celery sticks, chopped
4 garlic cloves, crushed
1 bay leaf
handful each fresh thyme and rosemary sprigs
½ tsp black peppercorns
½ tsp juniper berries
1 litre red wine

FOR THE FOIE GRAS
400 g piece foie gras
140 g Cognac
2–3 pinches of sugar

FOR THE FARCE
10 g white bread
30 ml cream, well chilled
30 g hare trimmings, taken from the reserved shoulders of the hare
30 g hare offal, taken from the hare
1 egg, well chilled
140 g pork belly, well chilled
100 g streaky bacon, chopped and well chilled
50 g veal trimmings, well chilled
80 g wild mushrooms, such as ceps, chanterelles or girolles, trimmed
30 g shallot, diced
small handful flat-leaf parsley leaves, finely chopped
65 g black truffles
20 ml white truffle oil
2 pinches of ground allspice

FOR THE HARE SAUCE
1 hare carcass, reserved from boning out the hare
4 tbsp vegetable oil
1 litre reserved marinade liquor, from marinating the hare
all the reserved vegetables and spices from marinating the hare
3 litres chicken stock or double chicken stock (page 285 or 286)
a little thickener (glossary)

TO MAKE THE HARE
300 g lardo di colonnata (glossary), frozen and thinly sliced
30 g butter
4 tbsp reserved hare sauce

TO SERVE
250 g cauliflower purée (page 233)
8 cooked cauliflower florets (page 276)
16 cooked cauliflower slices (page 276)
4 tbsp butter emulsion (page 278)
100 ml Parmesan cream (page 277)
2 tbsp Parmesan, freshly grated
20 ml red wine shallot essence (page 278)
30 g butter, diced
16 pieces dried cauliflower (page 278)
25 g black truffle

SERVES 8

HARE

Take the shoulders off the hare and make up 30 g of trimmings to use in the farce. Set aside until needed. Remove the heart, lungs, kidneys and liver. Discard the heart and reserve the rest to use in the farce – you'll need 30 g in total. Set aside until needed. Debone the rest of the hare: start with a sharp boning knife at one side of the hare and work around the carcass, over the backbone to the other side, lifting the meat off the bone as you go, being careful not to cut through the flesh. Put the meat into a casserole with the vegetables, herbs, spices and wine, and leave to marinate for 24 hours in the fridge. Reserve the carcass to use in the sauce.

FOIE GRAS

Devein the foie gras and spread out in a tray. Sprinkle with the sugar and season with salt and black pepper. Flambé the Cognac and leave to cool. Pour over the foie gras and leave to marinate for 3 hours, then roll into a long cylinder the length of the hare. Wrap tightly in clingfilm and chill for another 6 hours to firm up the shape.

FARCE

Soak the bread in the cream and put through a mincer with the reserved hare trimmings and offal, egg, pork belly, bacon, veal, mushrooms, shallot, parsley and black truffles. Mix in the truffle oil and allspice, then season with salt and black pepper. Take the hare out of the marinade and spread on a clean work surface. Strain the marinade through a colander into a clean pan and reserve. Reserve the drained vegetables, herbs and spices to use in the sauce. Unwrap the foie gras and discard the clingfilm. Spread the farce down the middle of the hare in a line approximately 10 cm wide and place the marinated foie gras in the middle of this. Use the sides of the hare to fold the farce around the foie gras and then wrap the hare around so that the foie gras and farce are in the middle.

HARE SAUCE

Roughly chop the reserved hare carcass with a heavy knife and sauté in a pan in half of the oil until well browned. Bring the reserved marinade liquor to the boil for 2–3 minutes to solidify any impurities. Pass the liquid through a fine chinois. Sauté the reserved marinated vegetables, herbs and spices in the rest of the vegetable oil in a large pan until well caramelised. Add the hare bones, solidified marinade liquor and chicken stock, and bring to a simmer for 40 minutes. Pass through a chinois into a clean pan and bring back to the boil, reducing to 300 ml. Thicken with the thickener, a pinch at a time, and pass through a double layer of muslin – you will need 300 ml for the sauce and an additional 4 tablespoons to reheat the hare.

TO MAKE THE HARE

Cover a large sheet of greaseproof paper with the thinly sliced lardo and place the rolled hare on one side. Use the paper to roll the hare in the lardo, then roll it tightly in clingfilm and tie the ends. Tie the roll tightly with butcher's string at 2 cm intervals and vacuum pack. Preheat a water bath to 55°C. Cook the hare in the water bath for 9 hours, then transfer to an ice bath to cool completely. When cool, cut 8 × 4 cm portions and vacuum pack 4 in a single layer in 2 bags, each with a knob of butter and 2 tablespoons of the reserved hare sauce.

SERVING

Heat a water bath to 60°C and preheat a grill. Heat the hare portions in the water bath for 10 minutes. Warm the cauliflower purée and florets in a small pan and heat the cauliflower slices in the butter emulsion in a separate pan. Spoon the cauliflower purée onto the left-hand side of each warmed serving plate into 2 × 4–6 ml oval moulds. Cover generously with Parmesan cream and sprinkle over the grated Parmesan, then gratinate under the grill. Heat the hare sauce in a small pan with the red wine shallot essence and whisk in the butter. When warm, add the hare portion on the right-hand side and pour over a little of the hare sauce. Finish each one with 2 cauliflower slices and 2 pieces of dried cauliflower, and then shave some black truffle over the top.

BREAST of PHEASANT *with a* LIGHT MORTEAU SAUSAGE STUFFING *and* LEG GLAZED *with a* BLACK PUDDING *and* WALNUT CRUST, FRIED CABBAGE *and a* BURNT ONION STUFFED *with* CRUSHED JERUSALEM ARTICHOKE, PHEASANT SAUCE *and* SAGE JUICE

FOR THE PHEASANT
4 pheasants, plucked and cleaned
zest of 1 orange
1 each fresh rosemary and thyme sprigs
8 g Lucky duck spice mix (glossary)
30 g rock salt
500 g duck fat

FOR THE BLACK PUDDING CRUST
100 g shelled walnuts
350 g Jack McCarthy's black pudding, casing removed and roughly chopped
100 g fine white breadcrumbs
150 g unsalted butter, at room temperature

FOR THE PHEASANT STUFFING
1 slice white bread
75 ml milk
25 g cooked ham, chopped
60 g pork belly, chopped
40 g pancetta, sliced
25 g lardo di colonnata (glossary)
25 g Morteau sausage (glossary), chopped
1 egg
30 g Parmesan, freshly grated
1 tbsp chopped fresh flat-leaf parsley

FOR THE CRUSHED JERUSALEM ARTICHOKES AND EMULSION
1 onion, finely chopped
100 g smoked bacon or bacon rind
2 fresh thyme sprigs
20 ml olive oil
400 g Jerusalem artichokes
300 ml milk
500 ml cream
5 drops white truffle oil (glossary), optional

FOR THE ROASTED ARTICHOKES
4 Jerusalem artichokes, scrubbed, evenly sized
125 g unsalted butter

FOR THE BURNT ONIONS
100 g butter
1 tsp sugar
pinch of onion powder (glossary)
4 small white onions, peeled and cut in half lengthways

TO SERVE
8 x 40 g portions pommes Dauphine (page 280)
vegetable oil, for deep-frying
400 ml pheasant sauce (page 285)
40 g butter
2 tbsp melted pheasant fat, optional, this can be reserved from making pheasant stock (page 286)
2 tbsp aged sherry vinegar
8 fried cabbage leaves (page 279), Savoy
30 ml sage juice (page 279)
about 1 tsp onion powder (glossary)

SERVES 8

Pheasant is a real festive dish which appears on our menu in November. It is a really popular item, but it needs to be hung for 14–17 days at least, then you get a lovely, rounded gamey flavour to match all the other great flavours of Christmas.

PHEASANT

Remove the wings from the pheasants, take the breasts off the bone and trim down, then reserve. Remove the legs and then cut off the thighs to use for the confit. (The wings and drumsticks can be used for pheasant sauce, page 285.) Pulse the orange zest with the herbs, spice mix and salt in a blender. Rub into the pheasant thighs, cover with clingfilm and refrigerate overnight. The next day, preheat the oven to 140°C. Put the duck fat into a tray deep enough to hold the pheasant thighs as well and place in the oven to heat up. When the oil is hot, put in the pheasant thighs, ensuring they are completely submerged. Cook for 40 minutes – the thighs are cooked when the thighbone can be twisted and pulled out with no resistance. Leave to cool, and when they reach room temperature, remove the thighbones. Press the confit between 2 trays with a weight on top for 2 hours, then trim into a rectangular shape.

BLACK PUDDING CRUST

Blend the walnuts in a food processor, then add the black pudding and blend to a paste. Add the breadcrumbs and butter, and blitz everything together. Roll the black pudding paste out between 2 sheets of greaseproof paper to a 3 mm thickness, then cut into rectangles and use to cover the confit.

PHEASANT STUFFING

Soak the bread in milk, then drain. Using a mincer, finely mince all the ingredients together and mix well. Preheat a steam oven to 70°C. Carefully stuff the pheasant breasts in an even layer between the skin and breast. Place in a roasting tray and cook on 100 per cent steam for 12 minutes. Cool.

CRUSHED JERUSALEM ARTICHOKES AND EMULSION

Preheat the oven to 170°C. Sweat the onion, bacon and thyme in the oil in an ovenproof pan until softened, without colouring. Peel and slice the artichokes, and add to the pan with the milk and cream. Cover and place in the oven for 30 minutes until tender. Reserve 150 g of the cooked artichokes. Strain off the cooking liquid and reserve 500 ml. Reduce the rest of the liquid to a thick cream consistency, being careful not to let it catch. With the back of a fork, crush the cooked artichokes, adding back enough of the reduced liquid to make a chunky paste, then season with salt and black pepper, and add the white truffle oil if using. To make the emulsion, blend the reserved liquid with 150 g of the reserved artichokes until completely smooth. Pass through a fine chinois and season with salt and black pepper. Put into a foam gun, charge with 2 gas chargers and keep warm.

ROASTED ARTICHOKES

Bring a sauté pan up to a medium heat and add the butter. Move the pan constantly while the butter melts and then begins to turn brown. At this stage add the artichokes, maintaining a medium heat. Turn constantly and baste the artichokes with the brown butter until they are a deep golden brown and completely cooked through when tested with a knife; there should be no resistance at all. Cool.

BURNT ONIONS

Preheat the oven to 160°C. Heat an ovenproof sauté pan until hot. Melt the butter, then add the sugar, onion powder and salt, ensuring it is evenly distributed. Place the onions in the pan, cut side down, and cook without moving until the edges are caramelised a dark brown. Transfer to the oven and roast for 4 minutes until tender. Carefully separate the layers – you need 8 in total.

SERVING

Preheat an oven to 150°C and preheat the grill. Place the stuffed breasts skin side down in a large, cold, ovenproof sauté pan. Bring the pan up to a medium heat and cook until the skins are well caramelised and crispy, then transfer to the oven for 4 minutes. Leave to rest for 2 minutes on a cooling rack before carving in half lengthways. Put the thighs on a tray in the oven for 5 minutes. Place the black pudding crust on top and transfer to the grill for another 3 minutes to crisp up the crust and then place on each warmed serving plate with a carved breast. Meanwhile, slice the artichokes in half lengthways and warm through in the oven. Place a piece on each plate. Heat the crushed artichokes in a pan. Warm the onion shells under the grill. Fill each shell with the hot artichoke mixture and put on the plate. Roll the portions of Dauphine mixture and deep-fry at 190°C in the oil until golden brown. Drain on kitchen paper and season with salt and black pepper. Meanwhile, heat the pheasant sauce in a small pan and whisk in the butter with the pheasant fat if using. Stir in the aged sherry vinegar and keep warm. Finish by arranging a cabbage leaf and a pomme Dauphine on each plate, pour over the pheasant sauce and add some dots of sage juice. Pipe the artichoke emulsion onto the filled onion shells and dust with onion powder.

ARUN KAPIL IS AT THE HELM OF GREEN SAFFRON IN MIDLETON, COUNTY CORK. WE WORKED WITH HIM TO CREATE TWENTY UNIQUE BLENDS FOR OUR KITCHEN. HE IS AN EXPERT SPICE GRINDER, WHO USES THE HIGHEST GRADE SPICES FROM SMALL HOLDINGS IN HIS NATIVE INDIA. HE CONTINUES A MUCH OLDER TRADITION WHERE THE ENGLISH MARKET IN CORK BRINED AND SPICED MEATS FOR THE BRITISH EMPIRE.

CONFIT HALIBUT *with* JAPANESE SPICES *and* CITRUS FRUIT, ROASTED WHITE ASPARAGUS *and* SPIDER CRAB

FOR THE HALIBUT
3 litres light olive oil
10 garlic cloves, lightly crushed
zest of 1 orange
5 each fresh rosemary and thyme sprigs
5 bay leaves
1 tsp coriander seeds
10 star anise
8 x 200 g halibut tranches
1 tsp Japanese spices (glossary), optional
2 tbsp vegetable oil

FOR THE WHITE ASPARAGUS PURÉE
25 g butter
2 shallots, sliced
1 bunch white asparagus, peeled and woody stalks removed, chopped into small pieces
100 ml milk
100 ml water
½ tsp icing sugar
3–4 drops white truffle oil, optional
a little thickener (glossary)

FOR THE CRAB ESSENCE
1 kg live spider crabs
2 onions, sliced
2 carrots, sliced
1 celery head, sliced
2 fennel bulbs, sliced
2 tbsp extra virgin olive oil
2 bay leaves
200 ml Pernod
200 ml brandy
300 ml white wine
2 litres fish stock (page 286) or water
50 g semi-dried tomatoes (page 287)
40 g fresh basil leaves
a little xanthan powder (glossary)

FOR THE PICKLED WHITE ASPARAGUS
150 ml rice wine vinegar
2 tsp sugar
zest of ½ a lemon
4 white asparagus spears

TO SERVE
150 g potatoes, Rooster, cut into 1 cm dice
150 g cooked white crabmeat
12 fresh basil leaves, finely sliced
24 roasted white asparagus (page 284)
24 small broccoli leaves
4 tbsp butter emulsion (page 278)
100 ml lemon purée butter sauce (page 285)
1 blood orange, peeled, segmented and roughly chopped
½ lemon and ½ lime, peeled, segmented and roughly chopped
2 tsp dehydrated soy granules (glossary), optional

SERVES 8

What I love about this dish is how the Japanese spices combine with the citrus fruit and crab – it is a wonderful combination. Once you've used the aromatic oil for the confit, it can be strained and used again.

HALIBUT

Preheat the oven to 50°C. To make the aromatic oil, place the olive oil in a pan with the garlic, orange zest, herbs, coriander seeds and star anise. Simmer for 2 minutes and then pour into a deep tray large enough to hold the halibut fillets in a single layer – they need to be completely submerged in the oil. Place in the oven for 30 minutes. Season the halibut with salt and the Japanese spices if using, and pan fry briefly in a hot pan in the vegetable oil until lightly seared on both sides. Transfer to the preheated confit oil and cook for 20 minutes until the halibut is just cooked through and tender. Leave sitting in the oil.

WHITE ASPARAGUS PURÉE

Heat the butter in a pan and sweat the shallots until soft but not coloured. Add the asparagus and sweat gently for 8–10 minutes, without colouring. Add the milk and water, and simmer for 15 minutes until the asparagus is completely soft. Drain in a colander, reserving the liquid, then blend the shallot and asparagus mix with enough of the cooking liquid to make a smooth purée. Add the thickener a pinch at a time. Pass through a fine chinois and add the sugar, then season with salt, white pepper and truffle oil if using.

CRAB ESSENCE

Kill the crabs and place in a large bowl, then crush down to a paste with a rolling pin. Meanwhile, sauté the vegetables and bay leaves in the oil over a medium heat until well caramelised. Add the alcohol and reduce by half, then add the crab mixture with the stock or water. Bring to the boil and simmer for 40 minutes. Remove from the heat, add the basil and leave for 10–15 minutes. Strain through a colander and then through a double layer of muslin into a clean pan. Return to the boil and reduce to 500 ml. Transfer to a blender and blitz with the semi-dried tomatoes. Pass through a fine chinois and thicken with the xanthan powder.

PICKLED WHITE ASPARAGUS

Boil the vinegar in a pan with the sugar, lemon zest and a pinch of salt until the sugar has dissolved, then cool. Meanwhile, shave the asparagus on a mandolin and sprinkle with a good pinch of salt. Leave for 20 minutes, then rinse and dry with kitchen paper. Add to the pickle and leave for 30 minutes.

SERVING

Preheat the grill. Cook the potato dice in boiling salted water until tender. Warm 250 ml of the white asparagus purée in a pan with the white crabmeat and cooked potato dice, then fold in the basil. Spread 2 tablespoons of the white asparagus purée onto each warmed serving plate and top with the crab and potato mix followed by the roasted asparagus. Cook the broccoli leaves in the butter emulsion. Warm the lemon purée butter in a separate pan and fold in the blood orange and the lemon and lime pieces, then allow to just warm through. Lift the halibut out of the confit oil and carefully remove the skin and bones, keeping the shape of the tranche intact. Flash under the grill on a tray for 2 minutes to warm through. Place on the plate and dress with the broccoli leaves and lemon purée butter. Add some dots of crab essence and 2 pieces of the pickled asparagus. If using, sprinkle over some dehydrated soy granules to finish each plate.

TERRY **BUTTERLY** OF COASTGUARD SEAFOODS
IS A VETERAN OF THE SEA, A RACONTEUR
AND A MAN WITH GENEROSITY AT HIS CORE.
NO LOBSTER OR CRAB IS SAFE FROM THIS MAN.

TURBOT COOKED *with* CITRUS SALT, BROCCOLI PURÉE *and* FRIED POLENTA, CRAB *and* YUZU DRESSING *with* DILL OIL

This combines the best of what the Atlantic has to offer. The turbot is a meaty, textural fish, and when combined with purple sprouting broccoli, it is an ideal dish for February and March. The yuzu, a strong Japanese citrus fruit, works well with the robust turbot, crab and brassica flavours, delivering a simple elegance to this dish.

FOR THE PICKLED BROCCOLI

25 ml white wine
25 ml white wine vinegar
25 ml water
25 g caster sugar
1 fresh thyme sprig
1 bay leaf
zest of ½ lemon and ½ orange
100 g broccoli stems

FOR THE POLENTA

1 tbsp light olive oil, extra for greasing
1 shallot, very finely diced
1 small garlic clove, very finely chopped
1 tsp fresh thyme leaves
750 ml chicken or crab stock (page 285 or 287)
125 g polenta
35 g cold pressed rapeseed oil (glossary)

FOR THE CRAB AND YUZU DRESSING

200 ml ice filtered crab stock (page 287)
2 g yuzu salt (glossary)
20 ml fresh yuzu juice (glossary) or use lemon juice
a little thickener (glossary)

FOR THE BROCCOLI PURÉE

1 tbsp light olive oil
50 g broccoli trimmings
250 g broccoli stems, sliced
1 shallot, finely sliced
½ garlic clove, finely chopped
1 anchovy fillet, drained and finely chopped

FOR THE TURBOT

40 ml vegetable oil
8 × 160 g turbot fillets, skinned and boned
35 g butter, diced
35 ml vermouth or white wine
squeeze of lemon juice
2 tsp citrus salt (page 284)

TO SERVE

4 tbsp vegetable oil
100 g purple sprouting broccoli, small florets and leaves
2 tbsp butter emulsion (page 278)
2 tsp dill oil (page 281)

SERVES 8

PICKLED BROCCOLI

Bring all the ingredients, except the broccoli, to the boil, stirring to dissolve the sugar, and then cool. Meanwhile, use a Japanese mandolin to finely shave the broccoli stems. Blanch in a pan of salted water until just cooked. Refresh in a bowl of iced water. When cool, drain and dry with kitchen paper. Put into a bowl and pour over the pickling liquid. Chill overnight.

POLENTA

Heat the oil in a pan and gently fry the shallot, garlic and thyme until soft but not coloured. Add the stock and bring to a simmer, then add the polenta in a thin stream and cook over a low heat, stirring frequently, until the polenta is completely soft. Add the rapeseed oil and season with salt and black pepper. Pour the polenta into an oiled tray, lined with greaseproof paper – the polenta needs to be 2–3 cm deep. Chill for 3–4 hours until set (overnight is fine too). Turn out the set polenta onto a chopping board and cut into 16 × 1 × 3 cm pieces. Cover with clingfilm and chill until needed.

CRAB AND YUZU DRESSING

Warm the stock in a small pan. Whisk in the yuzu salt and yuzu juice, then whisk in the thickener, a pinch at a time, to thicken slightly. Chill until needed.

BROCCOLI PURÉE

Heat the olive oil in a frying pan and gently fry the broccoli trimmings, shallot, garlic and anchovy until soft, but not coloured. Boil the broccoli stems in a pan of salted water until well cooked and soft. Blend with the broccoli trimmings and mix until smooth. Pass through a chinois into a bowl set over another boil of ice to preserve the colour, and season with salt and black pepper. Chill.

TURBOT

Heat the oil in a frying pan and fry the turbot fillets on both sides for 2–3 minutes until the fish is golden brown, then add knobs of the butter and a splash of vermouth or wine. Allow the liquid to thicken, and use to baste and coat the fish as it cooks. When just cooked, add the lemon juice. Lift the fish onto a tray and sprinkle with the citrus salt. Keep warm.

SERVING

Heat the oil in a sauté pan and fry the polenta pieces in batches until golden brown and crispy. Drain on kitchen paper. Blanch the purple sprouting broccoli in a pan of boiling salted water and refresh in a bowl of iced water, then drain. Heat in the butter emulsion and season with salt and black pepper. Warm the crab and yuzu dressing in a small pan. Warm the broccoli purée in a pan and drag lines of it across the right-hand side of each warmed serving plate, then top with the crispy polenta pieces. Place the turbot on the left-hand side, add 8 pieces of pickled broccoli and scatter over the purple sprouting broccoli. Drizzle over the dressing and dot the dill oil.

HOTPOT of HEREFORD PRIME BEEF with JELLIED CONSOMMÉ and SPRING VEGETABLES

FOR THE BRAISED BEEF
1.8 kg top rib of beef on the bone
1 onion, sliced
1 large carrot, roughly chopped
2 celery sticks, roughly chopped
½ garlic bulb, sliced in half
1 bay leaf
small handful each fresh thyme, sage and rosemary sprigs
1 litre red wine
50 ml vegetable oil
1 litre chicken stock (page 285)

FOR THE BEEF CONSOMMÉ
50 ml vegetable oil
2 kg boneless beef shin, cut into 2.5 cm dice
2 large onions, finely chopped
4 large carrots, finely chopped
3 celery sticks, finely chopped
8 garlic cloves, lightly crushed
375 ml Madeira
5 litres double chicken stock (page 286)
1 tbsp tomato purée

TO CLARIFY THE CONSOMMÉ
200 g beef trimmings
6 egg whites
2 carrots, roughly chopped
1 onion, roughly chopped
3 celery sticks, roughly chopped
1 bunch fresh tarragon
a little thickener (glossary)

FOR THE MUSTARD SAUCE
200 ml mayonnaise (page 280)
2 tbsp wholegrain mustard
1 tbsp creamed horseradish (glossary)
1 tsp lemon juice

FOR THE OX TONGUE
1 pickled Hereford ox tongue
1 large onion, sliced
3 carrots, sliced
3 celery sticks, chopped
3 garlic cloves, lightly crushed
1 bay leaf
handful each fresh thyme and rosemary sprigs
1 tsp each black peppercorns and coriander seeds
100 ml white wine vinegar

FOR THE BABY VEGETABLES
200 g prepared baby vegetables (selection of carrots, turnips, purple sprouting broccoli, broad beans and baby leeks, whatever is in season)

FOR THE PAIN DE MIE DUMPLINGS
320 g pain de mie dough (see onion bread recipe, page 264)

TO SERVE
2 tbsp light olive oil
4 x 200 g Hereford beef fillet medallions
100 ml butter emulsion (page 278)
80 g velvet plopping mushrooms (glossary), trimmed and cut up if large, or use baby button mushrooms

SERVES 8

This is a dish I could stare into for hours. It is a reflection of the fat of the land, presented in a clean and wholesome way, with a feeling of nostalgia for anyone who has drawn comfort from a bowl of good stew.

BRAISED BEEF

Place the beef in a deep tray with the vegetables, herbs and wine, ensuring the meat is completely submerged. Chill for 24 hours. Preheat the oven to 90°C. Drain the meat in a colander over a clean pan and bring the liquid to the boil for 2–3 minutes to solidify any impurities. Pass through a fine chinois. Dry the beef with kitchen paper and heat half the vegetable oil in a pan. Sauté the beef until well caramelised all over, being careful not to burn it. Meanwhile, heat the rest of the oil in a pan large enough to hold the meat, vegetables and liquid. Add the vegetables and cook over a medium to high heat, stirring frequently, until well browned. Add the browned meat and pour over the reserved liquid and the stock. Cover the surface with greaseproof paper and wrap in 2 layers of foil, then cook in the oven for 9–10 hours until the beef is completely tender and the ribs can easily be pulled out. Cool to room temperature, then lift out the beef, take out the ribs and remove the connective tissue. Press the meat lightly between 2 trays with a weight on top until cold. Pass the cooking liquid through a fine chinois into a clean pan and reserve. When cold, slice the beef into 8 x 60 g portions. Chill until needed.

BEEF CONSOMMÉ

Heat half the oil in a large pan and thoroughly caramelise the diced beef shin, then remove from the pan and drain off the fat. Add the rest of the oil to the pan and sauté the vegetables until well browned. Remove from the pan and drain off the fat. Return the meat and the vegetables to the pan, cook for 5 minutes, then add the Madeira and simmer until reduced to a glaze. Pour in the stock and add the tomato purée. Bring to the boil, then reduce to a simmer and cook for 1 hour, skimming off any fat as it collects on the surface. Strain through a chinois, then through a double layer of muslin. Leave to cool.

CLARIFYING THE CONSOMMÉ

Put the beef trimmings in a blender with the egg whites, vegetables and tarragon, and blend to a rough purée. Pour the reserved beef stock into a pan and whisk in the beef and egg white mixture, then slowly bring back up to a very low boil. When the egg whites have solidified on top, pass through a double layer of muslin. Thicken, a pinch at a time, until lightly jellied, and season with salt and black pepper – you will need 2.6 litres. Chill.

MUSTARD SAUCE

Combine all the ingredients together in a bowl and then transfer to a squeezy bottle.

OX TONGUE

Place the tongue in a pan, cover with cold water and bring to the boil, then simmer for a few minutes to clean the tongue. Discard the water and clean the pan. Put the tongue into a clean pan with the vegetables, herbs, spices and vinegar, and cover with fresh water. Bring back to the boil and simmer for 3–4 hours, topping up the water as required. Cool the tongue in the liquid, then peel and cut 8 × 50 g portions. Chill.

BABY VEGETABLES

Scrub and trim the baby vegetables where necessary, then blanch separately in a pan of boiling salted water until just tender. Refresh in a bowl of iced water, then drain and chill until needed.

PAIN DE MIE DUMPLINGS

Break the dough into 16 × 20 g pieces and roll into dumplings. Arrange on a tray and leave to prove for 45 minutes in a warm place. Bring 500 ml of the beef consommé to a gentle simmer, drop in the dumplings and poach for around 10 minutes, turning occasionally, until the dough is cooked through. Keep warm.

SERVING

Preheat the oven to 160°C. Bring 500 ml of the beef consommé to a gentle simmer in a pan. Heat the oil in a sauté pan and season the beef medallions generously with salt and black pepper. Sear until they are well caramelised all over, then remove from the pan and drop into the gently simmering beef consommé for 4 minutes. Lift out of the consommé and leave to rest in a warm place for another 4 minutes, then trim and slice each piece in half. Warm the braised beef and tongue portions in a little of the reserved braised beef cooking liquor in a tray in the oven. Warm the blanched baby vegetables in the butter emulsion and season with salt and black pepper, then drain off any excess and keep warm. Bring 1.6 litres of the beef consommé to the boil in a large pan and cook the mushrooms for 1 minute. Arrange a piece of tongue, braised beef and medallion on each warmed serving dish with the baby vegetables, and then ladle over the consommé and mushroom mixture. Finish with a spoonful of mustard sauce and the dumplings.

MAURICE KETTYLE IS THE OWNER OF KETTYLE IRISH FOODS BASED IN THE FECUND COUNTRYSIDE OF COUNTY FERMANAGH. WE RELIED ON HIS EXPERT EYE IN HAND-PICKING THE IRISH ANGUS BEEF FROM THE SLANEY VALLEY FOR THE QUEEN'S DINNER.

ROASTED SQUAB PIGEON *with* PICKLED BABY SHIITAKE *and* MUSHROOM KETCHUP, ROASTED WHITE ASPARAGUS *with* ROCKET JUICE *and* ROCKET OIL

There is a lovely combination here between the sharp mushroom ketchup, the peppery rocket and the salty, smoky bacon with the squab. A light, aromatic counterfoil to the rich, dense meat.

FOR THE PIGEON

8 squab pigeons
zest of 1 orange
9 fresh thyme sprigs
1 fresh rosemary sprig
8 g Lucky Duck spice mix (glossary)
300 g duck fat
30 g rock salt
4 garlic cloves, crushed
8 tsp extra virgin olive oil

FOR THE MUSHROOM KETCHUP AND MUSHROOM JUICES

500 g Paris brown mushrooms
4 g salt
1 tsp Chardonnay vinegar
1 tsp Kikkoman soy sauce
4 g sugar
1 tbsp thickener (glossary)

TO SERVE

3 tbsp vegetable oil
40 g unsalted butter
100 ml pigeon glaze (page 279)
16 roasted white asparagus (page 284)
24–32 pickled shiitake mushrooms (page 282)
100 ml rocket juices (page 279), in a squeezy bottle
30 ml rocket oil (page 281), in a squeezy bottle
16 slices grilled yeast-cooked bacon (page 288)
handful fresh rocket leaves

SERVES 8

PIGEON

Remove the wings, legs and thighs from each pigeon (the wings and legs can be used for pigeon glaze, page 279). Take out the heart and liver, cover with clingfilm and chill until needed. Remove and discard the wishbone. Pulse the orange zest, 1 thyme sprig, the rosemary, spice mix and rock salt in a blender. Rub into the pigeon thighs, cover with clingfilm and refrigerate overnight. The next day, preheat the oven to 140°C and wash the salt mixture off the pigeon thighs. Put the duck fat into a tray deep enough to hold the pigeon thighs as well and place in the oven to heat up. When the duck fat is hot, add the pigeon thighs, ensuring they are completely submerged. Cook for 25 minutes – the thighs are cooked when the thighbones can be twisted and pulled out with no resistance. Leave to cool, and when they reach room temperature, remove the thighbones. Meanwhile, heat a water bath to 57°C. Vacuum pack each pigeon crown separately with the garlic, thyme and extra virgin olive oil, and cook in the water bath for 40 minutes. Lift out the bags and leave to cool completely in an ice bath. Chill until needed. Alternatively, preheat the oven to 160°C. Sear the pigeons in a sauté pan, then add the thyme and garlic, and roast for 8–10 minutes until just cooked through but still a little rare in the middle.

MUSHROOM KETCHUP AND MUSHROOM JUICES

Chop the mushrooms along with the salt in a food processor, then hang in a muslin bag overnight in the fridge. The next day, bring the juice to the boil in a pan, skimming off any scum that rises to the surface. Put 250 ml in a small pan, add the vinegar, soy sauce and sugar, and whisk in 2 teaspoons of the thickener, a pinch at a time, until thickened. Add to the rest of the mushroom juice and whisk in the remaining thickener, a pinch at a time, to thicken slightly. Pass through a fine chinois and put into a squeezy bottle. Chill until needed and then bring back to room temperature when ready to serve.

SERVING .

Preheat the oven to 180°C and preheat the grill. To finish the pigeon, heat half of the oil and the butter in a sauté pan until foaming and sear the pigeon crowns until golden. Transfer the pan to the oven for 3 minutes, then rest for a further 3 minutes. Warm the pigeon glaze and brush over the rested crowns, then carve off the breasts. Meanwhile, put the confit pigeon thighs on a tray and heat under the grill. Keep warm. Season the reserved livers and hearts, and sauté briefly in a hot pan with the rest of the oil so that they are browned but pink on the inside. Warm the pickled mushrooms and roasted white asparagus on a tray under the grill. Arrange the 2 carved pigeon breasts and confit thighs on each warmed serving plate with the liver and heart. Add 2 roasted white asparagus and 3–4 of the pickled mushrooms. Top each pickled mushroom with the mushroom ketchup and dot each plate with the rocket juice and rocket oil along with the mushroom juice. Finish with the bacon and rocket leaves.

ROASTED SKEAGHANORE DUCK *with* BLOOD ORANGE *and* GLAZED SALSIFY, CONFIT WING *and* GIZZARD *with* PURPLE SPROUTING BROCCOLI

FOR THE DUCK

4 Skeaghanore ducks, wings and gizzards intact
1.2 litres water
200 ml white wine vinegar
100 g golden syrup
8 fresh thyme sprigs
8 garlic cloves, lightly smashed
4 bay leaves
2 oranges, halved
zest of 1 orange
1 sprig fresh rosemary
8 g Lucky Duck spice mix (glossary)
30 g rock salt
500 g duck fat

FOR THE DUCK SAUCE

1 tbsp vegetable oil
2 shallots, quartered
1 carrot, roughly chopped
2 tbsp brown sugar
1 tsp honey
small handful fresh thyme sprigs
1 bay leaf
5 whole cloves
250 ml port
125 ml blood orange juice
100 ml sherry vinegar
250 ml double chicken stock (page 286)
125 ml Madeira jus (page 279)
50 ml blood orange purée (page 283)
a little thickener (glossary)
32 x 3 cm square pieces confit orange (page 276)
32 pieces chopped blood orange segment

FOR THE PURPLE SPROUTING BROCCOLI

8 purple sprouting broccoli spears, trimmed

FOR THE ORANGE GLAZE

juice of 4 blood oranges
25 g sugar
1 tsp blood orange purée (page 283), optional

FOR THE GLAZED SALSIFY

8 salsify roots (glossary)
a little lemon juice
2 tbsp vegetable oil
50 g butter
150 ml Madeira

TO SERVE

4 tbsp olive oil emulsion (page 278)
10 g confit orange (page 276), cut into small dice

SERVES 8

There is nothing as nice as duck cooked on the bone, the only problem is trying to resist eating it when you are carving it. We start this dish the day before it is ready to serve. The legs are not needed for this but they can be confited along with the wings and gizzards and used in another dish.

DUCK

Take the gizzards out of the ducks, put on a plate and cover with clingfilm in the fridge until needed. Bring 200 ml of the water to the boil in a pan with the vinegar and syrup, then leave to cool. In a separate pan, bring the rest of the water to the boil, ladle 2–3 ladlefuls over the duck to open the pores of the skin, then brush the syrup mixture onto the skin of the ducks. Stuff the cavity of each duck with an equal amount of thyme (reserving a sprig to use in the confit), garlic, bay leaf and orange, then truss or tie them, sealing the cavity, and place on a draining tray. Chill overnight. Remove the legs and wings from the ducks, and reserve (the legs are not needed for this recipe but can be confited and used in another dish). Pulse the orange zest with the reserved thyme sprig, rosemary, spice mix and salt in a blender. Rub into the wings and reserved gizzards, cover with clingfilm and refrigerate overnight. The next day, preheat the oven to 140°C. Put the duck fat into a tray deep enough to hold the wings and gizzards as well, and place in the oven to heat up. When the duck fat is hot, put in the wings and gizzards, ensuring they are completely submerged. Cook for 1 1/2 hours until cooked through. Cool to room temperature, then remove from the fat and debone the wings. Trim into a neat shape and chill everything until needed.

DUCK SAUCE

Heat the oil in a large pan and sauté the shallots and carrot over a high heat until slightly burnt. Add the honey and brown sugar, and cook for another few minutes until well caramelised, then add the thyme, bay leaf, cloves and port, and reduce over a high heat to a syrup consistency. Pour on the blood orange juice and reduce by half, then add the sherry vinegar and continue to reduce to a syrup consistency. Pour in the stock and Madeira jus, and simmer for 30 minutes, then whisk in the blood orange purée. Pass through a fine chinois and then through a double layer of muslin into a clean pan. Thicken, a pinch at a time, to a sauce consistency.

PURPLE SPROUTING BROCCOLI

Blanch the broccoli in a large pan of boiling salted water until just tender, then refresh in a bowl of iced water. Drain, cover with clingfilm and chill.

ORANGE GLAZE

Reduce the blood orange juice in a small pan to around 50 ml, then add the sugar and heat until dissolved. Remove from the heat and add the blood orange purée if using.

GLAZED SALSIFY

Scrub the salsify roots under cold running water, peel with a sharp knife and place in a bowl of water with the lemon juice. Heat the oil in a sauté pan and add the salsify. Cook until starting to brown, then add the butter (the butter will foam and turn brown), and season with salt and white pepper. Continue to cook until the salsify is almost soft, then pour off the fat. Return the pan to the heat and add the Madeira . Reduce until it forms a glaze, turning the salsify roots regularly, until they are well coated and glossy. Drain off any excess liquid and keep warm.

SERVING

Preheat the oven to 190°C. Season the ducks generously with salt and black pepper, and place in a tray. Roast for 22–25 minutes, basting several times, until just cooked through but still pink – the core temperature should be 60°C when probed. Leave the ducks to rest for 10 minutes, then carve and brush with the orange glaze. Alternatively, steam the ducks first at 100°C for 5 minutes, then roast for 16 minutes as above, reducing the oven temperature to 180°C. Warm a little duck sauce in a pan and use this to heat the confit gizzards. Place the confit wings on a tray and heat in the oven for 5–6 minutes until hot. Keep warm. Heat the olive oil emulsion in a pan and use to warm the purple broccoli spears. Season with salt and black pepper, then drain off any excess liquid. Heat 200 ml of the duck sauce in a pan, stir in the confit orange and orange pieces, and allow to warm through. Carve the breasts off the glazed ducks and cut each one into 2 pieces. Arrange on warmed serving plates and add a confit wing and half a confit gizzard. Add the salsify and purple sprouting broccoli. Finish with the duck sauce, putting roughly 4 pieces of the confit orange and blood orange segment on each plate.

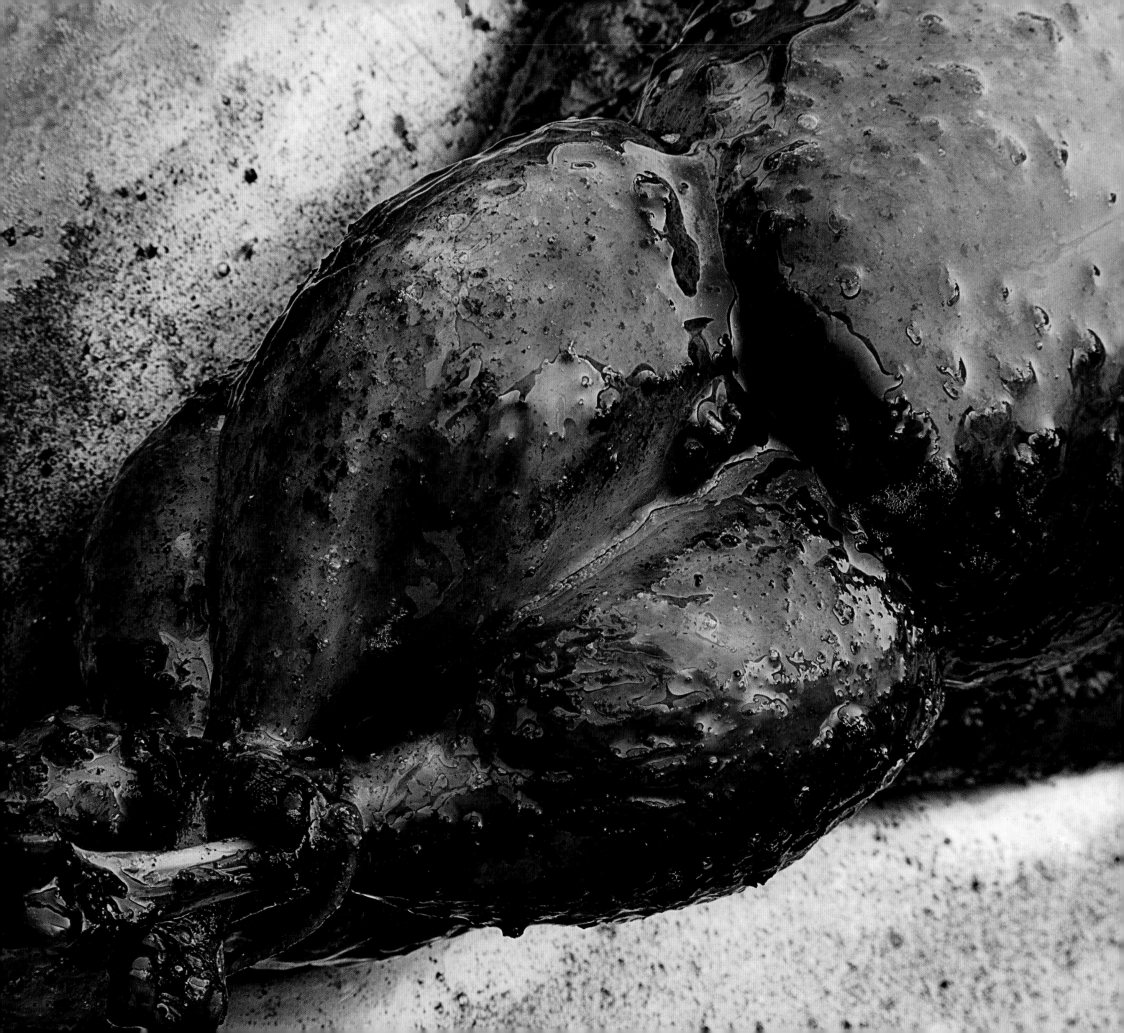

STEAMED CORNED MUTTON *and* CAPER PIE *with a* WHITE ONION PURÉE *and* MUSTARD CREAM SAUCE *with* GREEN VEGETABLES

This is perhaps a forgotten dish as it can be difficult to get mutton, but we shouldn't forget this important part of our culinary history. I could sit down and eat this dish every day. This can also be made with ordinary mutton, but it will need to be seasoned first whereas the corned mutton needs no extra seasoning.

FOR THE MUTTON FILLING AND SAUCE
4 tbsp vegetable oil
1 kg Coughlan Meats corned mutton, cut into 1 cm dice
150 ml Madeira
2 onions, sliced
4 carrots, sliced
4 celery sticks, sliced
3 garlic cloves, finely chopped
1 bay leaf
small handful fresh thyme and rosemary sprigs
1.5 litres double chicken stock (page 286)
50 ml tarragon vinegar reduction (page 287)
a little thickener (glossary)
35 g caper sprout purée (page 283), optional
1 tbsp Dijon mustard
70 g rinsed capers

FOR THE SUET PASTRY
680 g self-raising flour, extra to dust
340 g beef suet
10 g fresh chervil leaves, very finely chopped
200 ml milk
200 ml water
1 egg, beaten

FOR THE MUSTARD CREAM SAUCE
20 g butter
150 g shallots, diced
1 fresh thyme sprig
1 bay leaf
500 ml double chicken stock (page 286)
25 ml tarragon vinegar reduction (page 287)
300 ml cream
2 tbsp wholegrain mustard
1 tbsp Dijon mustard
a little thickener (glossary)

GREEN SPRING VEGETABLES
600 g green spring vegetables (selection of asparagus, purple sprouting broccoli, baby leeks, baby turnips, spring cabbage, broad beans, peas and celery)

TO SERVE
200 g white onion purée (page 284)
200 g butter emulsion (page 278)

SERVES 8

FOR THE MUTTON FILLING AND SAUCE

Preheat the oven to 110°C. Heat half the oil in a sauté pan and caramelise the diced mutton over a fairly high heat. Drain on kitchen paper to remove any excess fat. Deglaze the pan with the Madeira. Heat the rest of the oil in a large pan, add the vegetables and herbs, and cook for 8–10 minutes until tender, without colouring. Add the reduced Madeira with the mutton and the stock. Cover with a double layer of foil, transfer to the oven and cook for 4 hours or until the meat is soft but not falling apart. Strain the cooking liquid into a clean pan, return to the boil and reduce by half, discarding the vegetables and herbs from the meat. Add the tarragon vinegar reduction and thicken, a pinch at a time, to a heavy sauce consistency. Pass through a fine chinois and reserve 200 ml of the sauce to serve. Fold the mutton with enough of the remaining sauce to bind. Add the caper sprout purée if using, along with the mustard and capers. Season with salt and black pepper. Leave to cool and chill until needed.

SUET PASTRY

Blend the flour, 1 teaspoon of salt and the suet together in a food processor on the slowest speed or do this by hand in a bowl with a wooden spoon, then add the chervil and, with the machine running, slowly pour in the milk and water until a dough has formed. Tip onto a lightly floured work surface and knead together briefly, then wrap in clingfilm. Chill for 1 hour to allow the dough to rest. Roll out two-thirds of the pastry to a 2 mm thickness on a lightly floured board and use to line the 8 × 180 g pudding basins. Leave any extra pastry hanging over the sides. Roll out the remainder of the pastry and use to make the lids. Fill the pastry-lined pudding basins with the mutton mixture, brush the edges with the beaten egg and lay over the pastry lids. Press the edges together and trim off any excess pastry. Cover the tops with a pleated double layer of greaseproof paper and a layer of tin foil. Tie in place with string. Chill until needed.

MUSTARD CREAM SAUCE

Heat the butter in a pan and sweat the shallots, thyme and bay leaf until soft. Pour in the stock and reduce to a glaze, then add the tarragon vinegar reduction and cream, and briefly bring back to the boil. Pass through a fine chinois into a clean pan and whisk in the mustards. Thicken with the thickener, adding a pinch at a time.

GREEN SPRING VEGETABLES

Prepare each vegetable and then blanch them separately in a pan of boiling salted water until just tender. Drain and cool in a bowl of iced water. Drain again, peel the broad beans and chill all vegetables on a tray until needed.

SERVING

Cook the corned mutton pies in a steamer or steam oven at 100°C for 30 minutes. Heat the butter emulsion in a sauté pan and use this to warm the prepared green vegetables. Drain and season with salt and black pepper. Keep warm. Warm the white onion purée, mustard cream sauce and reserved mutton sauce in separate small pans. Put 2 tablespoons of white onion purée on one side of each warmed serving plate and swipe with the back of a spoon. Arrange the warmed green vegetables along this and place the mutton pie on the opposite side. Finish with a generous amount each of warm mustard cream and mutton sauce over the pie.

ALAN MURPHY OF COUGHLAN MEATS IN CORK'S
ENGLISH MARKET IS A FIFTH-GENERATION BUTCHER.
USING THEIR GREAT-GRANDFATHER'S RECIPE, THEY
CORN MUTTON FOR FOUR DAYS TO PRODUCE THEIR
HIGHLY LAUDED CORNED MUTTON

PORK CHEEK GRATINATED *with* JOWL, POTATO DUMPLINGS *and* BRANDON BAY COCKLES *with* CHARGRILLED WILD GARLIC

FOR THE PORK JOWL AND CHEEKS
2 carrots, finely chopped
2 onions, sliced
2 celery sticks, finely chopped
1 leek, finely chopped
6 garlic cloves, peeled and lightly crushed
handful fresh thyme sprigs
2 bay leaves
1 litre white wine
50 ml vegetable oil
16 medium pork cheeks, free range, about 2 kg in total
1 pork jowl, free range
70 g Highbank Farm apple sugar syrup (glossary)
700 ml double chicken stock (page 286)
10 g flat-leaf parsley leaves, finely chopped
15 g wild garlic stems, chopped
zest of 1/2 lemon
pinch of smoked salt
a little thickener (glossary)

FOR THE WILD GARLIC PURÉE
400 g wild garlic stems
3 shallots
50 g butter
200 ml cream, more if necessary
a little thickener (glossary)

TO SERVE
50 g butter
40 potato dumplings (page 281)
10 g Parmesan, freshly grated
2 tbsp olive oil, extra for brushing
2 tbsp Llewellyn's apple balsamic vinegar (glossary)
300 g cockles, scrubbed
16 wild garlic stems
1/2 tsp extra virgin olive oil
250 g white onion purée (page 284)

SERVES 8

Pork cheek and jowl with charred wild garlic leaf and salty flavoured cockles.
A magic marriage of the creatures from land and sea.

PORK JOWL AND CHEEKS

Put the vegetables, herbs and wine in a deep tray with the pork cheeks and jowl, and leave in the fridge for 24 hours. Preheat the oven to 160°C. Drain the pork in a colander set over a clean pan. Bring the liquid to the boil and boil for 2–3 minutes to solidify any impurities, then pass through a fine chinois. Heat a large sauté pan and fry the pork cheeks and jowl in batches in a little of the oil until golden all over. Deglaze the pan with a little of the reserved liquid. Heat the rest of the oil in an ovenproof casserole dish, add the drained vegetables and cook over a medium to high heat until they are well browned. Add the pork cheeks and jowl with the pan juices and apple sugar syrup. Pour over the reserved liquid and the stock, then wrap with a double layer of tin foil. Cook for 1½–2 hours or until the cheeks and jowl are all soft. Cool, then drain and pass the cooking liquid through a double layer of muslin into a clean pan. Put the cheeks and jowl on a tray, and chill for at least 2 hours. Reserve a little of the cooking liquid to use to finish cooking the pork cheeks when serving. Bring the rest to the boil and then reduce by half, skimming off the fat – you'll need 250 ml. Add a little thickener, a pinch at a time, until you have achieved a sauce consistency. When the jowl is cold, finely chop and combine with the parsley, wild garlic, lemon zest and smoked salt. Chill until needed.

WILD GARLIC PURÉE

Blanch the garlic stems for 30 seconds in a large pan of salted water and refresh in a bowl of iced water, then squeeze well to remove any excess water and put into a Pacojet. Freeze overnight, then blend the frozen garlic stems 3 times in the Pacojet. (Using the Pacojet intensifies the flavour but it is not essential if you do not have access to one.) Sweat the shallots in the butter until soft, then add the cream and heat until reduced by half. Leave to cool. Place in a blender with the blanched and squeezed wild garlic, and purée for 5 minutes until smooth, adding a little more cream if necessary. Pass through a fine chinois and add a little thickener, a pinch at a time, until you have achieved a purée consistency. Chill.

SERVING

Preheat the oven to 160°C and preheat the grill. Heat the pork cheeks in a pan with some of the cooking liquor and 2 tablespoons of the butter, then transfer to the oven for 5 minutes until heated through. Press a spoonful of the jowl mixture onto the top of 8 of the pork cheeks and gratinate under the grill. Meanwhile, drop the potato dumplings into a large pan of boiling salted water and simmer for about 2 minutes until they come back up to the surface, then drain. Heat the rest of the butter in a sauté pan with the water and toss in the drained dumplings. Sprinkle over the Parmesan and season with salt and black pepper. Keep warm. Bring the 250 ml of reserved pig cheek cooking liquor to the boil and whisk in the olive oil with the apple balsamic vinegar, then season. Tip in the cockles and cover with the lid. Allow to cook on a medium heat for 1–2 minutes until all of the shells have opened, then remove from the heat. Take half the cockles out of their shells and return them to the sauce, discarding the shells. Keep warm. Preheat a griddle pan and brush with a little olive oil, then briefly chargrill the garlic stems. Cut into pieces, dress with extra virgin olive oil and season with salt and black pepper. Warm the wild garlic purée in a small pan and put into a squeezy bottle. Heat the white onion purée and place two spoonfuls on each warmed serving plate, then top with one pork cheek glazed in the cooking liquor and wild garlic purée around the plates. Dot the potato dumplings and wild garlic purée around the plates. Spoon over the cockle sauce and finish each plate with pieces of the chargrilled wild garlic.

STEAMED WILD SEA BASS *with* ORGANIC CELERIAC, ROPE MUSSELS *in a* CRAIGIES CIDER DRESSING *and* TARRAGON JUICE *with* ROASTED

JERUSALEM ARTICHOKE

The mild but creamy flavour of the celeriac is a wonderful canvas on which to paint the other flavours of this dish, without overwhelming the queen of the sea, the wild sea bass. Unfortunately, now a rare treat.

FOR THE MUSSELS
200 ml water
1 kg mussels, scrubbed and beards removed

FOR THE VINAIGRETTE
400 ml dry cider
1 tbsp Llewellyn's apple balsamic cider vinegar (glossary)
100 ml grapeseed oil

FOR THE GLAZE
150 ml reserved mussel liquid
200 ml dry cider
1 tbsp grapeseed oil
1 tsp apple balsamic cider vinegar (glossary)

FOR THE SEA BASS
8 x 150 g wild sea bass escalopes, skinned and boned
1 tbsp softened butter

FOR THE CELERIAC RIBBONS
1 small celeriac, new season
500 ml fish stock (page 286)

FOR THE MONK'S BEARD
2 tbsp water
2 tbsp extra virgin olive oil
small handful of Monk's beard (glossary), trimmed, or use samphire or shaved asparagus

TO SERVE
4 small to medium roasted Jerusalem artichokes (page 284)
1 Granny Smith apple
250 ml celeriac purée (page 283)
small handful of fresh micro herbs
20 ml tarragon juice (page 279), in a squeezy bottle

SERVES 8

MUSSELS

Bring the water to boil in a large pan. Add the mussels, cover with the lid and cook over a medium to high heat for 3–4 minutes, shaking occasionally, until the shells have opened. Discard any that remain closed. Drain into a colander lined with a double layer of muslin set over a bowl, and reserve the liquid. Remove the mussel meat from the shells and chill until needed.

VINAIGRETTE

Take 200 ml of the reserved mussel liquid and reduce to 100 ml, then cool. In a separate pan, reduce the cider to

100 ml and cool. Combine both of the reduced liquids with the vinegar, then whisk in the oil, a little at a time, until emulsified.

GLAZE

Place 150 ml of the reserved mussel liquid and the cider in a pan, and reduce until slightly thick and sticky. Whisk in the vinegar and oil. Keep warm.

SEA BASS

Put each portion of sea bass on a square of buttered greaseproof paper. Season with salt and black pepper, and steam for 5 minutes until tender.

CELERIAC RIBBONS

Peel the celeriac and use a Japanese mandolin to cut into long ribbons. Bring the stock to the boil in a pan. Add the celeriac and cook for 30 seconds. Drain on kitchen paper and season with salt and black pepper. Keep warm.

MONK'S BEARD

Heat the water in a sauté pan. When it starts to boil, add the olive oil and continue to boil until emulsified. Add the Monk's beard and cook for a minute or so until wilted. Drain, then season with salt and black pepper. Keep warm.

SERVING

Preheat the oven to 160°C and warm the roasted artichokes in a small tray for 4–5 minutes, then cut in half. Peel the apple and cut into 2–3 mm dice. Heat the mussel meat with the diced apple in the vinaigrette. Warm the celeriac purée and put 2 tablespoons to the right of each warmed serving plate, then arrange the celeriac ribbons on top with the Monk's beard. Place a sea bass escalope on the other side of each plate and brush over the glaze. Scatter the micro herbs on top. Add the pieces of roasted Jerusalem artichokes and spoon around the mussels and apple vinaigrette. Finish with dots of the tarragon juice.

ED JOLLIFFE, SOMMELIER.

LATE SUMMER AT REDCROSS, COUNTY WICKLOW.

DESSERT COURSE

THE ART OF CHAPTER ONE

The word artisan is central to the work we do at Chapter One Restaurant, but it is a word that sometimes misleads. Irish artisans appear in many areas of human endeavour, so we consider not only the provenance of our food but also seek out craftspeople who make objects to hold our food, works to celebrate our food's unique Irishness and creations to adorn some of our quieter spaces. From bog oak sculptures and hand-crafted baskets to the bespoke charcuterie trolley made from Irish walnut, we make an effort to ensure that our entire restaurant celebrates the integrity of people who are masters of their craft.

Our kitchen and chef's table are monuments to the art of kitchen design. The smoked glass of the chef's table is a window into the world where I spend my days. Often, people are surprised by how quiet the kitchen is. There is a dichotomy of disciplines in my profession: the creative side that ignites the ideas for a dish, which then turns to what you might call the militaristic side where it is placed into the kitchen system. This requires extreme organisation, concentration, discipline and attention to detail. A sort of artist's studio but filled with people.

In 2012 we started commissioning artists to create seasonal artwork for the restaurant. The finished work appears on the menu cover and changes as each new commission is completed and the seasons change, and the original work then hangs in the restaurant. This is a unique way for the customer to engage with Irish talent and artists through the covers of our menus.

CARRAGEEN SET WEST CORK CREAM PUDDING *with* PAT CLARKE STRAWBERRIES *and* FRESH YOGHURT MOUSSE, SODA BREAD SUGAR BISCUITS *and* IRISH APPLE BALSAMIC VINEGAR MERINGUES

We created this dish for the State dinner at Dublin Castle, hosted by President McAleese, to honour the visit of Queen Elizabeth II to the Irish Republic. As it was the first ever visit by a reigning British monarch, we wanted the dish to entertain the diners visually as much as it would on the palate. The presentation looks like the setting for an Irish fairy tale and the flavours evoke childhood memories, yet they are matched by sophisticated textures and flavours. What a dainty dish to set before a queen.

FOR THE SODA BREAD SUGAR BISCUITS

100 g butter
300 g dark muscovado sugar
100 g plain flour
160 g egg whites
brown soda bread powder (page 289), for sprinkling

FOR THE CREAM PUDDING

700 ml milk
300 ml Glenilen cream
100 g sugar
5 vanilla pods
15 g gold leaf gelatine

FOR THE STRAWBERRY CONSOMMÉ

300 g strawberries
50 g sugar (1st)
juice of 1 lime
20 g sugar (2nd)
2 g gold leaf gelatine

FOR THE APPLE BALSAMIC VINEGAR MERINGUES

100 g egg whites
100 g caster sugar
pinch of cream of tartar
120 g icing sugar, sieved
50 ml apple balsamic cider vinegar (glossary)
5 g hy-foamer (glossary)

FOR THE YOGHURT AND VANILLA MOUSSE

1 g gold leaf gelatine
85 ml Glenilen cream
65 g sugar
2 vanilla pods, split in half and seeds scraped out
350 g Compsey Creamery Greek-style yoghurt

TO SERVE

75 ml Glenilen cream
4 fresh strawberries, cut into slices, ends discarded
24 dried strawberry pieces (page 289)
10 ml raspberry vinegar (glossary)

SERVES 8

SODA BREAD SUGAR BISCUITS

Melt the butter in a pan and add the sugar, stirring to dissolve. Remove from the heat and tip in the flour and egg whites, then whisk until smooth. Pass through a sieve and chill for 24 hours. The next day, preheat the oven to 170°C. Spread the tuile mix on a baking tray lined with a Silpat. Using a 4 × 2 cm template, make 8 tuiles and sprinkle with an even layer of the brown soda bread powder. Bake for 9 minutes until they have turned a rich brown colour. Leave for 1 minute to set and then transfer to a rack to cool completely.

CREAM PUDDING

Bring the milk and cream to the boil. Add the sugar and vanilla pods, and leave to infuse for 30 minutes. Soak the gelatine in cold water for 10 minutes, then squeeze out the excess liquid. Return the milk and cream mix to the heat, and bring to a simmer. Whisk in the soaked gelatine until dissolved, then strain through a fine chinois. Chill for 3–4 hours. Line the base of a 10 × 2 cm ring mould with clingfilm and fill to just over halfway up the sides. Chill for at least another hour.

STRAWBERRY CONSOMMÉ

Place all the ingredients in a bowl, except the second amount of sugar and the gelatine, and cook in a bain-marie set over a pan of simmering water for 2 hours. Strain through a fine chinois and chill for at least an hour. Take 130 ml of the strawberry consommé, add the second amount of sugar and bring to the boil. Meanwhile, soak the gelatine in water for 10 minutes, then squeeze out the excess liquid and whisk into the strawberry juice until dissolved. Leave to cool, then pour a thin layer of jelly over the top of each set cream pudding and chill for 1 hour. Reserve 200 ml of the consommé to make the strawberry cream for serving.

APPLE BALSAMIC VINEGAR MERINGUES

Preheat the oven to 70°C. Whisk the egg whites in a KitchenAid with a whisk attachment on a slow speed until frothy. Pour in the sugar, add the cream of tartar and hy-foamer, and continue to whisk until glossy and stiff. Add the sieved icing sugar and balsamic vinegar, and whisk for 1 minute. Put into a piping bag with a no. 1 nozzle and pipe 8 meringues onto a baking tray lined with silicone paper, then cook for 3 hours.

YOGHURT AND VANILLA MOUSSE

Soak the gelatine in cold water for 10 minutes, then squeeze out the excess liquid. Meanwhile, bring the cream, sugar and vanilla seeds to the boil. Whisk in the gelatine until dissolved. Remove from the heat and whisk in the yoghurt. Put into a foam gun and charge with 1 gas charger. Chill for at least 2 hours.

SERVING

Take the reserved 200 ml of strawberry consommé and stir in 75 ml of cream. Using a hot knife, unmould the cream puddings onto serving plates and then pour around the strawberry cream to flood each plate. Arrange fresh strawberry slices on each pudding, followed by pieces of dried strawberries and pieces of soda bread sugar biscuit. Add an apple balsamic vinegar meringue to each one and some dots of the raspberry vinegar. Finish with a dome of the yoghurt mousse.

VALERIE KINGSTON OF GLENILEN FARM, WHERE ARTISAN STANDARDS ARE NOT COMPROMISED DESPITE THE GROWING SUCCESS OF THE DAIRY PRODUCE. THEIR DOUBLE CREAM USED IN THE QUEEN'S DESSERT, TASTES OF OUR RICH IRISH TERROIR.

RASPBERRY MILLE FEUILLE *with* MASCARPONE MOUSSE *and* ARLETTE BISCUITS, CARAMELISED RASPBERRY SAUCE *with* WHITE CHOCOLATE *and* COFFEE BEAN ICE CREAM

There is nothing more visually engaging than raspberries standing tall and proud, glistening in their red coat of armour. The combination here is all about the white chocolate and coffee bean with the raspberries, though there are crunchy and light textures from the pastry too. It's a classic fantastic.

FOR THE MASCARPONE MOUSSE

125 g icing sugar
70 g egg yolks
250 g mascarpone cheese
1 vanilla pod, split in half and seeds scraped out
25 g gold leaf gelatine
300 ml cream, whipped

FOR THE WHITE CHOCOLATE AND COFFEE BEAN ICE CREAM

100 ml milk
10 coffee beans
40 g egg yolks
30 g caster sugar
20 g inverted sugar (glossary)
20 g white chocolate, broken into squares
2 g super neutrose (glossary)
100 ml cream

FOR THE RASPBERRY GLAZE

50 ml raspberry purée (glossary)
50 ml neutral glaze (glossary)
50 ml water

FOR THE PUFF PASTRY

200 g T55 flour, extra for dusting
60 g butter, melted
6 g salt
100 ml water
160 g butter, softened
icing sugar for dusting the Arlette biscuits

TO SERVE

48 raspberries
100 ml caramelised raspberry sauce (page 289)
shards of tempered white chocolate, to decorate (page 289)

SERVES 8

MASCARPONE MOUSSE

Whip the icing sugar and egg yolks in a KitchenAid fitted with a whisk attachment to create as much volume as possible. Add the mascarpone and vanilla seeds, and whip again until it stiffens up. Soak the gelatine in water for 10 minutes, then squeeze out the excess liquid. Heat 50 ml of the cream and add the soaked gelatine, whisking until dissolved. Quickly beat this into the mascarpone mix, then fold in the rest of the cream. Pour into a 25 cm frame lined with silicone paper and freeze. When frozen, cut into 8 pieces of 10 × 15 cm rectangles and refreeze until needed.

RASPBERRY GLAZE

Bring the raspberry purée and neutral glaze to the boil in a pan. Slowly add enough of the water to make the glaze fluid enough to lightly coat the raspberries.

WHITE CHOCOLATE AND COFFEE BEAN ICE CREAM

Bring the milk to 80°C and whisk in the coffee beans. Set aside to infuse for 30 minutes, then strain out the coffee beans and discard. Whisk the egg yolks, caster sugar and inverted sugar in a KitchenAid fitted with a whisk attachment for 5 minutes until pale. Pour in a quarter of the infused milk and then add back into the rest of the milk. Continue to heat, stirring to 84°C until the mixture coats the back of a wooden spoon. Meanwhile, melt the chocolate over a pan of simmering water. Strain the custard through a fine chinois and put in a food processor. Blitz with the super neutrose, cream and melted chocolate until smooth. Chill for 6–8 hours and then freeze in Pacojet tins.

PUFF PASTRY

Mix all the ingredients together, except for the softened butter, in a KitchenAid fitted with a dough attachment until a pastry is formed, then chill for 1 hour. Cut the pastry in half and roll each half into 2 × 1 mm thick sheets on a lightly floured work surface and then add 80 g of the softened butter to each one. Fold the pastry around the butter to form a rough envelope. Roll out again to a 1 mm thickness, then fold from the top to the middle, then from the bottom to the top of the fold. Rest for 30 minutes, then roll again and repeat 6 times, chilling for another 30 minutes after each roll. Finally chill for 2 hours to allow the pastry to rest and then use to make Arlette biscuits. Preheat the oven to 190°C. Thinly roll out the puff pastry to a 0.5 mm thickness, dust with icing sugar and cook on baking trays lined with silicone paper for 10 minutes until crisp and golden brown. Remove from the oven and cut into 24 pieces of 10 × 2 cm rectangles – nearly the same size as the mascarpone mousse rectangles. Leave to cool on a wire rack until needed.

SERVING

Sandwich a mascarpone mousse between 2 Arlette biscuits and place one on each serving plate, then decorate with 2 swipes of the raspberry glaze. Dip the raspberries in the glaze and arrange 5–6 on top of each one, then cover with a third Arlette biscuit and drizzle around a little of the caramelised raspberry sauce. At the top right-hand corner of each plate, put a quenelle of white chocolate and coffee bean ice cream, and decorate with the shards of tempered white chocolate.

CHEF'S TABLE.

GLENILEN MILK *and* LANNLÉIRE HONEY

FOR THE MILK ICE CREAM

400 ml organic milk
250 ml cream
50 g caster sugar
40 g inverted sugar (glossary)
80 g milk powder (glossary)
10 g super neutrose (glossary)

FOR THE BITTER CHOCOLATE AND ALMOND GANACHE

125 g Valrhona Caraïbe plain dark chocolate, broken into squares
50 g honey
250 ml cream
125 g whole blanched almonds
100 g caster sugar
30 ml water

FOR THE HONEYCOMB

140 g caster sugar
50 g honey
50 g glucose
30 ml water
8 g bread soda

FOR THE DRIED ALMOND MILK PIECES

70 g whole blanched almonds
250 ml organic milk
40 g glucose
5 g hy-foamer or lecithin powder (glossary)

FOR THE TOASTED SALTED ALMONDS

100 g whole blanched almonds
15 g Maldon sea salt

TO SERVE

2 g Maldon sea salt
8 tsp honey

SERVES 8

MILK ICE CREAM

Bring all the ingredients, except the super neutrose, to the boil in a heavy-based pan, whisking continuously as the milk powder can catch and burn quite easily. When it comes to the boil, add the super neutrose and continue to whisk for 3 minutes while it is still boiling. This will cook out the milk powder and the mix will get quite creamy and thick. Remove from the heat and blend with a hand blender for 1 minute. Chill for 6 hours, then freeze in a Pacojet container or churn in an ice cream machine according to instructions. When churned, pipe the milk ice cream into 8 × 7 cm silicone dome moulds 5 mm in depth. Refreeze when filled.

BITTER CHOCOLATE AND ALMOND GANACHE

Melt the chocolate in a bowl set over a pan of simmering water. Caramelise the honey in a heavy-based pan and heat the cream in a separate pan. Once the honey is caramelised and golden brown, deglaze with the cream. When it is all incorporated, boil for 1 minute. Add to the melted chocolate in 3 stages to create an emulsion, then blend with a hand blender for 1 minute. Transfer to a plastic container and cover with clingfilm. Leave to crystallise for 24 hours before use. The next day preheat the oven to 120°C and put the almonds on a baking tray. Roast for 20 minutes until golden brown. Meanwhile, place the sugar and water in a heavy-based pan, and simmer undisturbed until you have achieved a golden caramel. Remove the almonds from the oven and add to the pan, stirring quickly on the heat for 1 minute. Remove from the heat and spread thinly on a piece of silicone paper. When cold, blend to a rough crumb in a food processor. The next day fold this through the chocolate ganache and use to fill a piping bag fitted with a no. 2 nozzle.

HONEYCOMB

Place all the ingredients, except the bread soda, in a heavy-based pan, mix with a wooden spoon and bring to a caramel stage, which is approximately 160°C. Remove from the heat and whisk in the bread soda. The reaction will be fast and explosive so whisk fast until the soda is dispersed. Pour onto a large piece of silicone paper and allow to cool. When cool, break into pieces and store in a tightly sealed plastic container.

This reminds me of a fallen angel and it tastes like one too. The genesis of this dish came out of our desire to work a dessert from two great Irish products: Glenilen organic milk and Lannléire Bell Heather Honey, so it is the confluence of two fantastic foods creating a magical result.

DRIED ALMOND MILK PIECES

Preheat the oven to 170°C and toast the almonds for 15 minutes until golden brown. Remove from the oven and crush in a blender until coarse. Add to the milk and put in a sealed plastic container for 1 hour to infuse. Strain through a fine chinois and discard the almonds. Heat the strained milk and the glucose in a pan, and bring to just under the boil, then add the hy-foamer or lecithin and remove from the heat. Whisk for 5 minutes, then leave to rest for 1 minute. The foam on the top should be light and plentiful because the milk solids should have fallen to the bottom of the pan. Line a tray with silicone paper, then using a large spoon, place large dollops of the foam onto the tray. Continue with this process of heating and whisking until all the milk is used. Preheat the oven to 60°C and place the tray with the foam in the oven for 12 hours to dry out completely. Leave to cool and store in a tightly sealed container. These will last for 5 days.

TOASTED SALTED ALMONDS

Preheat the oven to 170°C and toast the almonds and salt in a baking tray for 20 minutes. Leave to cool, then remove the almonds and salt, and blitz in a Thermomix to a coarse crumb.

SERVING

Remove the ice cream domes from the freezer and roll each one in the salted almond crumb. Arrange on a tray for 15 minutes before serving. Pipe 35 g of the bitter chocolate and almond ganache on each serving plate, and place an almond-crumbed ice cream dome on top, making sure to hide the ganache. Decorate each one with 2 pieces of the honeycomb and 2 of the dried almond milk pieces. Break some of the dried almond milk pieces and honeycomb to a crumb, and sprinkle over the top. Finish each plate with a sprinkling of the Maldon salt and drizzle with the honey.

IRELAND'S PATRON SAINT OF BEES IS **EOGHAN MAC GIOLLA CODA** OF LANNLÉIRE HONEY, A BEEKEEPER WORKING WITH THE NATIVE IRISH HONEY BEE, IDEALLY SUITED TO IRELAND'S COOL, DAMP CLIMATE. MY FAVOURITE IS THE BELL HEATHER HONEY WHICH WE USE IN THE RESTAURANT FOR ITS SINGLE CRU ESSENCE.

POACHED MERINGUE STUFFED WITH LEMON CURD,
CHERRY ANGLAISE AND PISTACHIO BRITTLE, PAGE 212.

POACHED MERINGUE STUFFED *with* LEMON CURD, CHERRY ANGLAISE *and* PISTACHIO BRITTLE

Everybody loves poached meringue. It is a homely dessert, but in this dish we have re-imagined it in a sophisticated way. The surprise is the lemon curd and the floating fresh cherries slowly sinking beneath the surface. The pistachio brittle is a perfect match with the cherries and lemon. The softness of this dessert reminds you of childhood ingredients like custard and cream. One of our most basic recipes but deeply appealing.

FOR THE CHERRY ANGLAISE

250 ml milk
250 ml cream
200 g egg yolks
150 g sugar
400 ml cherry purée (glossary)

FOR THE POACHED MERINGUE

300 ml milk
50 g caster sugar (1st)
1 vanilla pod, halved and seeds scraped out
100 g egg whites
150 g caster sugar (2nd)
pinch of cream of tartar

FOR THE LEMON CURD

2 g gold leaf gelatine
100 ml lemon juice
60 g sugar
60 g egg yolks
80 g eggs
60 g butter, softened

FOR THE PISTACHIO BRITTLE

75 g shelled pistachios
50 g butter
50 g sugar
50 g glucose

TO SERVE

36 fresh cherries, halved
40 shelled pistachios

SERVES 8

POACHED MERINGUE

Bring the milk, the first amount of sugar and the vanilla seeds to 85°C in a pan. Whisk the egg whites in a KitchenAid fitted with a whisk attachment on a medium speed until frothy, then pour in the second amount of sugar and add the cream of tartar, then whisk at medium to high speed until glossy and semi-stiff. Spoon a dollop of the meringue into a small ladle and smooth to a dome shape with a palette knife. Dip the ladle into the heated milk mix, then gently stick a palette knife down the back of it and it should pop out. Poach for 2 minutes on either side. Take out and chill – you'll need 8 in total.

LEMON CURD

Soak the gelatine in water for 10 minutes. Put all the other ingredients, except the butter, in a heavy-based pan. Bring to the boil, whisking continuously, and allow to boil for 10 seconds. Squeeze out the excess water from the gelatine and add to the pan. Remove from the heat and blend with a hand blender. When the mix reaches 40°C, blend in the softened butter and pass through a fine chinois. Chill until needed.

PISTACHIO BRITTLE

Preheat the oven to 160°C. Blitz the pistachios in a food processor until roughly crushed. Place in a small pan with the butter, sugar and glucose, and heat for 5 minutes, whisking until smooth. Remove from the heat and spread between 2 sheets of greaseproof paper set on a baking tray. Leave to cool, then peel back the top piece of greaseproof paper and cook for 10 minutes until caramel brown. Leave to cool and break into shards. Store in an airtight container until needed.

SERVING

Put the lemon curd into a piping bag with a no. 3 nozzle. Blitz the cherry Anglaise with a hand blender to aerate and then use to cover the bottom of each chilled glass serving bowl. Using a small melon baller, scoop a hole out of the bottom of each poached meringue and fill this with the lemon curd. Carefully put one on top of each pool of cherry Anglaise. Decorate each one with cherry halves and pistachios, and finish with shards of the pistachio brittle.

CHERRY ANGLAISE

Bring the milk and cream to 80°C in a heavy-based pan. Whisk the egg yolks and sugar together for 5 minutes, then pour in a quarter of the milk mix. Pour back into a clean pan and cook to 84°C, stirring continuously, until the custard coats the back of a wooden spoon. Strain through a fine chinois and chill for 6 hours, then blitz in the cherry purée with a hand blender and pass through a fine chinois. Chill until needed.

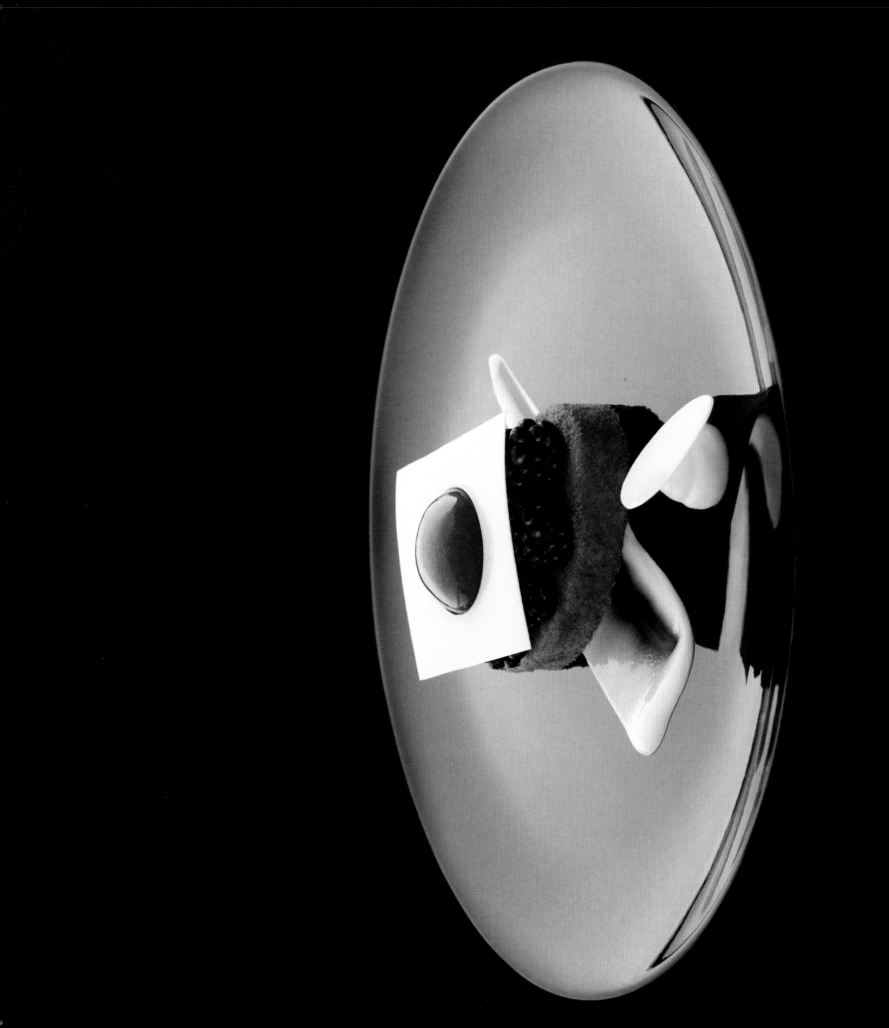

FRESH BLACKBERRIES *with* BAKED CUSTARD *and* GINGERBREAD CRUMB, LIME CURD *and* BLACKBERRY BOMBE

FOR THE BAKED CUSTARD

4 g gold leaf gelatine
125 ml milk
125 g egg yolks
25 g caster sugar
100 g maple syrup
375 ml cream

FOR THE LIME CURD

1.5 g gold leaf gelatine
125 ml fresh lime juice
75 g caster sugar
70 g egg yolks
130 g eggs
75 g unsalted butter, softened

FOR THE BLACKBERRY BOMBE

5 g gold leaf gelatine
250 ml blackberry purée (glossary)
25 g caster sugar

FOR THE BLACKBERRY BOMBE COATING

12 g gold leaf gelatine
100 ml water
25 ml blackberry purée (glossary)
25 g caster sugar
few drops purple food colouring

FOR THE BLACKBERRY AND YOGHURT SAUCE

25 ml blackberry purée (glossary)
50 g natural yoghurt
¼ vanilla pod, split in half and seeds scraped out

FOR THE WHITE CHOCOLATE DECORATIONS

100 g tempered white chocolate (page 289), broken into squares

TO SERVE

28 fresh blackberries
250 g gingerbread crumb (page 289)

SERVES 8

I love the combination of flavours and mouthfeel from the rich, creamy baked custard to the gingerbread crumbs and the elevation of flavours in the blackberries. Beautiful, light blackberries – acidic and fruity, some are really sweet – and a little bit of tempered white chocolate add texture and a nice homely flavour.

BAKED CUSTARD

Place the gelatine in a bowl of cold water and set aside for 10 minutes to soak, then squeeze dry. Heat the milk in a pan to 80°C and add the soaked gelatine, then whisk until dissolved. Whisk the egg yolks, caster sugar and maple syrup together for 5 minutes until pale. Stir in the cream with the milk mixture and strain through a fine chinois into a large jug. Cover with clingfilm and chill for 3 hours. Preheat the oven to 100°C. Pour the chilled custard into 8 × 50 g oval Silpat moulds, or use a mould or ramekin that is the same size, and place on a baking sheet. Bake for 25 minutes until the custard is cooked but still has a slight wobble in the centre. Leave at room temperature for 1 hour, then freeze for at least 6 hours or up to 4 weeks. Remove the custards 1 hour before serving.

LIME CURD

Place the gelatine in cold water and set aside for 10 minutes to soak, then squeeze dry. Place the lime juice in a heavy-based pan with the caster sugar, egg yolks and eggs. Bring to the boil, whisking continuously, and then allow to boil for 10 seconds. Add the soaked gelatine, remove from the heat and blend with a hand blender. When the mixture reduces to 40°C, blend in the soft butter. Pass through a fine chinois into a bowl. Cover with clingfilm and chill for at least 1 hour, then put into a squeezy bottle.

BLACKBERRY BOMBE

Place the gelatine in a bowl of cold water and set aside for 10 minutes to soak, then squeeze dry. Place the blackberry purée and sugar in a pan, and bring to the boil. Add the soaked gelatine, then remove from the heat and whisk until dissolved. Pour into a jug and leave to cool completely, then freeze in 8 × 30 g semi-sphere moulds and place on toothpicks in the freezer.

BLACKBERRY BOMBE COATING

Place the gelatine in a bowl of cold water and set aside for 10 minutes to soak, then squeeze dry. Bring the water, blackberry juice and caster sugar to the boil in a pan, and add enough of the purple colouring until a glossy blackberry colour is achieved. Remove from the heat and whisk in the soaked gelatine until dissolved, then strain through a fine chinois into a bowl. Leave to cool for 6 hours until it has reached below room temperature and then dip the bombes from the freezer in 3 times, allowing the coating to set for a couple of seconds each time. Remove the toothpicks and place the bombes on a tray lined with clingfilm. Place in the fridge until needed.

BLACKBERRY AND YOGHURT SAUCE

Place all the ingredients in a bowl and whisk until well combined. Pass through a fine chinois and put into a small squeezy bottle, then chill.

WHITE CHOCOLATE DECORATIONS

Spread the tempered white chocolate in a thin even layer on a sheet of acetate paper. When the chocolate turns matt and is just beginning to set, cut out 8 × 7 cm squares and stamp out 8 × 4 cm discs from the middle of each one. Arrange the squares and stamped-out discs on a lined baking tray and chill until ready to serve.

SERVING

Cut the fresh blackberries in half. Pipe a line of blackberry and yoghurt sauce on each serving plate, and then with the back of a small palette knife, create a swipe to the other side of the plate. Roll each baked custard in the gingerbread crumb and place in the centre of each plate. Then pipe a dot of lime curd in the centre of the baked custard and decorate with 7 blackberry halves. Place a bombe on top of each one, then place a square of the white chocolate sheet on top, again making sure the bombe is peeking through. Just to the top right of the custard pipe a dot of the lime curd, then put the disc of white chocolate over the top at an angle to finish.

DARREN CAMPBELL, HEAD WAITER.

CARAMELISED ELSTAR APPLE *and* MOLASSES SPONGE *with* SPICED PUMPKIN ICE CREAM

Everybody remembers a sweet, hot baked apple dessert from their childhood and this one reminds me of that. There is a lovely twist with the molasses which brings in a deep, rich flavour to the classic Irish apple. The pumpkin is seasonal too making it a celebration of seasonality. A heart-warming and slightly decadent version of the old fashioned baked apple sponge.

FOR THE SPICED ROAST PUMPKIN ICE CREAM

250 g peeled and seeded pumpkin, roughly chopped
1 star anise
½ cinnamon stick
250 ml milk
75 g egg yolks
25 g honey
50 g caster sugar
100 ml cream
20 g inverted sugar (glossary)
2 g super neutrose (glossary)

SERVES 8

FOR THE MOLASSES SPONGE

150 g eggs
170 g dark muscovado sugar
170 ml milk
250 g plain flour
75 g ground almonds
10 g baking powder
5 g ground cinnamon
5 g ground nutmeg
150 ml olive oil

FOR THE CARAMELISED APPLES

20 g caster sugar
2 Elstar apples
pinch of salt
10 g unsalted butter, extra to grease
light demerara sugar, to dust

FOR THE TREACLE SAUCE

100 g treacle
100 ml cream
15 g unsalted butter

SPICED PUMPKIN ICE CREAM

Preheat the oven to 200°C. Place the pumpkin in a tray with the spices. Cover with foil and bake for 40 minutes until the pumpkin is soft. Take off the foil, pour in the milk and return to the oven for another 2 minutes. Leave to cool, then cover with clingfilm and place in the fridge for 24 hours. The next day, strain through a fine chinois into a bowl. Whisk the honey and sugar into the egg yolks until pale and creamy. Heat the infused milk in a heavy-based pan to 45°C and then add in the inverted sugar, stirring to dissolve. Add the egg yolk and sugar mixture, and cook until the custard coats the back of a wooden spoon and has reached 84°C, then pour in the cream. Strain through a fine chinois into a bowl and add the super neutrose, then blend with a hand blender. Cover with clingfilm and chill for 12 hours, then freeze in a Pacojet tin.

MOLASSES SPONGE

Place the eggs and sugar in a KitchenAid fitted with a whisk attachment, and whisk on a medium speed for 8–10 minutes until light brown and fluffy. Pour in the milk and whisk for another minute. Sieve the dry ingredients in a bowl and then fold into the egg and milk mixture. Finally fold in the oil until just combined.

CARAMELISED APPLES

Heat a heavy-based frying pan over a high heat. Sprinkle the caster sugar over the base and leave it to caramelise undisturbed. Peel the apples and cut into 2 mm dice, discarding the cores. When the sugar has caramelised and become golden brown, add the apples to the pan with a pinch of salt and caramelise for 1 minute, then add the butter and cook for another minute, tossing to coat evenly. Remove from the heat. Using a pastry brush, butter 8 × 150 g heatproof glass moulds, then dust with the demerara sugar. Spoon 40 g of the caramelised apple into the bottom of each one and then cover with 45 g of the sponge mix. Cover with clingfilm and set aside for up to 4 hours until needed.

TREACLE SAUCE

Bring the treacle and cream to the boil in a pan, then simmer for 1 minute. Whisk in the butter and remove from the heat. Chill until needed.

SERVING

Preheat the oven to 185°C. Arrange the prepared sponges on a baking sheet and bake for 9 minutes until they have risen and turned golden brown. Bring the treacle sauce to the boil and spin the pumpkin ice cream in the Pacojet for a really smooth finish. Take the sponges out of the oven and quickly pierce the top of each sponge 5 times with a knife, then pour two dessertspoons of the treacle sauce into each one. Put a separate dish with a quenelle of pumpkin ice cream alongside.

DAVID LLEWELLYN'S ORCHARD, A SMALLHOLDING IN THE FERTILE COUNTRYSIDE OF NORTH COUNTY DUBLIN, PRODUCES A FINE RANGE OF APPLES, CIDERS AND VINEGARS. THEIR OUTSTANDING BALSAMIC CIDER VINEGAR IS MADE FROM THE FINEST OF IRISH APPLES.

FRESH BLACK FIGS *with a* BUTTERMILK CHANTILLY, PISTACHIO MOUSSE *and* GOAT'S MILK SORBET *with* ROSE WATER JELLY

FOR THE FIG JAM
250 g fig purée (glossary)
25 g sugar
zest and juice of ½ orange
6 g yellow pectin

FOR THE PISTACHIO MOUSSE
3 g gold leaf gelatine
100 ml cream
40 g sugar
70 g 100% pistachio paste (glossary)
300 ml cream, whipped

FOR THE BUTTERMILK CHANTILLY
5 g gold leaf gelatine
150 ml cream (1st)
105 g sugar
125 ml cream (2nd)
300 ml buttermilk

FOR THE ROSE WATER JELLY
75 g sugar
225 ml water
10 g rose syrup (glossary)
5 g rose water essence (glossary)
0.75 g agar agar powder (glossary)
7 g gold leaf gelatine
juice of ½ lime
1 vanilla pod, halved and seeds scraped out

FOR THE GOAT'S MILK SORBET
100 ml water
50 g sugar
20 g inverted sugar (glossary)
2 g super neutrose (glossary)
330 ml goat's milk

TO SERVE
4 fresh black figs
4 Irish oat biscuits (page 289), broken in pieces

SERVES 8

I love a combination of a heartfelt Irish ingredient such as buttermilk with something unexpected like figs and rose water jelly. It is like the mundane with the exotic. When we think of Ireland we think of buttermilk; it is almost the quintessence of Irishness, but rose water and figs reflect an Arabic tradition. For this to work it is absolutely essential to use the very ripest and the very best figs.

FIG JAM

Place all the ingredients, except for the zest and pectin, in a heavy-based pan. Bring to the boil, then slowly whisk in the pectin and boil for 10 minutes. Turn down the heat and simmer for 30 minutes. Remove from the heat and mix in the zest. Chill for 3 hours.

PISTACHIO MOUSSE

Soak the gelatine in cold water for 10 minutes, then squeeze out the excess liquid. Bring the cream and sugar to the boil, add the soaked gelatine, whisking until dissolved. Using a spatula, add the cream and gelatine mix to the pistachio paste in 3 stages to create an emulsion, mixing vigorously at each stage. Blend with a hand blender to ensure a smooth finish. Fold in the whipped cream and chill for at least 1 hour.

BUTTERMILK CHANTILLY

Soak the gelatine in a bowl of cold water for 10 minutes, then squeeze out the excess liquid. Bring the first amount of cream and the sugar to the boil, then add the soaked gelatine. When the mix cools to 40°C, add the second amount of cream and the buttermilk. Blend with a hand blender until smooth. Cover and chill overnight. Just before use, whip in a KitchenAid fitted with a whisk attachment to soft peaks. Chill until needed.

ROSE WATER JELLY

Bring the sugar, water, rose syrup and rose water essence to the boil. Add the agar agar and boil for 2 minutes to hydrate it. Soak the gelatine in a bowl of cold water for 10 minutes, then squeeze out the excess liquid. Add the lime juice to the syrup with the vanilla seeds and then whisk in the gelatine until dissolved. Pass through a fine chinois. Line the base of a 20 cm frame with clingfilm and pour the jelly in to a depth of 1 cm. Leave at room temperature for 1 hour and then chill for at least 2 hours. Just before use cut the jelly into 1 cm cubes and then in half to make triangles.

GOAT'S MILK SORBET

Boil the water, sugar and inverted sugar for 2 minutes. Add the super neutrose and boil for another minute. Blend with a hand blender. Allow to cool until 40°C and stir in the goat's milk. Chill for 6 hours and then freeze in Pacojet tins.

SERVING

Place the pistachio mousse and buttermilk Chantilly in separate piping bags with a no. 2 nozzle. Place a dessertspoon of the fig jam in the middle of each large, shallow serving bowl. Cut each fig into quarters and place two fig quarters on top of each one, then pipe 3 dots of pistachio mousse and 3 dots of buttermilk Chantilly around each bowl. Randomly place 5 triangles of the rose water jelly and a couple of pieces of the Irish oat biscuit. Finish each one with a quenelle of goat's milk sorbet.

PEARS COOKED *in* SAUTERNES INFUSED *with* ORANGE *and* CINNAMON *with a* LIGHT SPONGE, HAZELNUT CREAM *and a* MILK CRUMB *with* PEAR ICE CREAM

What's there not to like about beautiful, ripe, autumn pears, especially Pear Williams poached in the finest of dessert wines? When matched with a very light sponge, a mild, creamy hazelnut flavour and a slightly salty milk crumb, the result is simple but with an elegant mouthfeel.

FOR THE HAZELNUT SPONGE

60 g skinned hazelnuts
100 g egg whites
40 g egg yolks
85 g caster sugar
20 g T55 flour
10 ml Frangelico liqueur

FOR THE MILK CRUMB

45 g T55 flour
12 g cornflour
15 g caster sugar
2 g salt
40 g milk powder (1st) (glossary)
50 g unsalted butter, melted
100 g white chocolate drops
40 g milk powder (2nd) (glossary)

FOR THE POACHED PEAR BALLS

60 g caster sugar
60 ml Sauternes wine
3 ml orange blossom water (glossary)
3 strips of orange zest
200 ml water
4 Pear Williams

FOR THE PEAR PURÉE

50 ml water
1 cinnamon stick, split in half
1 vanilla pod, split in half and seeds scraped out
4 pears, Pear Williams
leftover pear from the poached balls (see above)

FOR THE PEAR ICE CREAM

100 ml cream
30 g egg yolks
40 g caster sugar
15 g inverted sugar (glossary)
4 g super neutrose (glossary)
200 g pear purée (see above)

FOR THE HAZELNUT CREAM

2 g gold leaf gelatine
70 ml cream
100 g praline paste (glossary)
200 ml cream, semi-whipped

SERVES 8

HAZELNUT SPONGE

Blend all the ingredients in a blender for 1 minute, then pour into a foam gun, charge with 2 gas chargers and chill for 3 hours. Shake well before use and fill a regular plastic drinking cup a third of the way full and microwave for 40 seconds – the sponge will be fully cooked. Turn out on a rack to cool. Repeat until you have 8 sponges in total and store in a sealed plastic container until needed.

MILK CRUMB

Preheat the oven to 120°C. Put the flour, cornflour, sugar, salt and the first amount of the milk powder into a bowl and mix with your hands. Add the melted butter and mix with your fingertips until the mix resembles crumbs. Spread out on a baking tray lined with silicone paper and cook for 12 minutes. Leave to cool. Melt the white chocolate in a bowl set over a pan of simmering water. Add the second amount of milk powder and mix well to combine – it will become extremely thick but this is normal. Add the crumb to the chocolate and mix well until the chocolate has created different-sized crumbs. Place on a tray lined with silicone paper and chill for 1 hour. When chilled, put into a sealed plastic container and chill again until needed.

POACHED PEAR BALLS

Bring the sugar, Sauternes, orange blossom water, zest and water to the boil in a pan, and boil for 1 minute. Peel the pears and use a melon baller to quickly make pear balls. The remainder of the pear flesh can be used for the pear purée. Drop all the pear balls into the syrup and boil for 5 minutes. Turn off the heat and allow to cool in the syrup. The pears should be fully cooked and turn translucent. When cool, keep in the syrup and chill until needed.

PEAR PURÉE

Place the water, cinnamon and vanilla in a pan, and bring to a simmer. Quickly remove the stalks from the pears and peel, then cut into thin slices, including the cores. Slice the leftover pear from the poached pear balls in the same way. Add both lots of pears to the pan containing the water and spice mix, and cover with a cartouche. Cook for 5 minutes on a high heat, stirring occasionally. (The reason you have to work quickly is because there is an enzyme in pears called polyphenol oxidase that has to be cooked above 100°C to ensure the pears do not brown, so by doing this you will get a white purée without adding ascorbic acid or lemon juice, therefore maintaining the pure flavour of the pear itself.) After 5 minutes, remove the cinnamon and vanilla pod, and discard. Place the contents of the pan in a blender and blend until very smooth, then pass through a fine chinois. Cover with a layer of clingfilm touching the surface of the purée and chill down. When chilled, set 200 g aside for ice cream and transfer the rest to a small squeezy bottle. Chill until needed.

PEAR ICE CREAM

Heat the cream in a heavy-based pan. Meanwhile, whisk the egg yolks, caster sugar and inverted sugar in a bowl using a hand blender. When the cream is hot, pour some into the egg and sugar mix, whisking to combine, then pour back into the pan, continuously whisking. Add the super neutrose and bring the mix up to 82°C using an electronic probe. Take off at 82°C and whisk for another 2 minutes, then blend in the pear purée with a hand blender for 2 minutes. Pass through a fine chinois and then chill the mix for 6 hours. Freeze in Pacojet containers or churn in an ice cream machine according to instructions.

HAZELNUT CREAM

Soak the gelatine in cold water for 10 minutes, then squeeze out the excess liquid. Bring the cream to a simmer in a small pan and whisk in the soaked gelatine until dissolved. Put the praline paste in a bowl and pour over the cream and gelatine mix in 3 stages, mixing well each time to create an emulsion. Fold in the semi-whipped cream, put into a sealed plastic container and chill until needed.

SERVING

Fill a piping bag fitted with a no. 2 nozzle with the hazelnut cream. Spoon 30 g of the milk crumb onto the base of each large, shallow serving bowl and pipe 3 large domes of hazelnut cream at the top. Then to the right and at the bottom of the bowl, pipe 3 large pools of the pear purée in between the cream and put 5 of the poached pear balls around the bowl. Place a large quenelle of the pear ice cream in the centre of each serving and tear 3 large pieces of the hazelnut sponge and arrange around each quenelle of ice cream to finish.

FROZEN NOUGAT PARFAIT *with* CALAMANSI VINEGAR JELLY *and* POACHED PEAR, CHOCOLATE *and* HAZELNUT COVERED LIME CHANTILLY, YUZU SALT CARAMEL

FOR THE BASE
50 g milk chocolate, broken into squares
75 g praline paste (glossary)
50 g Irish oat biscuits, crushed (page 289)
50 g feuilletine (glossary)

FOR THE PARFAIT
30 g pine nuts
30 g skinned hazelnuts
30 g whole blanched almonds
30 g egg whites
20 g sugar (1st)
pinch of cream of tartar
90 g egg yolks
20 g sugar (2nd)
50 g honey
50 ml fresh pear purée (glossary)
150 g cream, whipped

FOR THE CALAMANSI VINEGAR JELLY
7 g gold leaf gelatine
200 ml fresh pear purée (glossary)
25 g Calamansi vinegar (glossary)
25 g sugar
0.75 g agar agar powder (glossary)

FOR THE POACHED PEARS
200 ml white wine
400 ml water
50 ml lemon juice
300 g sugar
1 cinnamon stick, lightly crushed
1 star anise, lightly crushed
zest of 1 orange and 1 lemon
4 firm ripe pears

FOR THE LIME CHANTILLY
4 g gold leaf gelatine
100 ml cream (1st)
30 g caster sugar
80 ml lime juice
200 ml cream (2nd)
zest of 2 limes

FOR THE CHOCOLATE COATING
100 g 70% plain chocolate, broken into squares
50 g cocoa butter (glossary)
75 g skinned hazelnuts

FOR THE CHOCOLATE DÉCOR
150 g tempered milk chocolate (page 289)

FOR THE YUZU CARAMEL SAUCE
150 g sugar
150 ml cream
8 g yuzu salt (glossary)

SERVES 8

The key to this dish is the vinegar jelly which sits on top of the nougat. There is a combination of beautifully poached balls of pear with the Calamansi vinegar, cutting through the sweetness of the nougat. The milk chocolate ball has a lime Chantilly which runs along with the salt caramel and over the sweet fruit flavours. A modern creation of ancient flavours.

BASE

Melt the chocolate and praline in a bowl over a pan of simmering water. Add the crushed Irish oat biscuit and feuilletine, and mix well. Spread thinly into a 30 × 70 cm cake tray lined with clingfilm and freeze.

PARFAIT

Preheat the oven to 155°C. Roast all the nuts in a baking tray for about 20 minutes until just golden brown. Cool and blitz in a blender until coarse. With an electric whisk, beat the egg whites on a medium speed until frothy, then slowly add the first amount of sugar with the cream of tartar and continue to whisk until stiff peaks have formed. Cover with clingfilm and chill. Place the egg yolks, the second amount of sugar, the honey and the pear pureé in a bowl set over a pan of simmering water. Whisk until the temperature hits 82°C. Remove from the heat and transfer to a KitchenAid fitted with a whisk attachment. Whisk on the highest speed until the bowl is cold to the touch. Put the chilled meringue in a large bowl using a spatula. Fold in the coarsely ground nuts and then fold in the egg mix from the KitchenAid followed by the cream. Pour into the frozen cake base and refreeze for another 6 hours until solid.

CALAMANSI VINEGAR JELLY

Soak the gelatine in cold water for 10 minutes, then squeeze out the excess liquid. Meanwhile, bring the pear purée, vinegar and sugar to the boil. Add the agar agar and boil for 2 minutes to hydrate the agar agar. Remove from the heat and stir in the soaked gelatine until dissolved. Pour into a 20 cm tray that is 2 mm deep and lined with clingfilm. Leave at room temperature for 1 hour, then chill for at least 2 hours.

POACHED PEARS

Bring all the ingredients, except the pears, to the boil and boil for 2 minutes. Meanwhile, peel the pears and add to the pan, then turn the heat off or keep the syrup at 85°C if possible. Make a cartouche and place on top, turning the pears with a large spoon every 15 minutes. The pears are cooked when a knife goes through without resistance – this should take about 45 minutes. Remove from the heat and chill the pears in the syrup overnight. This will make them go translucent.

LIME CHANTILLY

Soak the gelatine in cold water for 10 minutes, then squeeze out the excess liquid. Bring the first amount of cream, sugar and lime juice to the boil, then add the soaked gelatine, stirring to dissolve. Allow to cool to 50°C and then add the second amount of cream with the zest. Chill for 12 hours, then whip in a KitchenAid with a whisk attachment until semi-stiff peaks appear. Freeze 16 × 20 g semi-sphere moulds, then when frozen, stick together to create 8 spheres. Stick a toothpick into one end of each sphere and put back in the freezer.

CHOCOLATE COATING

Preheat the oven to 160°C. Heat the chocolate and cocoa butter in a bowl over a pan of simmering water until melted. Roast the hazelnuts in a baking tray in the oven until golden brown. Leave to cool, then crush in a blender until coarse. Set aside.

CHOCOLATE DÉCOR

Thinly spread the tempered milk chocolate on acetate sheets, and when the chocolate is nearly set, cut into 8 × 1.5 × 10 cm bars. Place another sheet of acetate on top, weigh down with a heavy book to keep flat and leave to crystallise for 6 hours before using.

YUZU CARAMEL SAUCE

Put the sugar in a heavy-based pan and caramelise undisturbed until the sugar is a rich golden colour. At this point bring the cream to the boil and add to the caramel in 2 stages with a wooden spoon, then boil for 2 minutes. Remove from the heat and blend in the salt with a hand blender, then pass through a fine chinois. Leave in a container covered with clingfilm to set at room temperature overnight.

TO FINISH THE DISH

Heat the chocolate coating to 40°C 1 hour before serving, then dip in each lime Chantilly sphere, making sure it is completely covered. Sprinkle over the roasted crushed hazelnuts to cover completely. Arrange on a tray lined with greaseproof paper and leave at room temperature to defrost. Cut the parfait into 8 × 3 × 10 cm rectangles and put back in the freezer, then do the same with the jelly but leave at room temperature.

SERVING

With a melon baller, make 40 poached pear balls. Place a parfait in a straight line to the right of each serving plate, then cover with a Calamansi vinegar jelly. Carefully put 5 of the poached pear balls in a line on top, followed by a bar of the chocolate décor. To the top right-hand corner of the plate, place a chocolate and hazelnut coated lime Chantilly sphere. Put the yuzu caramel sauce into a small squeezy bottle, then pipe 3 dots of the sauce in a crescent shape, increasing in size each time, to finish.

HOT VALRHONA GUANAJA CHOCOLATE SOUFFLÉ

Soufflé is the dish of choice for dessert lovers, the ultimate dessert. I like that it is decadent and has beautiful chocolate transfer yet it is light too. Needless to say it is one of the most popular dishes on the menu. A classic dish where the ingredients are part of the magic.

FOR THE CHOCOLATE SOUFFLÉ
300 g Guanaja 70% plain chocolate, broken into squares
300 ml milk
20 g cornflour
200 g egg whites
80 g caster sugar
pinch of cream of tartar
60 g egg yolks
softened unsalted butter, to grease
demerara sugar, to dust

SERVES 8

CHOCOLATE SOUFFLÉ

Melt the chocolate in a bowl set over a pan of simmering water, being careful not to heat it over 50°C. Set aside at room temperature to cool a little. Meanwhile, place the milk and cornflour in a large pan, and whisk until smooth. Place on the heat and slowly bring to the boil, whisking continuously. Allow it to boil for 5 seconds – the mixture should be shiny and thickened. Remove from the heat and pour in the melted chocolate. Using a balloon whisk, beat vigorously until thick and glossy. Set aside and leave to cool to 45°C. Place the egg whites in a KitchenAid fitted with a whisk attachment and whisk on a medium speed until fluffy, then slowly add the caster sugar and cream of tartar, and continue to mix until semi-stiff peaks appear. Using a spatula, mix the egg yolks into the cooled chocolate mixture until smooth and then gently fold in the meringue until just combined. Using a pastry brush, butter 8 × 150 ml soufflé moulds or ramekins, brushing upwards to ensure the best rise, then dust with the demerara sugar. Divide the chocolate mixture among them and smooth the top with a palette knife. If you are using a traditional soufflé ramekin with a rim, gently run your thumb around the edge to help release the mixture before baking. These can be chilled and left to sit for 1 hour before baking.

SERVING

Preheat the oven to 185°C. Arrange the moulds on a baking tray and bake for 9 minutes until well risen but with a slight wobble in the middle. Bring to the table immediately.

MANJARI CHOCOLATE *and* ESPRESSO MOUSSE CAKE *with* ORANGE PURÉE *and* TARRAGON GEL, CHOCOLATE CRUMB *and* CARAMEL ICE CREAM

Essentially this is a play on a chocolate orange, making it a beautiful interplay between that classic combination and the notes of tarragon and coffee. All the flavours work in harmony creating a rich symphony. A real winter dessert.

FOR THE CHOCOLATE CRUMB

20 g ground almonds
20 g light demerara sugar
20 g plain flour
16 g bitter cocoa powder, 84% cocoa solids
1 g salt
12 g unsalted butter, diced and well chilled

FOR THE MANJARI CAKE BASE

30 g Manjari 64% plain chocolate, broken into squares
60 g praline paste (glossary)
40 g cooked chocolate crumb (see above)
40 g feuilletine (glossary)

FOR THE CHOCOLATE AND TARRAGON MOUSSE

8 g gold leaf gelatine
80 g Manjari 64% plain chocolate, broken into squares
70 ml milk
20 g bunch fresh tarragon
100 ml cream, whipped to soft peaks

FOR THE ESPRESSO MOUSSE

3.5 g gold leaf gelatine
30 g egg yolks
20 g eggs
40 g caster sugar
24 ml water
8 g coffee essence (glossary)
700 ml cream, whipped to soft peaks

FOR THE TARRAGON AND ORANGE GEL

80 ml freshly squeezed orange juice, sieved
10 g fresh tarragon sprigs
10 g caster sugar
10 g glucose
0.5 g agar agar powder (glossary)

FOR THE ORANGE PURÉE

3 oranges, diced
150 g caster sugar
90 ml water
1 vanilla pod, split and seeds scraped out

FOR THE CARAMEL ICE CREAM

3 g coffee beans
200 ml milk
60 g egg yolks
40 g sugar (1st)
12 g inverted sugar (glossary)
20 g sugar (2nd)
1.5 g super neutrose (glossary)
100 ml cream

FOR THE CHOCOLATE CAKE GLAZE

22 g gold leaf gelatine
50 g Guanaja 70% plain chocolate, broken into squares
120 g pâte à brune (glossary)
60 g caster sugar
70 ml water
14 g glucose
15 g dried milk powder (glossary)
7 g bitter cocoa powder, 84% cocoa solids
70 ml cream

SERVES 8

CHOCOLATE CRUMB

Put all the dry ingredients in a KitchenAid with a paddle attachment and mix on a medium speed. Slowly add the diced butter and continue to mix until the mixture resembles granola. Chill for at least 1 hour. Preheat the oven to 160°C, place the chilled crumbs on a lined baking tray and cook for 15 minutes, then take out of the oven and crush gently with the a metal scraper to even out the mix.

MANJARI CAKE BASE

Melt the chocolate and praline in a bowl over a pan of simmering water. Add the cooked chocolate crumb and feuilletine, and mix well. Spread thinly into a 20 × 20 cm cake tray lined with greaseproof paper and freeze.

CHOCOLATE AND TARRAGON MOUSSE

Soak the gelatine in cold water for 10 minutes. Melt the chocolate over a bain-marie. Meanwhile, bring the milk to the boil, add the tarragon and cover with clingfilm, then leave for 1 hour to infuse. Strain the milk into a clean pan and bring to 80°C. Gently squeeze out the gelatine, add to the milk and whisk until dissolved. Pour over the chocolate in 3 stages, mixing with a spatula to create a shiny emulsion, and blitz with a hand blender. When the chocolate mix is at 45–50°C, fold in the cream, pour on top of the frozen cake base and refreeze.

ESPRESSO MOUSSE

Soak the gelatine in cold water for 10 minutes. Whisk the yolks on a medium speed and eggs in a KitchenAid fitted with a whisk attachment to a light ribbon stage. When this starts to happen, bring the water and sugar to the boil, and cook to 121°C, then pour into the egg mix, whisking continuously. Whisk for 10–15 minutes until cold. Gently squeeze out the excess water from the gelatine. Bring the coffee essence to the boil and add the soaked gelatine, whisking to dissolve. Transfer to a large bowl and beat in 2 dessertspoons of the egg mix. Gently fold in the rest of the mix followed by the cream, pour on top of the frozen chocolate mousse and refreeze. When frozen, use a hot knife and cut 8 × 7 × 3.5 cm rectangles, then freeze again.

TARRAGON AND ORANGE GEL

Bring the orange juice and tarragon to the boil, and leave for 30 minutes, then strain into a clean pan. Add the sugar and glucose, and return to the boil. Tip in the agar agar and boil for another 2 minutes to hydrate the agar agar. Pass through a fine chinois and leave at room temperature for 2 hours. Just before serving, blend with a hand blender and transfer to a small squeezy bottle.

ORANGE PURÉE

Place all the ingredients in a large pan and bring to the boil. Boil for 5 minutes and then simmer for 40 minutes. Blend until smooth, then pass through a fine chinois and chill.

CARAMEL ICE CREAM

Preheat the oven to 190°C and roast the coffee beans for 3 minutes in a tray, then crack the beans lightly in a small blender. Heat the milk to 80°C in a heavy-based pan with the lightly cracked coffee beans and set aside to infuse. Whisk the yolks and the first amount of sugar together, then whisk in the inverted sugar. Put the second amount of sugar in a heavy-based pan and caramelise. When the caramel is a rich caramel colour, add the hot infused milk in 2 stages, mixing vigorously with a large whisk. Pour a quarter of the milk into the yolk mixture and whisk back into the pan, then cook to 84°C, until it coats the back of a wooden spoon. Pass through a fine chinois and whisk in the super neutrose, then blend with a hand blender and add the cream. Leave to cool and then chill for 6–8 hours to rest. Freeze in Pacojet tins.

CHOCOLATE CAKE GLAZE

Soak the gelatine in cold water for 10 minutes. Melt the chocolate and pâte à brune in a bowl over hot water. Bring the sugar, water, glucose, milk powder, cocoa powder and cream to the boil. Boil for 2 minutes and then simmer for 15 minutes, stirring occasionally. Squeeze out the excess moisture from the gelatine and whisk into the pan until dissolved. Pour over the chocolate mixture in 3 stages, mixing with a spatula to create a shiny emulsion, then blend with a hand blender and pass through a fine chinois.

SERVING

Heat the chocolate cake glaze to 40°C in a small pan and use to glaze each Manjari cake in an even layer. Leave at room temperature for 40 minutes to an hour to defrost. Take a serving plate and pipe a dot of the orange purée at one end, then with the back of a spoon, swipe the purée to create a rough C-shape. Place a cake in the middle of each plate and put 1 1/2 dessertspoons of the chocolate crumb at one end of the cake. Pipe dots of the orange and tarragon gel starting at the top of the plate. Finish each plate with a quenelle of caramel ice cream on top of the chocolate crumb.

MANJARI CHOCOLATE AND ESPRESSO MOUSSE CAKE WITH ORANGE PURÉE AND TARRAGON GEL, CHOCOLATE CRUMB AND CARAMEL ICE CREAM, **PAGE 232.**

TOONSBRIDGE BUFFALO RICOTTA CHEESECAKE *with* CRUSHED IRISH OAT BISCUIT *and* PASSION FRUIT CURD, PASSION FRUIT *and* THYME SORBET

This is a simple yet playful take on cheesecake and is made with Irish buffalo ricotta. The dish has varying textures and flavours, and I love the contrast of the creaminess of the ricotta and the texture of the oats, with the exotic twist of passion fruit.

FOR THE CHEESECAKE
10 g gold leaf gelatine
70 ml cream
35 g sugar
70 g honey
220 g buffalo ricotta
220 g cream cheese
350 ml cream, whipped
zest of 1 lemon

PASSION FRUIT CURD
1 g gold leaf gelatine
70 ml passion fruit purée (glossary)
50 g sugar
40 g egg yolks
50 g eggs
50 g butter, softened

PASSION FRUIT GEL
100 ml passion fruit purée (glossary)
35 g sugar
30 g glucose
½ lemon grass stalk
1 g agar agar powder (glossary)

PASSION FRUIT AND THYME SORBET
200 ml water
100 g sugar
125 ml passion fruit purée (glossary)
12 g inverted sugar (glossary)
4 g fresh thyme sprigs
2 g super neutrose (glossary)
100 ml sparkling water

FOR THE DEHYDRATED LEMONADE
50 ml water
50 g sugar (1st)
100 ml lemon juice
200 ml bottled still water
50 g sugar (2nd)
1.2 g xanthan powder (glossary)
5 g methocel (glossary)

FOR THE NOUGAT TUILES
100 g glucose
40 ml water
125 g sugar
25 g pâte à glace (glossary)
50 g flaked almonds

TO SERVE
200 g crushed Irish oat biscuit (page 289)

SERVES 8

CHEESECAKE

Soak the gelatine in water for 10 minutes. Bring the cream, sugar and honey to the boil until the sugar has dissolved. Squeeze out the excess water from the gelatine and add to the pan, whisking until dissolved. Cream the ricotta and cream cheese together in a KitchenAid with a paddle attachment. When the honey mixture is at 45°C, add to the cheese mix and blend smooth. Fold in the whipped cream and lemon zest. Pipe into 8 × 30 g semi-sphere moulds and freeze.

PASSION FRUIT CURD

Soak the gelatine in water for 10 minutes. Place the passion fruit purée in a heavy-based pan with the sugar, yolks and eggs, and cook, whisking continuously until it thickens and becomes jelly-like. Boil for 10 seconds and remove from the heat. Squeeze out the excess liquid from the gelatine and blend into the egg mix with a hand blender until dissolved. When the mix cools to 40°C, blend in the butter and chill for 1 hour.

PASSION FRUIT GEL

Place all the ingredients in a pan except the agar agar. Bring to the boil and leave to infuse for 15 minutes. Remove the lemon grass, bring the mix back to the boil, then add the agar agar and boil for 2 minutes to hydrate the agar agar. Pass through a fine chinois and leave at room temperature for 1 hour. Blend in a blender, then put into a squeezy bottle and chill for at least 1 hour.

PASSION FRUIT AND THYME SORBET

Bring all the ingredients to the boil except the super neutrose and sparkling water. Infuse for 1 hour. Strain through a chinois into a clean pan and bring to the boil. Add the super neutrose and boil for 1 minute. Remove from the heat and blend for 30–45 seconds, then chill. When chilled, add the sparkling water and freeze in Pacojet tins.

DEHYDRATED LEMONADE

Boil the water and the first amount of the sugar together for 2 minutes. Strain through a fine chinois and add the lemon juice. Chill for 1 hour, then stir in the bottled water and chill again for another hour. Place 300 ml of the lemonade in a large jug, and using a hand blender, blend in the second amount of the sugar with the powder and methocel for 5 minutes. Transfer to a KitchenAid fitted with a whisk attachment and whisk until stiff peaks have formed. Put into a piping bag with a no. 1 nozzle and pipe into small spheres. Dehydrate at 50°C for 12 hours.

NOUGAT TUILES

Preheat the oven to 190°C. Caramelise the glucose, water and sugar in a heavy-based pan undisturbed. When the mix is a rich caramel colour, add the pâte à glace and almonds. Remove from the heat and thinly spread onto greaseproof paper. When cold, blend to a fine powder, and with a fine sieve, sprinkle onto a baking tray lined with Silpat, then stamp out 8 tuiles with a 5 cm ring cutter. Bake for 2–3 minutes until glossy and shiny.

SERVING

Spread 1 ½ tablespoons of the crushed Irish oat biscuit into a rough circle on each serving plate. Place a cheesecake on top, upside down, and put a nougat tuile on each one, then pipe over 35 g dollops of the passion fruit curd. Pipe 3 dots of the passion fruit gel in between the curds and place 3 pieces of the dehydrated lemonade on the curd. Finish each plate with a quenelle of the passion fruit and thyme sorbet.

SEAN FERRY (LEFT), THE CHEESE MAKER, AND **JOHN LYNCH** (RIGHT), THE BUFFALO FARMER, WORK WITH TOBY SIMMONDS, FAMED ARTISAN ACTIVIST OF TOONSBRIDGE DAIRY IN MACROOM, COUNTY CORK. THERE YOU'LL FIND, SINCE OCTOBER 2009, IRELAND'S FIRST BUFFALO MOZZARELLA AND BUFFALO RICOTTA BEING MADE FROM THE MILK OF THE HAPPILY GRAZING ITALIAN WATER BUFFALO HERD.

CLAUDIO CORALLO 100% CHOCOLATE SORBET *with* ESPRESSO CRUMB *and* ORANGE

I don't think there is anyone in the world who takes making chocolates as seriously as Claudio Corallo does. His 100% chocolate is extraordinary as it has almost no bitterness, which is nearly impossible for chocolate with such a high cocoa content. This is a celebration of his 100% chocolate in a sorbet. It is pure, pure chocolate and what a fantastic mouthfeel.

FOR THE CHOCOLATE SORBET
200 g Claudio Corallo 100% chocolate
210 g sugar
460 ml water

FOR THE ESPRESSO CRUMB
60 g butter
10 g barley malt
50 g ground almonds
70 g malted flour, mixed grain
50 g demerara sugar
10 g freshly ground coffee

TO SERVE
40 g confit orange (page 276)
gold leaf, to decorate, optional

SERVES 8

CHOCOLATE SORBET

Put the chocolate, sugar and water in a pan, and heat to 65°C, mixing well, until the chocolate and sugar have dissolved. Freeze the mixture to -22°C and then put it into the Pacojet. Before it has frozen, the cocoa butter has a tendency to separate and to both rise and fall, so whisk thoroughly to emulsify. Store at -21° or -22°C.

ESPRESSO CRUMB

Melt the butter and barley in a small pan. Mix all the dry ingredients in a large bowl and add the butter and barley mix, then rub with your fingertips until a fine crumb is formed. Chill for 1 hour. Preheat the oven to 160°C. Spread out the crumb on a baking tray lined with silicone paper and cook for 15 minutes until cooked through. Leave to cool at room temperature.

SERVING

Spoon 1½ tablespoons of the espresso crumb into each small serving dish and top each one with a quenelle of the chocolate sorbet. Sprinkle over the confit orange and, if using, decorate with the gold leaf to finish.

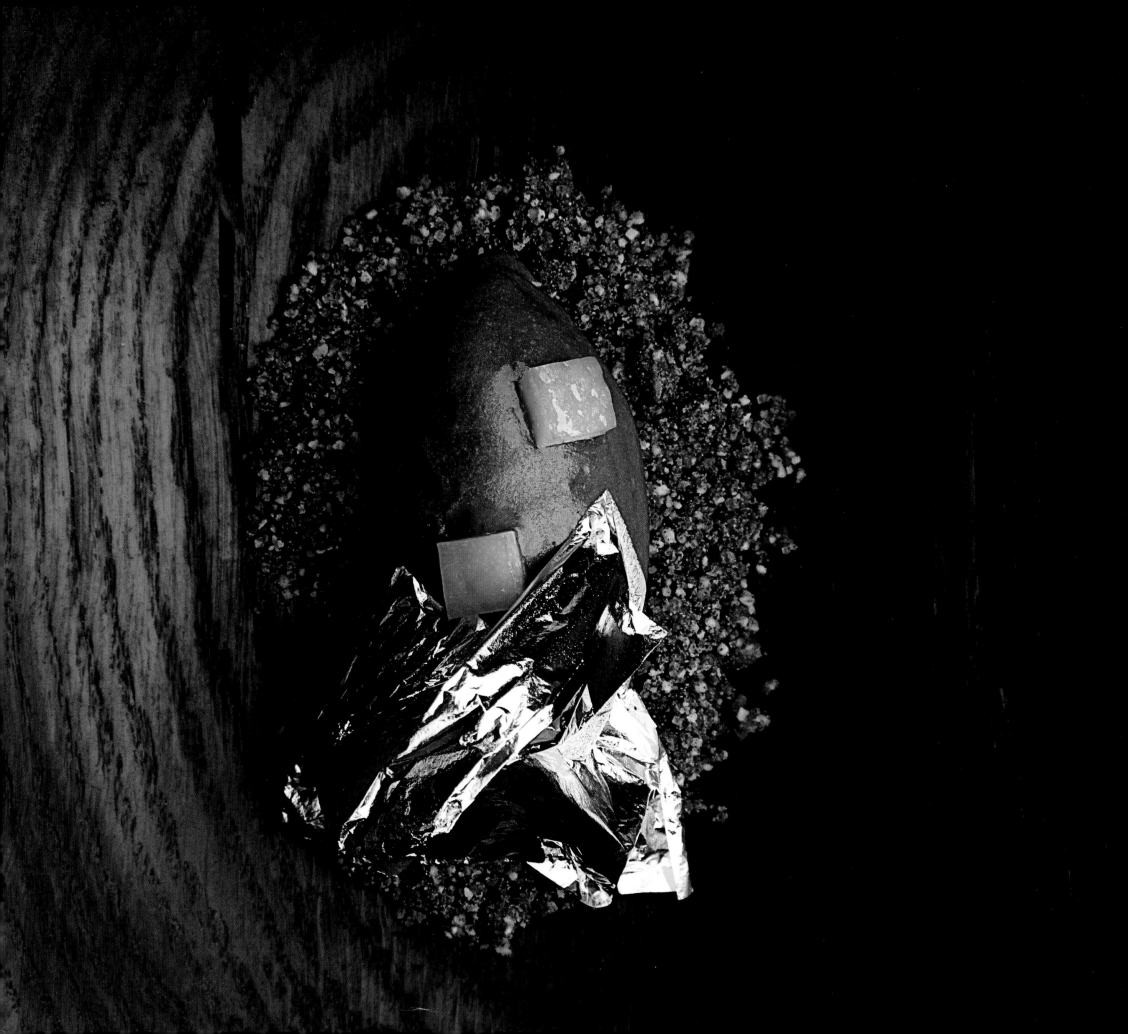

EARL GREY TEA SOAKED PRUNES *with a* GINGER GEL *and* CLEMENTINE COMPÔTE, LEMON TEA SORBET *with* MASCARPONE MOUSSE *and* GINGER BISCUITS

Prunes are an old favourite and this is a take on prunes with cream and biscuits. This is essentially something very simple taken to a new level by the muscovado brown sugar biscuits, which give it a sort of liquorice twist and textural crunch, contrasted with the softness from the prunes and mascarpone mousse.

FOR THE MUSCOVADO BISCUITS

35 g butter
100 g dark muscovado sugar
30 g plain flour
60 g egg whites
20 g gingerbread powder (page 289)
20 g demerara sugar

FOR THE TEA SOAKED PRUNES

500 ml water
175 g sugar
1 orange, sliced
2 star anise
2 bay leaves
5 g root ginger, sliced
2 Earl Grey tea bags
16 ready-to-eat Agen prunes

FOR THE TEA AND LEMON SORBET

125 g sugar
125 ml water
15 g inverted sugar (glossary)
3 g super neutrose (glossary)
½ lemon, sliced
5 g root ginger, sliced
1 bay leaf
2 Earl Grey tea bags
200 ml sparkling water

FOR THE MASCARPONE MOUSSE

40 g sugar
0.5 g xanthan powder (glossary)
2.5 g hy-foamer (glossary)
125 ml milk
125 ml cream
250 g mascarpone cheese

FOR THE GINGER GEL

50 g root ginger, peeled and sliced
100 g sugar
100 g glucose
200 ml water

FOR THE CLEMENTINE COMPÔTE

2 Clementines, quartered
150 g sugar
20 g glucose
½ vanilla pod
300 ml water

TO SERVE

4 gingerbread biscuits (see above), broken into 24 shards
1 tsp orange powder (page 289)

SERVES 8

MUSCOVADO BISCUITS

Melt the butter in a pan, then add the sugar and mix to a paste. Remove from the heat and mix in the flour and egg whites. Pass through a tamis or drum sieve into a clean bowl and leave to rest overnight in the fridge. The next day, preheat the oven to 170°C. Spread the biscuit mix on a Silpat using a 2 × 4 cm template and sprinkle over the gingerbread powder and demerara sugar. Bake for 9 minutes until crisp and golden brown. Transfer to a wire rack and leave to cool completely.

TEA SOAKED PRUNES

Bring all the ingredients, except for the prunes, to the boil. Allow to boil for 2 minutes and then pour over the prunes. Leave at room temperature to soak for at least 12 hours.

TEA AND LEMON SORBET

Bring the sugar and water to the boil until the sugar has dissolved. Add the inverted sugar and super neutrose, and boil for 1 minute. Add the lemon, ginger and bay leaf, and boil for another minute. Remove from the heat, add the tea bags and then cool to room temperature. Stir in the sparkling water and then pass through a fine chinois. Freeze in Pacojet containers for 12 hours or churn in an ice cream machine.

MASCARPONE MOUSSE

Mix together the sugar, xanthan powder and hy-foamer. In a separate bowl, mix the cream and milk, and then with a hand blender start to blend to create a vortex, slowly adding the sugar mixture, blending for 2 minutes. Put the mascarpone in a liquidiser and blend with the milk and cream mix. Pass through a fine chinois and then use to fill a foam gun three-quarters of the way full. Charge with 1 gas charger and shake well to combine. Leave to rest for 1 hour.

GINGER GEL

Place all the ingredients in a pan and bring to the boil, then reduce the heat and simmer for 3 hours. Pour into a Thermomix and blend on full power for 3 minutes, then pass through a fine chinois and allow to cool. Transfer to a squeezy bottle and chill until needed.

CLEMENTINE COMPÔTE

Put the Clementines in a small pan and cover with water. Bring to the boil and strain. Do this one more time, then strain off the liquid and place the Clementines back in a clean pan with the sugar, glucose, vanilla and water. Bring to the boil, then reduce the heat to a low simmer and simmer for 12 hours. Leave to cool, then chop into fine dice. Chill until needed.

SERVING

Drain the prunes and put 5 in each large, shallow serving bowl. Put a teaspoonful of the Clementine compôte in 3 random positions between the prunes and drizzle with the ginger gel. Place a quenelle of the tea and lemon sorbet on top of each one, and pipe on a generous amount of mascarpone mousse from the foam gun so that it is almost covering. Decorate each mousse with 3 shards of gingerbread biscuit and finish with the orange powder.

ANDY TURNER, HEAD CHEF.

HOT CHOCOLATE MOUSSE *with* WHIPPED LEMON JELLY *and* PRALINE CREAM, VANILLA ICE CREAM *and* CONFIT ORANGE *with* SPICED BREAD BISCUIT

This has been on the menu for many years and it is a real crowd pleaser. We would never dare take it off the menu so we rotate it with different flavours depending on our mood and the seasons. What people love is the contrast between textures, temperatures and flavours, all in the one dish. A real workhorse of a dish which we still love in the kitchen.

FOR THE CHOCOLATE MOUSSE
200 g 55% plain chocolate, broken into squares
150 ml cream
150 g egg whites

FOR THE WHIPPED LEMON JELLY
100 g sugar
120 ml lemon juice
zest of 2 lemons
150 ml water
4 g green cardamom seeds
1 lemon grass stalk
10 g gold leaf gelatine

FOR THE PRALINE CREAM
2 g gold leaf gelatine
50 ml cream
125 g praline paste (glossary)
250 ml cream, whipped

FOR THE VANILLA ICE CREAM
200 ml milk
2 vanilla pods, split in half and seeds scraped out
60 g egg yolks
40 g sugar
10 g inverted sugar (glossary)
2 g super neutrose (glossary)
1 litre cream

TO SERVE
80 g confit orange (page 276)
16 spiced bread croûtons (page 289)

SERVES 8

CHOCOLATE MOUSSE

Preheat a water bath to 60°C. Melt the chocolate in a bowl over a pan of simmering water. Bring the cream to the boil in a separate pan and then pour over the melted chocolate, whisking until smooth. When cool, add the egg whites. Use the mixture to fill a foam gun three-quarters of the way full and charge with 3 gas chargers. Put into the water bath for at least 30 minutes before serving. It will keep in the water bath for up to 3 hours.

WHIPPED LEMON JELLY

Bring all the ingredients, except the gelatine, to the boil and leave to infuse for 1 hour. Soak the gelatine in water for 10 minutes and then squeeze out the excess liquid. Strain the infusion and then add the soaked gelatine, whisking until the gelatine has dissolved. Chill overnight. The next day put the jelly in a KitchenAid fitted with a whisk attachment and whisk on a high speed until it trebles in volume. Fill a disposable piping bag and pipe the aerated jelly into 8 glass serving dishes, filling each one a quarter of the way up. Chill for at least 45 minutes to set.

PRALINE CREAM

Soak the gelatine in water for 10 minutes, then squeeze out the excess liquid. Meanwhile, bring the cream to the boil and add the soaked gelatine, whisking until dissolved. Pour over the praline paste in 3 stages, mixing with a spatula to create a glossy emulsion. Fold in the whipped cream and put into a piping bag, then chill.

VANILLA ICE CREAM

Bring the milk to 80°C in a heavy-based pan and whisk in the vanilla seeds. Leave to infuse for 30 minutes. Whisk the egg yolks, sugar and inverted sugar together for 5 minutes until pale, then pour a quarter of the milk into the egg mixture. Pour back into the milk and cook, stirring continuously, until the mixture coats the back of a wooden spoon and is 84°C. Strain through a fine chinois, then blend with the super neutrose and cream. Chill for 6–8 hours and then freeze in Pacojet tins.

SERVING

Pipe 50 g of the praline cream over each set whipped lemon jelly. Using the foam gun, pipe the warm chocolate mousse two-thirds of the way up each serving glass. Place a quenelle of the vanilla ice cream on each one. Finish with a sprinkle of the confit orange and 2 spiced bread croûtons.

WHITE CHOCOLATE GANACHE *with* OKITSO MANDARIN SORBET *and* BERGAMOT LEMON CREAM, BERGAMOT HONEY COATED CHIBOUST *and a* HAZELNUT TUILE

This is a celebration of the relationship between the fragrant and aromatic Bergamot lemon and the perfumed and mild Japanese-style mandarin sorbet. The white chocolate is thickened with agar agar giving it a sort of fudge-like texture and the hazelnut adds a further contrast at the end.

FOR THE WHITE CHOCOLATE GANACHE

4 g gold leaf gelatine
225 g white chocolate, broken into squares
155 ml cream
30 ml water
12 g glucose
1.5 g agar agar powder (glossary)

FOR THE WHITE CHOCOLATE POWDER

100 g white chocolate, broken into squares
50 g absorbit (maltodextrin) powder (glossary)

FOR THE BERGAMOT LEMON CREAM

100 ml Bergamot lemon juice
75 g sugar
55 g egg yolks
60 g eggs
60 g butter, softened

FOR THE LEMON GEL

50 ml lemon juice
25 ml water
25 g sugar
10 g glucose
1 g agar agar powder (glossary)

FOR THE OKITSU MANDARIN SORBET

45 g sugar
45 g inverted sugar (glossary)
90 ml water
1 g super neutrose (glossary)
90 ml Okitsu mandarin juice (glossary)
30 ml sparkling water

FOR THE HAZELNUT TUILE

20 g glucose
20 g sugar
20 g praline paste (glossary)

FOR THE ITALIAN MERINGUE

30 g egg whites
30 g caster sugar (1st)
10 ml water
10 g caster sugar (2nd)

FOR THE LEMON CHIBOUST

30 ml Bergamot lemon juice
25 ml cream
30 g egg yolks
12 g sugar
5 g cornflour
2 g gold leaf gelatine

FOR THE BERGAMOT HONEY DIP

50 g Bergamot honey (glossary)
75 ml water
½ vanilla pod, split in half and seeds scraped out
0.4 g kappa (glossary)

SERVES 8

WHITE CHOCOLATE GANACHE

Melt the white chocolate in a bowl over a pan of simmering water. Soak the gelatine in water for 10 minutes and then squeeze out the excess liquid. Meanwhile, bring the cream, water and glucose to the boil in another pan, then add the agar agar and boil for a further 2 minutes. Remove from the heat and add the soaked gelatine, whisking until dissolved. Create an emulsion with the liquid and the chocolate by adding the cream mixture into the chocolate in 3 stages, finish with a hand blender, then set in a non-stick 25 cm square frame. Leave at room temperature for 1 hour, then chill for 1 hour. Using a hot knife, cut into 8 strips, each 18 × 2 cm. Chill until needed.

WHITE CHOCOLATE POWDER

Melt the white chocolate in a bowl over a pan of simmering water. Place in a Thermomix with the absorbit, then mix at 50°C until a powder is formed. Pass through a sieve and store in an airtight container for up to 3 days.

BERGAMOT LEMON CREAM

Place all the ingredients, except for the butter, in a heavy-based pan. Bring to the boil, whisking constantly, then allow to boil for 5 seconds . Remove from the heat and pour into a bowl. Allow to cool to 50°C and then blend in the butter. Place in a piping bag with a no. 2 nozzle and chill until needed.

LEMON GEL

Bring all the ingredients, except the agar agar, to the boil in a pan. Add the agar agar and boil for a further 2 minutes. Pass through a fine chinois and leave at room temperature for 1 hour, then blitz in a blender and pass through a fine chinois again. Fill a small squeezy bottle and chill.

OKITSU MANDARIN SORBET

Bring the sugars and water to the boil. Add the super neutrose and boil for 1 minute. Remove from the heat and cool to room temperature. Using a hand blender, blend in the mandarin juice and sparkling water. Freeze in a Pacojet or churn in an ice cream machine. Store in the freezer until needed.

HAZELNUT TUILE

Preheat the oven to 150°C. Place the glucose and sugar in a heavy-based pan, and heat to 155°C, then add the praline, stirring until well combined. Roll between 2 sheets of greaseproof paper to a 2 mm thickness. Place in the oven for 2–3 minutes to soften, then pull off random shards and cut with a scissors. Store in an airtight container until needed.

ITALIAN MERINGUE

Slowly whip the egg whites in a KitchenAid with a whisk attachment. Put the first amount of sugar in a pan with the water and start to bring to the boil. By the time this reaches 110°C, the egg whites should be frothy, then add the second amount of sugar and increase the speed to medium. When the syrup reaches 120°C, remove from the heat, pour into the egg white mix and turn the speed up to high.

LEMON CHIBOUST

Whisk all the ingredients, except the gelatine, in a heavy-based pan. Put the gelatine in water for 10 minutes. Bring the ingredients in the pan to the boil, whisking constantly. Squeeze out the excess liquid from the gelatine and add to the pan, whisking until dissolved. Once the mixture has reached a boil, remove from the heat. The Italian meringue should be ready by now, fold this directly into the chiboust and continue to fold until shiny and glossy. Pipe into 8 × 30 g semi-sphere silicon moulds and freeze.

BERGAMOT HONEY DIP

Whisk all the ingredients in a pan and bring to the boil. Boil for 1 minute and then pass into a clean pan. Unmould the chibousts, and using a toothpick, dip each one into the honey dip to cover in a thin film. Arrange on a Silpat to defrost in the fridge.

SERVING

Place a strip of the white chocolate ganache on each plate in a rough S-shape, then pipe around 5 dots of the Bergamot lemon cream. Pipe 7 randomly sized dots of the lemon gel around each plate. Place a hazelnut tuile in the centre of each ganache and sprinkle generously with the white chocolate powder. Place a quenelle of the mandarin sorbet at one end of the plate and a coated chiboust at the other end of the plate to finish.

MALTED BANANA CREAM with SALTED CARAMEL and PEANUT TUILE, GINGER MILK and COCONUT SORBET

FOR THE MALTED BANANA CREAM
80 g caster sugar (1st)
50 g barley malt
1 cinnamon stick
2 star anise
6 bananas
70 g caster sugar (2nd)
30 ml water
20 g caster sugar (3rd)
50 g egg whites
10 g gold leaf gelatine
200 ml cream

FOR THE COCONUT SORBET
20 g inverted sugar (glossary)
30 g caster sugar
50 ml water
200 g Capfruit coconut purée (glossary)
3 g super neutrose (glossary)

FOR THE GINGER MILK
125 ml cream (1st)
60 g caster sugar
10 g root ginger, sliced
3 g gold leaf gelatine
80 ml cream (2nd)
170 ml milk

FOR THE COCONUT AND CHOCOLATE POWDER
30 ml coconut oil
30 g Valrhona Caraïbe plain chocolate, broken into squares
30 g adsorbit (maltodextrin) powder (glossary)

FOR THE SALTED CARAMEL SAUCE
100 g caster sugar
100 ml cream
10 g Maldon sea salt

FOR THE PEANUT TUILES
110 g fondant (glossary)
75 g glucose
25 g roasted unsalted peanuts

TO SERVE
40 g gingerbread powder (page 289)

SERVES 8

MALTED BANANA CREAM

Preheat the oven to 160°C. Caramelise the first amount of sugar with the barley malt in a heavy-based sauté pan to a deep dark caramel. Add the cinnamon and star anise. Cut the bananas in half lengthways with the skin still on and put into the caramel, skin side up, and cook for 1 minute. Transfer to the oven for 15 minutes, then remove from the oven, and while still hot, carefully remove the cinnamon, star anise and banana skins. Put the caramelised bananas and caramel into a blender, and blend to a purée. Pass through a fine chinois. Put the second amount of sugar and the water in a small pan, and bring to 120°C. When the syrup hits 109°C, set up a KitchenAid fitted with a whisk attachment and start to whisk the egg whites on a medium speed. When the mixture starts to become frothy, add the third amount of sugar and turn the speed up high. The syrup should nearly be the correct temperature at this stage. When it hits 120°C, turn the speed of the KitchenAid down and pour in the syrup in one go, then turn the speed back up to high and whip for about 10 minutes. Soak the gelatine in cold water for 10 minutes, then drain and squeeze out the excess liquid. Put 250 g of the banana purée in a pan and gently warm, then add the gelatine and stir to dissolve. Remove from the heat. Whip the cream to semi-soft peaks and set aside. Transfer the banana and gelatine mix to a bowl and fold in the meringue from the KitchenAid, then fold in the cream. Line a tray or mould that is 30 cm square and 1.5 cm deep with silicone paper. Add the malted banana cream and smooth off evenly with a palette knife. Freeze for 3 hours.

COCONUT SORBET

Bring all the ingredients to the boil except the coconut purée and super neutrose. When it just hits the boil, add the super neutrose and boil for another minute, whisking continuously. Remove from the heat and blend with a hand blender. When it cools to 40°C, add the coconut purée and blend again, then pass through a fine chinois. Chill for 6 hours, then freeze in a Pacojet container or churn in an ice cream machine according to instructions.

In the bleak mid-winter this is a visual treat for tired eyes. The first taste reveals the harmony of its muted, sweet creaminess, then along come bundles of textures and exotic overtones.

GINGER MILK

Bring the first amount of cream, sugar and ginger to the boil, stirring until the sugar has dissolved. Remove from the heat and infuse for 1 hour, then strain through a fine chinois. After an hour, soak the gelatine in cold water for 10 minutes, then squeeze out the excess liquid. Heat a little of the infused cream in a small pan and whisk in the gelatine until dissolved, then pour back into the rest of the infused cream. Stir in the second amount of cream and milk, and transfer to a plastic container. Cover with clingfilm and chill for 24 hours to set. The next day, whip in a KitchenAid fitted with a whisk attachment until semi-stiff peaks appear, then fill a piping bag with a no. 1 nozzle. Chill until needed.

COCONUT AND CHOCOLATE POWDER

Gently heat the coconut oil in a small pan, then add the chocolate and remove from the heat. Mix until smooth, then transfer to a Thermomix and add the absorbit. Blend on medium speed until you have achieved a fine powder. Pass through a fine sieve for a fluffier powder. Store tightly wrapped in a plastic container in the fridge.

SALTED CARAMEL SAUCE

Caramelise the sugar in a heavy-based pan to a rich deep caramel colour. Bring the cream to the boil and very carefully add the caramelised sugar in 3 stages with a wooden spoon. Allow to boil for 1 minute, then add the salt. Remove from the heat and blend with a hand blender for 30 seconds, then strain through a fine chinois and allow to crystallise overnight at room temperature before using. Transfer to a squeezy bottle.

PEANUT TUILES

Bring the fondant and glucose to 150°C, stirring occasionally. While this is happening, blitz the peanuts to a fine crumb. When the fondant mix hits 150°C, remove from the heat and add the peanuts, mixing well to combine. Spread onto a piece of silicone paper as thinly as possible and allow to cool quickly. When cool, blend to a fine dust. Preheat the oven to 250°C. Line a baking tray with a Silpat, and using a fine sieve, dust the whole tray generously with the peanut mix. Cut into 32 × 8 × 6 cm triangles. Turn off the oven and put the tray into the oven. When the mix becomes glossy and shiny, remove from the oven and allow to cool completely. This should take about 3 minutes. Gently take off the peanut tuiles and store in a tightly sealed plastic container.

SERVING

Take the malted banana cream out of the freezer and cut into 7 × 5 cm triangles – you will need 16 in total. Sandwich together with the peanut tuiles on either side and allow to defrost for 20 minutes. Put 2 banana cream and peanut tuile sandwiches on each serving plate – 1 lying down and 1 standing up at opposite sides of the plate. Spoon 20 g of the coconut and chocolate powder onto the centre of each plate and top with a quenelle of the coconut sorbet. Pipe 2 large dots of salted caramel at the top and bottom of each plate, then pipe 3 × 15 g domes of the ginger milk around the plate. Sprinkle with the gingerbread powder to finish.

RHUBARB POACHED *in* BLACK PEPPER *with* SABLÉ BISCUITS, CRÈME FRAÎCHE *and* GINGER CREAM *with* ROSE WATER JELLY *and* SWEET CELERY

Rhubarb, black pepper, celery and ginger: possibly these very different ingredients shouldn't work together, yet they gather into a magical sum far greater than the parts.

FOR THE POACHED RHUBARB LIQUOR

100 ml freshly squeezed orange juice
200 g caster sugar
400 ml water
10 cracked peppercorns
1 star anise
1 vanilla pod, split in half and seeds scraped out
8 Irish rhubarb stalks

FOR THE RHUBARB SORBET

350 g rhubarb stalks
65 ml water
40 g caster sugar
25 g inverted sugar (glossary)
3 g super neutrose (glossary)

FOR THE ROSE AND RHUBARB JELLY

160 ml water
25 g caster sugar
2 g rose water (glossary)
50 g rhubarb purée (see above)
2.5 agar agar powder (glossary)

FOR THE CRÈME FRAÎCHE AND GINGER CREAM

100 g caster sugar
100 ml water
20 g root ginger, sliced
1 slice of orange
5 g green cardamom, blitzed
1 star anise
250 g crème fraîche

FOR THE BLACK PEPPER SABLÉ BISCUIT

90 g egg yolks
120 g caster sugar
180 g T55 flour
4 g baking powder
5 g salt
5 g cracked black pepper
120 g unsalted butter, softened

TO SERVE

2 celery sticks, new season

SERVES 8

POACHED RHUBARB LIQUOR

Bring all the ingredients, except the rhubarb, to the boil and allow to boil for 3 minutes, then turn off the heat. Trim the rhubarb and cut into 10 cm lengths, then add to the liquor and poach at 80°C for 20 minutes until a knife goes through with little resistance. Remove with a slotted spoon onto a tray with silicone paper to absorb the excess juices and chill until needed. Reserve the cooking liquor to use in the sorbet.

RHUBARB SORBET

Trim the rhubarb and cut into small pieces, 2 × 2 cm, and put in a bowl. Bring the reserved cooking liquor to the boil and add the rhubarb. Boil for 5 minutes, then turn off the heat and allow to sit for 20 minutes. Strain off the rhubarb through a fine chinois and then blend the rhubarb in a liquidiser until smooth – you will need 250 g of the purée for the sorbet and 50 g for the jelly. Bring the water, sugar and inverted sugar to the boil. Add the super neutrose and then boil for 2 minutes, whisking continuously. Remove from the heat, add 250 g of the rhubarb purée and blend with a hand blender for 1 minute, then pass through a fine chinois. Transfer the sorbet to a Pacojet container and freeze to -22° or churn in an ice cream machine according to instructions and store in the freezer.

ROSE AND RHUBARB JELLY

Bring the water, sugar, rose water and reserved 50 g of rhubarb purée to the boil. Add the agar agar and boil for 2 minutes to activate the agar agar, whisking continuously. Place one 30 × 21 cm acetate sheet on a flat baking tray and pour the liquid onto the sheet. Quickly spread the mixture as thin as possible with a palette knife and allow to set; it will set very fast so you have to work quickly. Chill for 30 minutes, then take out and cut into 2 × 21 cm strips – you will need 8 strips in total. Arrange on a tray lined with clingfilm and chill until needed.

CRÈME FRAÎCHE AND GINGER CREAM

Bring the sugar, water, ginger, orange, green cardamom and star anise to the boil, and boil for 8 minutes to get a good syrup consistency. Strain through a fine chinois and chill for 1 hour. When the syrup is chilled, whisk in the crème fraîche and then chill.

BLACK PEPPER SABLÉ BISCUIT

Whisk the egg yolks and sugar in a KitchenAid with a whisk attachment on high speed for about 10 minutes until it is pale, fluffy and has doubled in volume. Meanwhile, pass the flour and baking powder through a fine sieve twice. Stir in the salt and pepper. Change the whisk to the paddle attachment and add the flour mix in 3 stages to the egg yolks and sugar mixture while mixing on a low speed. When the flour is just combined, add the butter all at once and mix on a medium speed until combined and there are no specks of butter visible. Line a baking tray with silicone paper and remove the sablé from the KitchenAid and spread out to a 1 cm thickness. Chill for 30 minutes. Preheat the oven to 155°C and cook for 7 minutes, then turn around and cook for another 7 minutes. Remove from the oven and cut into rough 4 × 4 cm squares, then return to the oven for 5 more minutes (this ensures even cooking). Remove from the oven and cool on a rack, then transfer to a plastic container and wrap in clingfilm until needed.

SERVING

Using a vegetable peeler, pare 24 strips from the celery sticks and set aside to use for decoration. Cut the poached rhubarb into 1 × 2 cm batons – you will need 48 pieces in total. Starting at the top of each large, shallow serving bowl, arrange the rhubarb, creating a rough zigzag pattern, then place a quenelle of the rhubarb sorbet near the top of the bowl in between the first and second piece of rhubarb. Break the sablé biscuit into rough pieces and put 5 pieces on the rhubarb at various positions. Peel off the jelly strips and cover the rhubarb in a rough S fashion, then decorate each one with 3 celery strips. When serving, flood the right side of the bowls with the crème fraîche and ginger cream to finish.

BRENDAN GUINAN AND **DONNACHA DONNELLY,** THE LADS WHO HEAD UP THE IN SEASON FARM IN NORTH COUNTY DUBLIN. THEIR BUSINESS ENSURES CHAPTER ONE HAS ACCESS TO A RANGE OF NATIVE AND VARIETAL FRUITS AND VEGETABLES, WHICH ARE UNAVAILABLE FROM CONVENTIONAL SUPPLIERS.

VERONICA STEELE,
A LEGEND AND THE
MATRIARCH OF IRISH
FARMHOUSE CHEESE,
THE CATALYST FOR THE
IRISH ARTISAN MOVEMENT.

KNOCKSINK WOODS IN ENNISKERRY, COUNTY WICKLOW.

BREADS

BROWN SODA BREAD

Preheat the oven to 200°C. Put all the ingredients, except the bread soda, buttermilk and treacle, in a KitchenAid fitted with a whisk attachment. Mix the dry ingredients with the whisk. Heat the treacle and buttermilk to 45°C (this enables the flour to take the liquid and to absorb quicker and more evenly). When the buttermilk and treacle mixture is heated, add the bread soda. Then add to the dry ingredients in the mixer and mix on a medium speed for 5 minutes, then on a high speed for 2 minutes. Transfer the dough to a greased 900 ml non-stick bread tin and cook

in the oven for 40 minutes. (We place a heavy tray on top of the tin to ensure an even-shaped bread for even slices.) Remove from the tin and cook for another 10 minutes, then transfer to a metal rack to cool. Leave to cool for 2 hours before slicing as the treacle makes it quite sticky and difficult to cut while still warm.

MAKES A 900 ML LOAF

380 g wholemeal flour
230 g self-raising flour
140 g wheat bran
40 g jumbo porridge oats
40 g pinhead porridge oats
15 g salt
8 g sugar
25 g bread soda
1 litre buttermilk
40 g treacle
butter, to grease

MULTI SEED AND RAPESEED OIL BREAD

Preheat the oven to 160°C and place all the seeds in a small oven tray. Roast for 10 minutes to release a more rounded nutty flavour. Then put all the ingredients, except for the water, in a KitchenAid fitted with a dough hook, being careful not to let the salt and yeast touch. Heat the water to 37°C, then add to the mixer and mix on a medium speed for 8–10 minutes. (This is done to stretch the gluten in the flour, thus adding air which makes the bread lighter.) Then mix on a high speed for 2 minutes. Stop the machine, and with a dough scraper, remove the dough. Pour a little rapeseed oil into a large bowl and rub the oil up the sides; put the dough inside and fold it over on itself a couple of times to ensure it rises evenly. Wrap the bowl in clingfilm and place in a warm spot for 1 1/2 hours to rise. Carefully take the dough out of the bowl and place it onto a lightly floured surface. Using a floured dough scraper, form the dough into a rough rectangle, and from the top, fold the dough onto itself to the halfway mark of the dough. Then take the bottom of the dough and fold it back onto the top fold to create a layer (the folds should be away from you at this stage). Starting at one end of the dough, fold the dough

back towards you using your right hand, and with your left hand and thumb, move under the folds to almost create a tunnel (this creates air pockets). Seal the dough at either end and put into a 900 ml greased bread tin with the seal facing down. Put a warm damp cloth over the top of the tin and allow to prove for 45 minutes until the dough has risen over the top of the tin. Preheat a steam oven to 100°C. Put the dough in the oven and steam for 3 minutes, then without opening the oven, set to roast with no moisture at 240°C for 10 minutes. Turn the oven down to 180°C and cook for another 20 minutes. Remove from the tin and cook for another 10 minutes, then transfer to a metal rack to cool. Leave to cool for 1 hour before slicing.

MAKES A 900 ML LOAF

20 g flaxseeds
20 g linseeds
20 g sunflower seeds
20 g pumpkin seeds
625 g 755 flour, extra to dust
17 g salt
8 g sugar
18 g fresh yeast
20 ml rapeseed oil, extra to grease
425 ml water

ONION BREAD

To make pain de mie dough, refer to the onion bread recipe below but leave to rise without adding the 150 g caramelised onions. Then use as required.

MAKES A 900 ML LOAF

FOR THE CARAMELISED ONIONS
30 g butter
150 g onions, thinly sliced

FOR THE BREAD DOUGH (PAIN DE MIE DOUGH)
125 ml water
150 g caramelised onions (see above)
500 g T55 flour, extra for dusting
50 g caster sugar
12 g salt
20 g fresh yeast
100 g eggs
50 g butter, softened
groundnut oil, to grease

FOR THE GLAZE
1 egg
pinch of caster sugar

CARAMELISED ONIONS

Heat the butter in a pan and gently sauté the onions for 15–20 minutes until caramelised and browned. Leave to cool.

ONION BREAD

Heat the water to 37°C. Place the caramelised onions and the rest of the ingredients, except the butter, in a KitchenAid fitted with a dough hook, making sure that the salt and yeast are not touching. Mix on a medium speed for 5 minutes, then on a high speed for 3 minutes to stretch the gluten. After this, stop the machine and add the butter in all at once, then mix again on a medium speed for 5 minutes, making sure all the butter is mixed through. Remove the dough from the machine and put into a large bowl. Wrap in clingfilm and prove for 1½ hours. When proved, turn out the dough on a floured surface and then shape into a rough cylinder. Cut the dough into 6 × 170 g pieces, then roll each piece into a tight ball. Brush a 900 ml bread tin with groundnut oil to put the dough balls in, leaving a 1 cm gap between each one (this gives them the room to expand). Cover with a damp cloth to prevent a skin forming and prove for another 45 minutes. Preheat the oven to 170°C. Remove the damp cloth from the bread.

To make the glaze, whisk the egg in a bowl with a pinch of salt and the sugar, then gently brush a light coating onto the bread. (The egg wash protects the bread; the salt helps give the dough a crust as it dries it out; and the sugar gives the bread a glossy finish when it caramelises in the oven.) Sprinkle with sea salt and cook for 25 minutes, then remove from the tin and cook for another 10 minutes. Transfer to a wire rack to cool for 1 hour before cutting.

SPICED BREAD

MAKES 1 LOAF

150 g T55 flour
5 g ground cinnamon
1 g ground nutmeg
10 g baking powder
75 ml milk
150 g honey
1 vanilla pod, split in half and seeds scraped out
zest of 1 lemon and 1 orange
100 g eggs
30 g caster sugar

Preheat the oven to 160°C. Sift the flour, spices and baking powder together through a fine sieve and set aside. Warm the milk and honey to 50°C and add the vanilla and zests (warming this at above 40°C will ensure the flour absorbs easier). Place the eggs and caster sugar in a KitchenAid fitted with a whisk attachment and whisk on a high speed for 2 minutes. Add the milk and honey mixture, and mix for 1 minute, then add the rest of the ingredients and mix for 4 minutes on a medium speed. Pour the spiced bread mix into a 10 × 30 cm bread tin and bake for 50 minutes until a skewer comes out clean, ensuring it is cooked. Cool on a wire rack and then cut the bread into 8 cm logs. Wrap in clingfilm and freeze until needed.

WHOLEMEAL SOURDOUGH

You will need the ingredients for the daily feed of the starter every day.

MAKES 2 X 700 ML LOAVES

FOR THE STARTER
200 g wholemeal flour
200 g T55 flour
300 ml warm water

FOR THE DAILY FEED OF THE STARTER
200 g wholemeal flour
200 g T55 flour
300 ml warm water

FOR THE WHOLEMEAL DOUGH
720 g T55 flour
80 g wholemeal flour
480 ml warm water, plus 15 ml
4 g fresh yeast
160 g starter (see above)
20 g salt
groundnut oil, to grease

STARTER

To make a starter, a culture has to be made first. A culture is when flours are mixed with water, and the wild yeasts, bacteria and micro-organisms present in the air, flour, water and hands of the chef, which begin to ferment sporadically. Once the fermentation has started, the chef feeds the culture every day to turn it into a living starter. Mix the flours in a bowl with your hands until combined. Put the water in a bowl, and with your hands, mix in the flours until it resembles a thick batter – it is important to use your hands because of the bacteria present. Wrap this bowl in clingfilm and leave in a cool, shaded spot for 3 days. To do the first feeding after the 3 days, discard 80 per cent of your culture – this does not have to be exact. The remaining culture should just cover the bottom of the bowl.

DAILY FEED OF THE STARTER

Mix the flours and water into your starter having discarded 80 per cent of it as above. Do this every day; the morning time is best. Do not use for at least 1 week, although it takes 2–3 months to get the best results. The flavour will increase with the length of time you have your starter.

WHOLEMEAL DOUGH

Feed your starter 3 hours before use to ensure it is not too sharp. Put the water, yeast and starter in a KitchenAid fitted with a dough hook. Your starter should float in the water and this shows it is alive and breathing. Mix with your hands, then add the flours and mix with the hook for 7 minutes on a medium speed, then for 2 minutes on a high speed. Stop the machine, and leaving the dough hook inside, wrap the bowl in clingfilm for 40 minutes. Then remove the clingfilm, add the salt with the extra 15 ml of warm water and mix for 5 minutes on a medium speed. Stop the machine and take out the hook, then wrap the bowl in clingfilm and leave for 30 minutes. After 30 minutes, reach your hand under the dough and fold it onto itself, turning the bowl as you do this. Repeat this action 6 times, wrapping the bowl again – it should take 3 hours. When this process is finished, turn the dough out gently onto a floured surface. With a dough scraper, cut the dough in half and take 1 half in front of you, form the dough to a rough circle and stretch 1 end away from you and fold back to the middle. Turn the dough and repeat this four times – you should have a rough rugby ball shape. Then turn the dough over so that the smooth side is facing upwards, and with both hands, push the ends of the dough together underneath while turning the dough. Do this 3 times. (This captures the air inside and helps to create and seal in air pockets and bubbles.) Do the same to the other dough and put each dough into a 700 ml greased oval bread tin. Place in the fridge overnight to prove. The next morning allow the bread to come to room temperature for 30 minutes, then steam for 3 minutes, and without opening the oven, set to roast with no moisture at 240°C for 10 minutes. Turn the oven down to 200°C and cook for another 20 minutes. Remove from the tin and cook for another 10 minutes, then transfer to a metal rack to cool. Leave to cool for 1 hour before slicing.

DARREN HOGARTY, HEAD PASTRY CHEF.

IRISH SOURDOUGH BISCUITS

Preheat the oven to 60°C, spread the sourdough on a baking tray and put in the oven overnight to dry out. The next day, blend in a blender to a crumb. Melt the butter and allow to cool to 40°C. Place the sourdough crumbs in a KitchenAid with a paddle attachment and mix with the cornflour and icing sugar on a slow speed. Add the melted butter and mix for 1 minute, then add the egg and mix for 3 minutes. Take the mixture out onto a sheet of greaseproof paper, then place another sheet on top. Roll with a rolling pin as thin as possible. Preheat the oven to

170°C. Remove the top sheet of greaseproof paper and place the rolled mixture on a baking tray. Cook for 15 minutes until golden brown. Transfer to a wire rack to cool completely. When cool break into 10 × 25 g shards and store in a plastic container for up to 3 days.

MAKES ABOUT 10

150 g leftover sourdough bread, cut into
 rough cubes
30 g cornflour
45 g icing sugar
45 g butter
1 egg

MALTED SEED AND TREACLE BISCUITS

MALTED SEED BISCUITS

Put the dry ingredients into a KitchenAid with a paddle attachment and mix on a medium speed. Add the butter in 2 stages and then mix for another 3 minutes. Add the egg whites and mix for a final 2 minutes. Line a baking tray with greaseproof paper and spread the mix onto the tray as thin as possible – you want a fine, delicate biscuit. Leave to rest for 15 minutes at room temperature. Meanwhile, preheat the oven to 160°C and when rested, cook for 12 minutes until slightly golden. Transfer to a wire rack and leave to cool completely. Once cold, break into 10 × 25 g shards. Store in a plastic container for up to 3 days.

TREACLE GLAZE

Soak the gelatine in a bowl of cold water for 10 minutes. Heat the treacle, and when it comes to just before the boil, remove from the heat. Squeeze out the excess liquid from the gelatine and whisk into the treacle until smooth. Transfer to a plastic container for up to 1 day.

SERVING

Ten minutes before serving, arrange the biscuits on a baking tray lined with greaseproof paper. Using a pastry brush, brush a thin coating of the treacle glaze onto three-quarters of the biscuits, leaving a piece at the bottom clean to allow them to be picked up. Leave the biscuits to dry for 5 minutes at room temperature before serving.

MAKES ABOUT 10

FOR THE MALTED SEED
BISCUITS
50 g malt flour, multi seed (glossary)
50 g demerara sugar
50 g ground almonds
3 g salt
70 g unsalted butter
40 g egg whites

FOR THE TREACLE GLAZE
2 g gold leaf gelatine
50 g treacle

SODA BREAD AND DEMERARA SUGAR BISCUITS IN CHOCOLATE WITH SMOKED SEA SALT

MAKES 10–15

FOR THE BROWN BREAD
BISCUITS
35 g butter
100 g dark muscovado sugar
30 g plain flour
60 g egg whites
20 g brown soda bread powder
(page 289)
20 g demerara sugar

FOR THE CHOCOLATE
COATING
100 g 70% plain chocolate
50 g cocoa butter (glossary)
3–5 g smoked sea salt

BROWN BREAD BISCUITS

Melt the butter in a pan, then add the sugar and mix to a paste. Remove from the heat and mix in the flour and egg whites. Pass through a tamis or drum sieve into a clean bowl and leave to rest overnight in the fridge. The next day, preheat the oven to 170°C. Spread the biscuit mix on a Silpat using a 2 × 4 cm template and sprinkle over the brown soda bread powder and demerara sugar. Bake for 9 minutes until crisp and golden brown. Transfer to a wire rack and leave to cool completely.

CHOCOLATE COATING

Roughly chop up the chocolate and cocoa butter, and put into a bowl set over a pan of simmering water to melt. Allow to cool to 40°C. Break the biscuits into shards and dip three-quarters of the way into the chocolate, gently shaking off any excess. Place on a Silpat, sprinkle with the smoked sea salt to taste and allow to set for 1 hour at room temperature. When set, transfer to a plastic container and keep for up to 2 days before serving.

CHAPTER ONE JAMESON WHISKEY CHOCOLATES

MAKES 48

FOR THE FILLING
200 g 55% Callabaut plain chocolate
180 ml cream
75 ml Jameson whiskey
25 g butter

FOR THE CHOCOLATE
SHELLS
500 g Arcato l'Opera plain dark chocolate

FILLING

Melt the chocolate in a bowl over a pan of simmering water. Bring the cream to the boil and add to the melted chocolate in 3 stages to create an emulsion, then finish with a hand blender to ensure the perfect ganache. When the ganache cools to 50°C, blend in the whiskey and then the butter. Transfer to a suitable container and cover with clingfilm. Place in a cool spot for 24 hours to crystallise.

CHOCOLATE SHELLS

Temper the chocolate according to the instructions on the packaging (50–55°C, 27–28°C, 30–31°C). Using 2 × 24-section chocolate moulds, pour a large ladle of the melted chocolate into each mould and spread with a palette knife. Gently tap the moulds on the worktop to remove air bubbles, then turn over each mould to remove excess chocolate and tap the moulds again. Leave upside down on a metal rack to drain and set for a couple of minutes. When the chocolate is semi-set, scrape down each mould with a metal scraper to remove the edges. Put the moulds in the fridge for 30 minutes to allow the chocolate to set properly. When set, put the ganache in a piping bag fitted with a no. 2 nozzle and pipe into the chocolate shells, filling generously. Use a palette knife to smooth over the back, making sure it is clean and smooth. Re-melt the excess chocolate to 30°C, pour a generous amount on the back and smooth out to a clean, polished finish. Allow to set at room temperature, then wrap in clingfilm and place in the fridge overnight to allow crystallisation to occur. To unmould the chocolates, gently tap the mould onto a clean surface, then place the chocolates into a suitable container. Allow to come to room temperature for 45 minutes before serving.

CARAMELISED HONEY AND JAMESON WHISKEY CHOCOLATES

FILLING

Melt the chocolate in a bowl set over a pan of simmering water and set aside. Caramelise the honey in a heavy-based pan to a deep golden colour. Heat the cream and add to the caramelised honey in 3 stages, then boil for 1 minute. In a separate pan, heat the whiskey, then very carefully flambé. Allow the flame to burn out naturally. When this is done, add to the cream mixture. Blend with a hand blender for 1 minute to make a smooth glossy emulsion, then transfer to a suitable container and allow to rest at room temperature for 24 hours to ensure the crystallisation process is complete.

CHOCOLATE SHELLS

Temper the chocolate according to the instructions on the packaging (50–55°C, 27–28°C, 30–31°C). Using 2 × 24-section chocolate moulds, pour a large ladle of the melted chocolate into each mould and spread with a palette knife. Gently tap the moulds on the worktop to remove air bubbles, then turn over the moulds to remove excess chocolate and tap the moulds again. Leave upside down on a metal rack to drain and set for a couple of minutes. When the chocolate is semi-set, scrape down the moulds with a metal scraper to remove the edges. Put the moulds in the fridge for 30 minutes to allow the chocolate to set properly. When set, put the ganache in a piping bag fitted with a no. 2 nozzle and pipe into the chocolate shells, filling generously. Use a palette knife to smooth over the back, making sure it is clean and smooth. Re-melt the excess chocolate to 30°C, pour a generous amount on the back and smooth out to a clean, polished finish. Allow to set, then wrap in clingfilm and place in the fridge overnight to allow crystallisation to occur. To unmould the chocolates, gently tap the mould onto a clean surface, then place the chocolates into a suitable container. Allow to come to room temperature for 45 minutes before serving.

MAKES 48

FOR THE FILLING
150 g Manjari chocolate
90 g honey
225 ml cream
70 ml Jameson whiskey

FOR THE CHOCOLATE
SHELLS
500 g Divo l'Opera milk chocolate

BUTTERMILK AND MALTED BARLEY CHOCOLATES

FILLING

Melt the chocolate in a pan set over simmering water. Set aside to cool a little. Heat the cream and barley malt in a pan. Add the cream mix to the chocolate in 3 stages to make a glossy and shiny emulsion. Set aside to cool to between 40–50°C. Using a hand blender, blend in the butter followed by the buttermilk. Transfer to a suitable container and leave in the fridge overnight to allow the crystallisation process to occur.

CHOCOLATE SHELLS

Temper the chocolate according to the instructions on the packaging (50–55°C, 27–28°C, 30–31°C). Using 2 × 24-section chocolate moulds, pour a large ladle of the melted chocolate into each mould and spread with a palette knife. Gently tap the moulds on the worktop to remove air bubbles, then turn over the moulds to remove excess chocolate and tap the moulds again. Leave upside down on a metal rack to drain and set for a couple of minutes. When the chocolate is semi-set, scrape down the moulds with a metal scraper to remove the edges. Put the moulds in the fridge for 30 minutes to allow the chocolate to set properly. When set, put the ganache into a piping bag fitted with a no. 2 nozzle and pipe into the chocolate shells, filling generously. Use a palette knife to smooth over the back, making sure it is clean and smooth. Re-melt the excess chocolate to 30°C, pour a generous amount on the back and smooth out to a clean, polished finish. Allow to set at room temperature, then wrap in clingfilm and place in the fridge overnight to allow crystallisation to occur. To unmould the chocolates, gently tap the mould onto a clean surface, then place the chocolates into a suitable container. Allow to come to room temperature for 45 minutes before serving.

MAKES 48

FOR THE FILLING
200 g Divo l'Opera milk chocolate
100 ml cream
30 ml liquid barley malt (glossary)
20 g butter, softened
100 ml buttermilk

FOR THE CHOCOLATE
SHELLS
500 g Arcato l'Opera dark chocolate

PASSION FRUIT MILK CHOCOLATES

MAKES 48

FOR THE PASSION FRUIT GANACHE

150 g Divo l'Opera milk chocolate
70 ml cream
70 ml passion fruit purée (glossary)

FOR THE PASSION FRUIT JELLY

2 g gold leaf gelatine
100 ml passion fruit juice

FOR THE CHOCOLATE SHELLS

500 g Divo l'Opera milk chocolate

PASSION FRUIT GANACHE

Melt the chocolate in a pan set over simmering water. Set aside to cool a little. Heat the cream and passion fruit juice in a pan. When heated, add the cream and passion fruit mixture to the chocolate in 3 stages to make a glossy and shiny emulsion. Set aside to cool to between 40–50°C. Transfer to a suitable container and leave in the fridge overnight to allow the crystallisation process to occur.

PASSION FRUIT JELLY

Soak the gelatine in a bowl of cold water for 10 minutes, then squeeze out the excess liquid. Bring the passion fruit juice to the boil and add the squeezed out gelatine. Strain through a fine chinois and cool to between 35 and 40°C. When cool, transfer to a small squeezy bottle.

CHOCOLATE SHELLS

Temper the chocolate according to the instructions on the packaging (50–55°C, 27–28°C, 30–31°C). When tempered, using 2 × 24-section chocolate moulds, pour a large ladle of the melted chocolate into each mould and spread with a palette knife. Gently tap the moulds on the worktop to remove air bubbles, then turn over each mould to remove excess chocolate and tap the mould agains. Leave upside down on a metal rack to drain and set for a couple of minutes. When the chocolate is semi-set, scrape down each mould with a metal scraper to remove the edges. Put the moulds in the fridge for 30 minutes to allow the chocolate to set properly. When set, put the ganache into a piping bag fitted with a no. 2 nozzle and pipe to half full with passion fruit jelly and re-set in the fridge for a further 30 minutes. Use a palette knife to smooth over the back, making sure it is clean and smooth. Re-melt the excess chocolate to 30°C, pour a generous amount on the back and smooth out to a clean, polished finish. Allow to set at room temperature, then wrap in clingfilm and place in the fridge overnight to allow crystallisation to occur. To unmould the chocolates, gently tap the mould onto a clean surface, then place the chocolates into a suitable container. Allow to come to room temperature for 45 minutes before serving.

BASIC RECIPES

SAVOURY

BEURRE NOISETTE

Makes 200 g
250 g butter

Melt the butter in a pan, then continue cooking over a medium to high heat until the butter turns golden brown. Remove from the heat. If not using immediately, stop the cooking process by pouring into a clean cold pan or by setting the pan into a bowl of cold water. The beurre noisette will keep well for 1–2 weeks in a sealed container in the fridge.

FOIE GRAS BUTTER

Makes 200 g
115 g unsalted butter
125 g foie gras

Preheat the oven to 80°C. Put the butter and foie gras in a small tray or pan and place in the oven for 40 minutes, until the foie gras is dissolved and the fat has separated from the solids. Carefully pour the fat into a clean storage container, discarding the solids. Allow to cool, then wrap in clingfilm and refrigerate. This will keep for 1 week in the fridge and it also freezes well.

COOKED WHITE BEAN CASSOULET

Makes 8 portions
300 g coco de paimpol beans (glossary), shelled weight
1 small carrot, cut in half lengthways
½ celery stick
1 garlic clove, peeled and lightly crushed
1 bay leaf
30 g smoked bacon
1 onion, chopped
100 ml fish stock (page 286) or chicken stock (page 285)

Put the beans in a pan with the carrot, celery, garlic, bacon, onion and bay leaf. Add the fish or chicken stock and enough water to comfortably cover the beans. Simmer over a low heat until the beans are completely soft with no resistance at all. Remove the vegetables and bay leaf, and season with salt. The beans can be left to cool in the liquid. Refrigerate until needed but they will keep for several days.

CAULIFLOWER FLORETS AND SLICES

Makes 8–10 portions
1 cauliflower

Using a mandolin, cut slices approximately 2 mm thick from the larger cauliflower florets – you will need 2 of these for each plate. Cut the rest of the cauliflower into florets – you will need approximately 300 g. Blanch the cauliflower in boiling salted water until just tender, cooking the slices and florets separately. Refresh separately in a bowl of iced water and reserve until needed.

CONFIT ORANGE

Makes about 200 g
4 oranges
125 g sugar
250 ml water
2 star anise
4 allspice berries
2 juniper berries

Cut each orange in 4 and remove the skins with pith, and refrigerate the flesh for use in other dishes. Put the skins in a pan of cold water and bring to the boil, then refresh in a bowl of iced water. Repeat this 3 times. Bring the sugar, water and spices to the boil and add the orange skins, then boil for 2 minutes. Transfer to a vacuum pack bag and cook in a water bath at 70°C for 10–12 hours until soft. Allow to cool and cut up the oranges as specified in recipes. Use as required.

TOMATO CONSOMMÉ AND JELLY

Makes 750 ml

1 kg vine ripened tomatoes
1 kg cherry tomatoes
2 garlic cloves
25 g caster sugar
50 ml Chardonnay vinegar
4 gold leaf gelatine leaves
groundnut oil, for greasing

Blend all the ingredients, except for the gelatine, then transfer to a large muslin bag. Hang the bag over a bowl in the fridge overnight. The next day, bring the tomato liquid up to the boil and reduce by a quarter to make 750 ml in total. Season with salt and white pepper to taste. Put the gelatine into a bowl of cold water and set aside for 10 minutes. When the gelatine is soft, gently squeeze out the excess water and heat a ladleful of the consommé in a small pan until just below the boil. Whisk in the softened gelatine and then add back into the rest of the consommé. Pass through a fine chinois and pour into a small lightly oiled tray lined with clingfilm or into serving bowls and leave to set in the fridge for 2 hours, or pour into a piping bag after leaving to cool.

COOKED LOBSTER

The same method can be used for cooking crabs.

Makes 8 portions

2 x 600–800 g live lobsters
salt
splash of white wine vinegar

Bring a large pan of water to the boil. Heavily salt it using 40 g of salt to 1 litre of water, then add the splash of vinegar. Humanely kill the lobsters and break them down into claws and tails. Blanch the lobster parts in the hot water, 2 minutes for the claws and 3 for the tails, then transfer to a bowl of iced water. When cool, use the back of a heavy knife to gently crack the shells and remove the meat. Cut into pieces approximately 3 cm long and chill until needed.

COURT BOUILLON

Makes 2 litres

1.8 litres water
200 ml white wine
2 onions
1 celery stick
2 carrots, sliced
2 bay leaves
1 fresh thyme sprig
1 tsp black peppercorns
2 star anise
12 juniper berries
1 tbsp salt

Put all the ingredients in a pan and bring to a simmer. Use as required.

PARMESAN CREAM

Makes 350 g

500 ml cream
100 g Parmesan, freshly grated
2 egg yolks

Heat the cream in a pan and simmer until reduced by half. Remove from the heat and add the Parmesan, stirring continuously. Allow to cool completely, then whisk in the egg yolks. Keep at room temperature until needed. It does not refrigerate so make on the day you are serving.

ONION BREAD, RYE BREAD OR BRIOCHE CRISPS

Makes 8

½ loaf onion bread (page 264), rye bread or brioche bread, frozen
200 ml light olive oil

Preheat the oven to 160°C. Take the bread out of the freezer for 10 minutes before use. Using a meat slicer, cut 8 × 2–3 mm slices. Lay the slices on a heavy baking tray and oil generously with olive oil. Season lightly with the salt and then cover with another sheet of greaseproof paper and another heavy baking tray. Bake for 6–8 minutes or until golden brown. Remove from the trays and allow to cool. Use on the same day.

BRIOCHE OR RYE BREAD CROÛTONS

Makes 20 portions

100 g brioche or rye bread, crusts removed and cut into 1 cm dice
75 g butter

Heat the butter in a small sauté pan until foaming and add the brioche or rye bread cubes. Cook over a medium heat, tossing continuously until the bread is a uniform golden brown. Drain on kitchen paper and season with salt. Make on the day you need them.

DEEP-DRIED BEETROOT CRISPS

2 large beetroots
vegetable oil, for deep-frying

Peel the beetroots and thinly slice using a mandolin. Then cut out circles of the beetroot using a 45 mm cutter. In a dehydrator, dry the circles at 125°C for 3 hours. To serve, deep-fry the beetroot crisps at 150°C for 5–10 seconds until crispy and then drain on kitchen paper. Season with salt.

DEEP-FRIED PARSLEY ROOTS

2 flat-leaf parsley roots
vegetable oil, for deep-frying

Peel the parsley roots and remove the tops with a knife. Using a Y-peeler, peel long strips the length of the parsley root. Deep-fry in the vegetable oil at 140°C until golden brown and crisp. Drain on kitchen paper and season with salt.

DEEP-FRIED SAGE LEAVES

vegetable oil, for deep-frying
16 fresh sage leaves

Heat the oil in a deep-fat fryer to 140°C and cook the sage leaves for 30 seconds. Drain on kitchen paper and season with salt and pepper. Use immediately.

HAZELNUT DRESSING

If you are only using a small amount of this dressing, the rest can be stored in the fridge. It is very versatile and goes well with green salads.

Makes about 800 ml
200 ml sunflower oil or light olive oil
100 ml hazelnut oil
30 ml white truffle oil
80 ml black truffle vinegar (glossary)
80 ml port
80 ml hazelnut alcohol, optional
160 ml aged sherry vinegar
juice of ½ lemon
2 tbsp Dijon mustard
1 tbsp white truffle honey (glossary)
1 tbsp sugar

Put all the ingredients into a high speed blender and blend until fully emulsified. Season to taste and place in a squeezy bottle until needed.

MUSTARD AND WHITE TRUFFLE HONEY DRESSING

Makes 250 ml
2 tbsp Dijon mustard
2 tbsp white truffle honey (glossary) or any honey will suffice
20 ml black truffle vinegar (glossary) or balsamic vinegar
20 ml aged sherry vinegar
50 ml lemon juice
2 tbsp Amontillado sweet sherry
100 ml light olive oil
100 ml hazelnut oil

Whisk together the mustard and honey and all the vinegars. Then add the lemon juice and sherry, and gradually whisk in both oils. Season with salt and black pepper. Use as required.

DRIED CAULIFLOWER

Makes 50 g
200 g cauliflower

Using a mandolin, slice the cauliflower thinly. Spread on a tray and dry in a low oven or dehydrator at 55°C for 3–4 hours until crisp.

DRIED SWEETCORN

Makes 50 g
100 g sweetcorn kernels
200 ml olive oil

Mix the sweetcorn kernels with enough olive oil to lightly coat and a generous pinch of salt. Spread on a baking sheet and place in a preheated oven at 90°C. Roast for an hour or until the kernels are dried out and chewy. Use as required.

MUSHROOM DUXELLE

Makes 800 g
500 g mushrooms, trimmed
1 litre water
1 litre milk
30 g butter
100 g shallots, very finely diced
5 garlic cloves, crushed
150 ml port
100 ml cognac
200 ml cream
3 tbsp lemon juice

Place the mushrooms in a pan with the water and milk, and bring to a simmer for 10 minutes. Strain off the mushrooms and set aside. Melt the butter in a separate pan and sweat the shallots and garlic until soft without colouring. Add the port and cognac, reduce by 90 per cent, then add the cream and reduce again by 80 per cent until really thick. Finely chop the mushrooms, then add to the reduced cream and shallots. Stir until you get a rich creamy texture and then heat thoroughly before removing from the heat. Season with salt and black pepper, and add the lemon juice. Allow to cool. The duxelle will keep in the fridge for 2–3 days.

BUTTER OR OLIVE OIL EMULSION

Makes 200 g
100 g butter or 100 ml extra virgin olive oil
40 ml water

Place the butter or olive oil and water in a pan and bring to the boil to emulsify. Use as required.

RED OR WHITE WINE SHALLOT ESSENCE

Makes 750 ml
10 shallots, roughly chopped
750 ml red or white wine

Put the shallots and red or white wine in a blender and blend to a purée. Transfer to a bowl and cover in the fridge overnight. The next day, pass the liquid through a double layer of muslin and store in the fridge. This will keep well in the fridge for up to several weeks.

PATA NEGRA FARCE

Makes 250 g
25 g cooked ham
100 g lean pork meat
25 g pata negra ham or Parma ham will suffice
25 g lardo di colonatta (glossary)
25 g garlic sausage
1 egg
30 g Parmesan grated
1 slice of white bread soaked in milk
2 tbsp fresh flat-leaf parsley, chopped

Mince all the ingredients together in a medium-sized mincer. Use as required.

FRIED CABBAGE LEAF

Makes 8 portions

½ head cabbage, preferably Savoy or York
100 g foie gras butter (page 276) or beurre noisette (page 276)

Separate out the cabbage leaves and remove the central rib – you'll need 8 in total. Blanch in a pan of boiling salted water until just cooked, then refresh in a bowl of iced water. Dry on kitchen paper. Heat a large sauté pan until hot. Add the foie gras butter and fry the cabbage leaves until well browned and crispy. Drain on kitchen paper and use as required.

FRIED FLAT-LEAF PARSLEY

handful fresh flat-leaf parsley leaves
olive oil, for brushing

Wash and dry the parsley. Coat with olive oil, then stretch some clingfilm over a plate and put the parsley leaves on top. Place in a microwave for 3–4 minutes to fry the leaves.

GRELOT ONIONS

Makes 8

8 medium to large grelot onions, outer layer peeled and tops chopped off
40 g butter
pinch of sugar

Sauté the grelot onions in the butter over a medium heat, then add a pinch of sugar and baste the onions with the hot foaming butter. Transfer to a preheated oven at 160°C and cook for 10 minutes until soft. Remove from the oven and season with salt and pepper. They should be really brown and soft.

CRAB JUICE

Add a little thickener, a pinch at a time, to a crab stock until slightly thickened. Use as required.

PIGEON GLAZE

Makes about 200 ml

8 pigeon carcasses, including any bones and trimmings
50 ml olive oil
4 shallots, chopped
2 celery sticks, roughly chopped
2 carrots, roughly chopped
4 garlic cloves, lightly crushed
handful each fresh thyme and sage sprigs
1 bay leaf
2 g black peppercorns
1 star anise
1 tsp coriander seeds
3 juniper berries
1 tsp vadouvan spice (glossary)
150 ml Madeira
2 litres double chicken stock (page 286)
1 tsp thickener (glossary)
1 tsp aged sherry vinegar
40 g butter, diced and chilled

Roast the pigeon bones in a hot pan in the olive oil until well coloured. Add the onion, celery, carrots, garlic, herbs and spices, and cook over a medium heat until browned. Stir in the vadouvan spice, then pour in the Madeira and simmer to reduce by half. Cover with the chicken stock and bring to the boil. Reduce the heat and simmer gently for 2 hours, skimming off the fat as it collects on the surface. Pass the stock into a clean pan, return to the boil and reduce to 200 ml, then pass through a double layer of muslin. Use the thickener to thicken to a glaze consistency, adding a pinch at a time. When ready to serve, heat the sauce and stir in the aged sherry vinegar, then whisk in the butter.

FRESH BAY LEAF, SAGE, TARRAGON OR ROCKET JUICE

This needs to be started the day before it is needed.

Makes about 150 ml

4 large bunches of fresh herbs (fresh bay leaves, sage, tarragon or rocket)
1 tsp thickener (glossary)

Bring a large pan of water to a vigorous boil. Meanwhile, prepare a bowl of iced water. Blanch the herbs for ten seconds in the boiling water, lift out using a spider and put straight into the bowl of iced water. When cold, drain the herbs and put into a Pacojet. Place in the freezer and freeze overnight or until completely solid. Blend the herbs three times, then add an equal volume of ice cold water and mix well. Pass through a double layer of muslin, pressing well to extract all the juice. Thicken the herb juice with the thickener, a pinch at a time. Put into a squeezy bottle. These will keep for up to 1 week.

MADEIRA JUS

Makes about 1 litre

2 tbsp olive oil
2 onions, sliced
2 carrots, chopped
3 celery sticks, chopped
1 leek, sliced
6 garlic cloves, lightly crushed
handful fresh thyme sprigs
2 bay leaves
550 ml Madeira
5 litres double chicken stock (page 286)
1 tsp thickener (glossary)
40 g butter, diced and chilled

Heat the oil in a large pan and roast the vegetables and herbs over a high heat until well caramelised. Add 400 ml of the Madeira and the chicken stock, then bring to the boil and simmer for 20 minutes. Strain through a colander into a clean pan, bring back up to the boil and reduce to 1 litre. Remove from the heat and add the remaining 150 ml of the Madeira. Pass the sauce through a double layer of muslin and then thicken slightly with the thickener, a pinch at a time. When ready to serve, heat the sauce and whisk in the butter.

RABBIT JUS

Makes about 1 litre

4 rabbit carcasses
60 ml vegetable oil
3 onions, chopped
2 celery sticks, chopped
4 large carrots, chopped
6 garlic cloves, sliced in half
handful each fresh rosemary and thyme sprigs
2 bay leaves
500 ml white wine
3 litres double chicken stock (page 286)
a little thickener (glossary)

Discarding the rabbit heads, chop the carcasses into 5–10 cm pieces. Heat 30 ml of the oil and roast the bones, stirring frequently, until well coloured. Heat the rest of the oil in a stockpot, then add the onions, celery, carrots, garlic and herbs, and cook over a medium heat, stirring frequently, until well browned. Pour in the wine and simmer to reduce by half. Add the roasted bones and cover with the stock, then bring to the boil and simmer gently for 40 minutes, skimming off the fat with a ladle. Pass the stock into a clean pan, return to the boil and reduce to 1 litre. Pass through a double layer of muslin and thicken slightly with the thickener, a pinch at a time.

MAYONNAISE

Makes 420 ml

2 egg yolks
10 g mild mustard
20 ml white wine vinegar
pinch of cayenne pepper
400 ml light olive oil

Place the egg yolks, mustard, vinegar, cayenne pepper and a pinch of salt in a blender and mix briefly, then with the blender on a medium speed pour in the oil in a slow, steady stream until it is all incorporated and emulsified. If the mayonnaise is too thick, add a little warm water. Use as required.

EGG WHITE MAYONNAISE

Makes 450 ml

2 egg whites
10 g mild mustard
20 ml white wine vinegar
pinch of cayenne pepper
400 ml sunflower oil
40 ml warm water

Place the egg whites, mustard, vinegar, cayenne pepper and a pinch of salt in a blender and mix briefly, then with the blender on a medium speed pour in the oil in a slow, steady stream until it is all incorporated and emulsified. Then slowly blend in the warm water, which helps to better emulsify the mayonnaise. Use as required.

CHICKEN MOUSSE

Makes about 400 g

200 g skinless chicken breast fillet, diced and chilled
1 egg white, chilled
5 g salt
175 ml cream, chilled

Blitz everything together in a blender, then pass through a tamis or a drum sieve. Chill until needed. Use on the same day.

BUTTERMILK POTATO PURÉE

Makes about 400 g

2.5 kg potatoes, Skerries Native, to give 600 g plain mash, 150 g smoked mash and 2 whole potatoes
250 g unsalted butter, chilled and diced
salt
75 ml milk
75 ml buttermilk
50 g spring onions, finely sliced
2 tbsp Thick and Easy

Preheat an oven to 150°C, 50% steam. Combine the milk and spring onions in a small pan and warm through, being careful not to boil, then remove from the heat and leave to infuse. Bake the potatoes in the preheated oven for 30 minutes or until completely cooked through. Alternatively boil, with skins on, in salted water until tender. Whilst still warm, peel off the potato skins. Reserve two of the potatoes, and put an additional 300 g into the smoker over a medium heat for 10 minutes. Put the rest through a mouli. When the smoked potatoes are ready, put them through the mouli as well, and mix with 600 g of the plain steamed mash. Season the potato with salt to taste, and mix well. Pass the spring onion infusion through a chinois and whisk in the Thick and Easy. Pour onto the mash and transfer to a Thermomix. Blend at 40°C for around 5 minutes, adding in the cold butter and buttermilk a little at a time, then pass through a fine chinois. To serve, warm in a pan.

SMOKED POMMES DAUPHINE

Makes 2 kg

FOR THE SAVOURY CHOUX PASTRY
125 ml cold water
125 ml milk
130 g unsalted butter, diced
200 g plain flour, sieved
3 g salt
3 g sugar
4 eggs

FOR THE DAUPHINE
600 g baby potatoes
600 g savoury choux pastry, chilled (see above)
600 g smoked potato purée (page 284), chilled
60 g Parmesan, freshly grated, chilled
3 g salt
3 g cayenne pepper or smoked paprika
vegetable oil, for deep-frying

SAVOURY CHOUX PASTRY

Put the water, milk and butter together in a pan and bring to the boil. Whisk in the flour, salt and sugar, then continue to stir with a wooden spoon until the mixture comes together. Transfer to a KitchenAid fitted with a paddle attachment and mix on a medium speed. Add one egg and continue to mix until it is all incorporated, then continue adding the eggs, one at a time, until they are thoroughly mixed in and the mixture is smooth and glossy. Allow to cool, then transfer to the fridge and rest for 2 hours before making up the Dauphine.

DAUPHINE

Boil the baby potatoes in salted water until tender. When cool enough to handle, peel off the skins and crush. Allow to cool completely. Mix the chilled choux and smoked potato together, then add the Parmesan, salt and cayenne or smoked paprika. Fold together with the crushed baby potatoes. To serve, roll into balls of approximately 30 g each and deep-fry in vegetable oil at 180°C until golden brown. Drain on kitchen paper and season with salt.

POTATO DUMPLINGS

Makes 900 g

1½ kg potatoes, Rooster, scrubbed
80 g plain flour
4 egg yolks
1 tbsp thickener (glossary)
pinch of freshly ground nutmeg

Preheat the oven to 150°C – we use 50 per cent steam but an ordinary oven at 150°C will be ok. Bake the potatoes for 1 hour or until completely cooked through. While still warm, peel off the potato skins and put through a mouli, then pass through a fine sieve. Put on a tray, uncovered, in the fridge overnight to dry out. The next day, put the flour and 800 g of the potatoes into a bowl and rub together by hand, then add the egg yolks, thickener and nutmeg, and season with salt and white pepper. Knead to form a smooth dough, then roll out on a cold, lightly floured work surface into long rolls the thickness of a thumb and slice evenly into dumplings about 2 cm long. Roll into balls and put on a tray in the fridge until needed.

BLACK OLIVE OIL

Makes 200 ml

250 g black olives, pitted
150 ml extra virgin olive oil

Dry the olives for 3–4 days in a dehydrator until totally dry. Blitz to a powder in a Thermomix or blender, then pour on the olive oil and blend for 5 minutes. Pass through muslin. Use as required.

GARLIC OIL

Makes 1 litre

75 g garlic, crushed
1 litre olive oil

If you don't have a Pacojet, this method can also be used to make the herb oils, again cooking under 60°C.

Vacuum pack the garlic with the oil and cook in a water bath at 60°C for 2 hours. Be careful not to go over 60°C and you will get light fragrant oil without the breakdown of odorous garlic properties. Leave to cool, then strain through a fine chinois. This will keep for up to 2 weeks in the fridge.

DILL, CHIVE, BASIL, CORIANDER OR ROCKET OIL

Makes about 400 ml

500 g fresh herb leaves (dill, chive, basil, coriander or rocket)
400 ml light olive oil or any neutral oil like rapeseed

Blanch the herb sprigs in boiling unsalted water, lift out using a spider and refresh in a bowl of iced water. Drain and squeeze really tightly in a cloth, draining off as much of the water as you can. This will give you approximately150 g of blanched herb. Combine this with 400 ml of oil in a Pacojet container and freeze overnight. The next day, blend 2–3 times and hang in a muslin. The result is a deep green and strong herb-flavoured oil.

If you haven't got a Pacojet, half the quantities, so use 250 g of fresh herb sprigs and 200 ml light olive oil or any neutral oil like rapeseed. Blend together on a high speed for 3–4 minutes and hang in a muslin. Using a funnel, put into a squeezy bottle. These will keep for up to 1 week.

BEETROOT POWDER

Makes 50 g

300 g fresh beetroot

This can be made using the waste from juicing the beetroots to make the beetroot sauce. Spread on trays and dry in a dehydrator or low oven at 55°C until very dry. Blitz to a fine powder in a blender.

Peel the beetroot and then finely slice using a Japanese mandolin or meat slicer. Spread on trays and check after 3 hours – they should be completely dried out. Put the dried-out slices in a blender and blitz to a fine powder. This keeps for 3–4 days in an airtight container.

DRIED MUSHROOM SLICES OR POWDER

Makes 30 g

200 g mushrooms, any kind, we use large field mushrooms or Paris browns

Slice the mushrooms thinly on a Japanese mandolin. Spread on a tray and dry in a low oven or dehydrator at 55°C for about 2 hours until crisp. To make mushroom powder, blend the dried mushrooms to a fine powder. These keep for 3–4 days in an airtight container.

PICKLED BABY CUCUMBER

Makes 400 g

200 ml distilled malt vinegar
200 g sugar
100 ml water
2 coriander seeds
2 black peppercorns
1 star anise
1 small bay leaf
400 g baby cucumbers

Place the pickling ingredients in a pan and bring to the boil. Meanwhile, prick the cucumbers with a fork. When the pickle comes to the boil, add the cucumbers and cover with a lid to keep submerged, then remove from the heat. These are best made at least 2 days before you need them.

PICKLED CARROT STRIPS

Makes 15–20 strips

3 carrots
handful of salt
50 ml water
50 g sugar
100 ml apple balsamic cider vinegar (glossary)
2 tsp Japanese apple cider vinegar (glossary), optional
5 coriander seeds
½ star anise
1 tsp caraway seeds

Slice the carrots on a mandolin. Lay on a tray, sprinkle evenly with salt and leave for 20 minutes. Rinse and pat dry. Put the water, sugar and vinegars in a pan together with the spices and bring to the boil until the sugar has dissolved. Leave to cool, then pour over the carrots and pickle for 30 minutes.

PICKLED CAULIFLOWER

Makes 20 pieces

1/4 cauliflower, tough core removed
4 g salt, plus a handful for the cauliflower slices
600 g rice wine vinegar
40 g sugar
5 g lemon zest

Slice the cauliflower on a mandolin. Lay on a tray, sprinkle with salt and leave for 20 minutes. Rinse and pat dry. Bring the vinegar to the boil with the sugar, zest and salt. When the sugar is dissolved, allow to cool. Reserve 350 ml of the pickle for the pickled pumpkin and pour the rest over the cauliflower.

PICKLED CROWN PRINCE PUMPKIN SLICES

Makes 16 pieces of pickled pumpkin slices

1/4 small crown prince pumpkin
6 g salt, plus a handful for the pumpkin slices
250 ml Hondashi stock (glossary)
30 ml mirin
30 ml sake
5 g rice vinegar
30 ml dark soy sauce
350 ml reserved pickle liquid from the pickled cauliflower (see above) or any other vegetable

Peel the pumpkin and then slice on a mandolin. Lay on a tray, sprinkle with salt and leave for 20 minutes. Rinse and wring out in a clean tea towel to get rid of as much water as possible. Bring the stock, mirin, sake, vinegar and soy to the boil with the salt. Leave to cool, then mix with the 350 ml of reserved pickle. Pour over the pumpkin slices.

PICKLED KING OYSTER, SHIITAKE OR VELVET PIOPPINO MUSHROOMS

Makes 250 g

125 ml white wine
125 ml white wine vinegar
250 ml water
5 g salt
12 g caster sugar
1 garlic clove, crushed
1 small fresh thyme sprig
1 bay leaf
2 g coriander seeds
2 g black peppercorns
250 g mushrooms, king oyster, shiitake or piccioni
125 ml extra virgin olive oil

Put the white wine, vinegar, water, salt, sugar, garlic, herbs and spices into a pan and bring to the boil. Add the mushrooms and return the pan to the boil, then remove from the heat and allow to cool. When cold, drain off and discard three-quarters of the pickling liquid, then pour over the olive oil. These will keep for 2 weeks in the fridge.

PICKLED RED DULSE OR SEA SPAGHETTI

Makes 150 g

150 g red dulse or sea spaghetti
600 ml rice vinegar
4 g salt
40 g sugar
3 g lemon zest

Wash the red dulse or sea spaghetti and carefully sort through it, discarding any damaged pieces. Put the rice vinegar in a pan large enough to hold all the ingredients, and add the salt, sugar and lemon zest. Bring to the boil, stirring to dissolve the sugar, and add the red dulse or sea spagetti. Return to the boil and simmer for about 5 minutes until tender. Remove from the heat and allow to cool before serving.

PICKLED SHALLOT RINGS

Makes about 8 portions

100 ml apple balsamic cider vinegar (glossary)
25 g sugar
25 shallot rings from the middle and outer part of a shallot

Bring the vinegar and sugar to the boil, remove from the heat and allow to cool. Place the shallot rings in the solution for 1 hour before serving.

PICKLED WHITE RADISH

Makes 20 pieces

1/2 white radish, scrubbed
600 g rice wine vinegar
40 g sugar
5 g lemon zest
4 g salt
pinch of ascorbic acid

Finely slice the white radish on a mandolin. Bring the vinegar to the boil with the sugar, zest and salt. When the sugar is dissolved, remove from the heat and add the ascorbic acid, then leave to cool. Pour over the radish slices.

BASIL OR FLAT-LEAF PARSLEY PURÉE

Makes 700 ml

500 g fresh basil or flat-leaf parsley leaves
400 ml cream

Blanch the basil or flat-leaf parsley in boiling unsalted water, lift out using a spider and refresh in a bowl of iced water. Squeeze with a towel, draining all the moisture away. This will give you approximately 150 g of blanched herb. Put in a Pacojet and freeze overnight. The next day reduce the cream by half and allow to cool, then blend with the frozen basil to make the purée.

If you haven't got a Pacojet, just blend the blanched basil or flat-leaf parsley with the reduced cream in a high-speed blender until you get a smooth purée, adding a little more reduced cream if necessary. Using a funnel, put into a squeezy bottle.

BLOOD ORANGE PURÉE

Makes 150 ml

3 blood oranges or ordinary oranges, peeled, washed
  and roughly diced
150 g sugar
90 ml water
1 vanilla pod, split in half and seeds scraped out

Place all the ingredients in a large pan and bring to the boil for 5 minutes, then reduce the heat and simmer for 40 minutes. Transfer to a blender and purée until silky smooth, then pass through a fine chinois. Chill until needed.

CAPER SPROUT PURÉE

Makes 300 ml

200 g preserved caper flowers (glossary), drained and
  well rinsed
100 ml extra virgin olive oil

Blend the caper flowers with the extra virgin olive oil. Put into a squeezy bottle and chill until needed. This will keep for 1 week.

If you can buy caper flowers preserved in oil, just blend the whole jarful together.

CARROT AND BROWN BUTTER PURÉE WITH BLACK CUMIN

Makes 400 g

300 g carrots, very finely sliced
90 g beurre noisette (page 276)
10 g tarragon vinegar reduction (page 287)
pinch of ground black cumin

Cook the carrot slices in the beurre noisette over a medium heat until completely soft. Blend to a smooth purée in a blender, adding the tarragon vinegar reduction and finishing with a small pinch of the black cumin to taste. Refrigerate until needed.

CAULIFLOWER PURÉE

Makes 250 g

250 g cauliflower
80 ml milk
80 ml cream
1 fresh thyme sprig
1 tsp icing sugar, plus extra if needed
few drops white truffle oil, optional

Slice the cauliflower, including the core, but discard any leaves. Put in a pan with the milk, cream and thyme. Add the sugar, then cover and simmer until tender. When the cauliflower is cooked, strain the liquid into a clean pan and reduce to a cream consistency. Place the cooked cauliflower in a blender with enough of the reduced cooking liquid to make a thick, velvety purée. Season with salt and finish with the white truffle oil if using. Pass through a fine chinois and chill.

CELERIAC PURÉE

Makes 500 g

300 g celeriac, finely sliced
50 g unsalted butter
100 ml milk
50 ml cream

Sweat the celeriac in the butter in a medium pan until translucent. Add the milk and cream, and cover with a cartouche. Cook over a low heat until completely tender, then purée in a blender until smooth and velvety. Season with salt to taste and pass through a fine chinois. If not using immediately, chill the purée in the fridge, where it will keep for 3–4 days. To serve, heat in a pan and put into a squeezy bottle.

FENNEL PURÉE

Makes about 200 g

200 g fennel bulb
2 tbsp Pernod
50 ml extra virgin olive oil
2 star anise
1 tbsp lemon juice
7 g sugar
3 g salt
a little thickener (glossary)

Preheat a water bath to 85°C. Using a Japanese mandolin, thinly slice the fennel, reserving the green tops, and vacuum pack with the Pernod, oil, star anise, lemon juice, sugar and salt. Cook in the water bath for 18 hours, then drain the liquid into a clean pan, reserving the cooking liquid by half. Place the fennel in a blender with the reserved fennel tops and enough of the reduced cooking liquid, a little at a time, to make a smooth purée. Season with salt and white pepper, and thicken with thickener, adding a pinch at a time, while still mixing. Pass through a fine chinois. Cover with clingfilm and chill.

POTATO PURÉE

Makes about 900 g

700 g potato, Rooster, scrubbed
250 ml milk
200 g unsalted butter, diced and chilled
5 g salt

Preheat the oven to 150°C. We use 50 per cent steam but an ordinary oven at 150°C will be ok. Bake the potatoes for 30–40 minutes or until completely cooked through. While still warm, peel off the potato skins and put through a mouli. Heat the milk in a large pan and then add 450 g of milled potato, stirring with a wooden spoon. While still hot, beat in the diced cold butter, a couple of cubes at a time. Then pass through a tamis or a drum sieve. This should give you a very smooth potato purée. Season with the salt and white pepper.

SMOKED POTATO PURÉE

Use the same process as the potato purée except smoke half of the potatoes for about 10 minutes after baking and peeling. We use applewood chips and turf in our smoker.

WHITE ONION PURÉE

White onion purée is also known as sauce soubise.

Makes about 550 ml
50 g butter
325 g Cévennes onions or any premium-quality white onion, finely sliced
1 each fresh thyme and tarragon sprig
50 g smoked bacon or bacon trimmings
150 g crème fraîche

Melt the butter in a pan and add the onions, salt, pepper, thyme and bacon, and cook over a low heat until very soft. Add the crème fraîche and cook for 8–10 minutes, but add the tarragon just before taking it off the heat. Then strain and reserve the liquid. Heat the liquid in a small pan to reduce by half. Remove the bacon, thyme and tarragon and purée the onions in a blender. With the blender on a medium speed, add back enough of the reduced liquid to make a smooth purée. Pass through a fine chinois and chill until needed – this can be made a day ahead if necessary.

RED ONION RELISH

Makes 100 g
25 g sugar
125 ml water
1 tbsp red wine vinegar
100 g red onion, finely diced

Place the sugar, water and vinegar in a pan and heat to dissolve the sugar. Add the red onion and bring to a brisk simmer, then cook until the liquid has almost reduced to nothing. Use as required.

ROASTED BEETROOT

4 large red beetroots
2 large golden and candy beetroots
500 g coarse sea salt

Preheat the oven to 160°C. Fill the sea salt in a small baking tray to a depth of 2 cm. Add the beetroots and roast for 1–1½ hours or until tender. Allow to cool in the salt, then peel. Using a 45 mm cutter, cut the red beetroots into 5 mm discs and cut the golden and candy beetroots into rough dice of around 1.5 cm.

ROASTED CARROTS

Makes 16
16 medium carrots
20 ml vegetable oil
30 g beurre noisette (page 276)
2 tsp sugar
1 tsp aged sherry vinegar

Peel the carrots and cut off the tops, then heat the oil in a large sauté pan and fry over a medium to high heat until dark golden. Add the beurre noisette and continue to cook. Season the carrots with a pinch of salt and cook, turning frequently, until they are evenly caramelised. Pour off any excess fat and sprinkle over the sugar and vinegar, tossing until evenly coated in a glaze.

ROASTED JERUSALEM ARTICHOKES

Makes 8 portions
50 g butter
8 medium, even-sized Jerusalem artichokes, scrubbed

Heat the butter in a sauté pan with a lid, and as it starts to foam, add the artichokes and salt, then put on the lid. Cook over a medium heat, turning occasionally, until they are golden brown – this will take around 20 minutes. Remove from the heat and allow to cool in the pan – the artichokes should be completely cooked and tender. Use as required.

ROASTED WHITE ASPARAGUS

Makes 8 portions
500 ml water
½ tsp salt
30 g sugar
16 medium white asparagus spears, trimmed to approximately 10 cm
60 g butter

Bring the water to the boil and add the salt and sugar. Blanch the asparagus until tender, then refresh in a bowl of iced water. When ready to serve, sauté in a little butter in a hot pan until caramelised. Season with black pepper. Use as required.

CITRUS SALT

Makes 150 g
80 g lemon, lime and orange zest
50 g rock salt
15 g sugar
5 g Nepalese pepper or black or white pepper

Blanch the fruit zests 3 times using freshly boiled water each time. Leave to dry out in a dehydrator or in a warm place. When bone-dry, blend together with the other ingredients to a fine powder. Store in an airtight container and use as required.

BÉARNAISE SAUCE

Makes about 400 ml
40 ml tarragon vinegar reduction (page 287)
25 ml water
2 g salt
4 egg yolks
250 ml clarified butter (glossary)
2 tbsp fresh tarragon, chopped

Set a metal bowl over a pan of gently simmering water, making sure the bowl does not touch the water. Pour in 25 ml of the tarragon vinegar reduction, retaining 1 tablespoon for finishing the sauce, and add the water, salt and egg yolks, then whisk together until frothy. Continue whisking until the emulsion begins to thicken and is fully cooked. Gradually add the clarified butter, whisking continuously, until it is all incorporated. Pass through a fine chinois. Season with the remaining tablespoon tarragon vinegar reduction, salt and black pepper, and keep in a warm place until needed. Stir in the tarragon just before serving.

LEMON PURÉE BUTTER SAUCE

Makes 250 ml

2 lemon grass stalks
225 ml cider vinegar
125 ml lemon juice
50 g shallot, sliced
300 ml fish stock (page 286), or use leftover clam or mussel juice
2 tsp lemon purée (page 289)
200 g unsalted butter, diced
1 tsp Pernod
1 tbsp light soy sauce
½ tsp sugar

Crush the lemon grass stalks with the handle of a knife and chop roughly. Place in a small pan with the vinegar, lemon juice and shallot, and reduce until the liquid becomes a syrup. Add the clam stock and boil until the liquid is reduced by half. Pass off the liquid through a double layer of muslin and put 50 ml into a clean pan. Bring to the boil and add the lemon purée, then gradually whisk in the butter. Finish with the Pernod, soy sauce and sugar. Keep in a warm place until needed.

PHEASANT SAUCE

Makes 580 ml

2 kg pheasant carcasses, chopped, and/or drumsticks and any trimmings, about 500 g, or whatever you have
30 ml vegetable oil
2 onions, sliced
2 carrots, chopped
3 celery sticks, washed and chopped
1 leek, sliced
4 garlic cloves, lightly crushed
handful fresh thyme sprigs
2 bay leaves
300 ml Madeira
5 litres pheasant stock (page 286)
1 tsp thickener (glossary)

Preheat the oven to 200°C. Spread the chopped carcasses, drumsticks and trimmings on an oven tray and roast for 30–40 minutes until well caramelised. Heat the oil in a stockpot and put in the vegetables and herbs. Stir occasionally and cook over a high heat until well caramelised. Add 250 ml of the Madeira, then add the roasted bones and pour on the pheasant stock. Bring back to the boil and simmer for 1 hour. Strain through a colander and then through a double layer of muslin into a clean pan. Bring back to the boil again and boil to reduce to 500 ml. Finish with the rest of the Madeira and thicken slightly with thickener, a pinch at a time. This sauce will keep for 1 week in the fridge and it also freezes well.

LAMB SAUCE

Makes about 525 ml

4 kg lamb bones and trimmings, chopped into small pieces, ask your butcher to do this for you
30 ml vegetable oil
2 onions, sliced
2 large carrots, chopped
5 celery sticks, chopped
6 garlic cloves, slightly crushed
4 bay leaves
handful each fresh thyme, rosemary and sage sprigs
500 g tomatoes
300 ml white wine
5 litres chicken stock (page 285)
1 tsp thickener (glossary)

Preheat the oven to 200°C. Spread the lamb bones and trimmings on an oven tray and roast for 30–40 minutes until well caramelised. When cooked, there will be some fat in the tray, strain through a chinois into a container and cool. Meanwhile, heat the oil in a stockpot and sauté the vegetables and herbs until browned, then add the tomatoes and continue to cook until completely disintegrated. Pour in the wine and simmer for 1 minute. Add the browned bones to the pot and cover with the chicken stock. Bring to the boil and simmer gently for 4 hours. Strain through a colander and pass through a double layer of muslin into a clean pan. Bring back to the boil and simmer to reduce to 500 ml, skimming the fat off the surface as it reduces (this will take about an hour). Thicken slightly with thickener, a pinch at a time, and pass through muslin again. This will keep for 1 week in the fridge or for several weeks in the freezer.

RED WINE SAUCE

Makes 2 litres

1.5 litres red wine
750 ml port
1 litre chicken stock (page 285)
1 tsp thickener (glossary)

Put the red wine and port in a pan and simmer until reduced by half. Add the chicken stock and bring back to the boil. Reduce by half again and thicken, a pinch at a time, to a rich, thick consistency.

VENISON SAUCE

Makes 500 ml

3 kg venison bones, chopped into small pieces, ask your butcher to do this for you
1 kg venison trimmings
200 ml olive oil
2 onions, sliced
2 large carrots, chopped
4 celery sticks, chopped
8 garlic cloves, crushed
1 bay leaf
handful each fresh thyme and rosemary sprigs
2 tsp crushed juniper berries
1 tbsp black peppercorns
150 ml Madeira
150 ml port
5 litres chicken stock (page 285)
2 tbsp cranberry jelly (glossary)
1 tsp thickener (glossary)

Preheat the oven to 200°C. Spread the venison bones on an oven tray and roast for 30 minutes until well caramelised. Sauté the venison trimmings in a heavy-based pan over a high heat in some of the oil until well browned all over. Meanwhile, heat the rest of the oil in a stockpot and sauté the vegetables, herbs, juniper berries and peppercorns until browned. Add the Madeira and port, and simmer for 1 minute. Add the browned bones to the pot with the browned trimmings. Cover with the chicken stock and add the cranberry jelly, then bring to the boil and simmer gently for 3 hours. Strain through a colander and pass through a double layer of muslin into a clean pan. Bring back to the boil and simmer to reduce to 500 ml, skimming the fat off the surface of the stock as it reduces (this will take about an hour). Thicken with a little thickener, a pinch at a time, and pass through muslin again. This will keep for 1 week in the fridge or for several weeks in the freezer.

CHICKEN STOCK

Makes about 5 litres

4 kg chicken carcasses and/or chicken wings
10 litres water

Place the chicken bones in a large stockpot and cover with the water. Bring to the boil, then reduce the heat and cover with a lid. Simmer gently for 3 hours. Strain the stock through a colander and then through a double layer of muslin. This will keep for a week in the fridge and it also freezes well.

DOUBLE CHICKEN STOCK

Makes about 2–3 litres

5 litres chicken stock (page 285)
4 kg chicken carcasses and/or chicken wings

Place the chicken bones in a large stockpot and cover with the chicken stock. Bring to the boil, then reduce the heat and cover with a lid. Simmer gently for 3 hours. Strain the stock through a colander and then through a double layer of muslin. This will keep for a week in the fridge and it also freezes well.

DUCK NECK CONSOMMÉ

Makes about 3 litres

3 kg duck necks, chopped into pieces
500 g duck legs
25 ml vegetable oil
3 large onions, sliced
6 large carrots, roughly chopped
8 celery sticks, roughly chopped
10 garlic cloves, crushed
handful each fresh thyme sprigs and fresh rosemary sprigs
2 bay leaves
2 g black peppercorns
6 litres chicken stock (page 285)
75 ml dry Madeira
10 egg whites

Preheat the oven to 220°C. Put the duck necks in a single layer on a tray and roast in the oven for 30–40 minutes, turning once or twice, until well browned. Take the skins off the duck legs and smoke over a medium heat for 10 minutes, then take the meat off the legs and reserve for clarifying the stock. Meanwhile, heat the vegetable oil in a large pan and add the onions, carrots, celery, garlic and herbs, stirring frequently, until well browned. Add the browned duck necks and the smoked duck skins to the pan and cover with the chicken stock. Bring to the boil, then reduce the heat and simmer gently for 3 hours. At this point, add the Madeira and taste, adjusting the seasoning if necessary. Remove from the heat and allow to cool. When the stock is completely cold, put the duck meat into a blender with the egg whites and blend to a rough purée. Put the stock into a clean pan and whisk in the duck and egg white mixture, then bring the stock slowly back up to a very low boil. When the egg whites have solidified on top of the stock, carefully pass off the clarified liquid through a double layer of muslin. This will keep for 4–5 days in the fridge but is best frozen immediately where it will keep for several weeks.

PHEASANT STOCK

Makes about 2–3 litres

4 kg pheasant carcasses, chopped (including trimmings and skin)
30 ml vegetable oil
2 onions, sliced
2 large carrots, chopped
5 celery sticks, chopped
1/2 head of garlic, lightly crushed
1 bay leaf
handful each fresh thyme and rosemary sprigs
5 litres chicken stock (page 285)

Heat the oil in a large stockpot and sauté the vegetables and herbs, stirring occasionally, until browned. Sauté and brown the carcass bones separately. When browned, add to the stockpot and cover with the chicken stock. Bring to the boil and simmer gently for 3 hours. Strain through a colander and pass through a double layer of muslin. This will keep for up to a week in the fridge or for several weeks in the freezer. When cooked, there will be some fat in the tray and this can be used for the pheasant sauce. Strain this off through a fine chinois into a container, cool and then transfer to the fridge.

FISH STOCK

Makes about 2 litres

100 ml light olive oil
5 shallots, sliced or chopped
2 garlic cloves, crushed
1 bay leaf
1 fresh thyme sprig
4 medium-sized carrots, chopped
1 head of celery, chopped
2 fennel heads, sliced
zest of 1/2 lemon
2 star anise
150 ml Vermouth
200 ml dry white wine
2 kg fish bones (turbot, sole or brill), roughly chopped
3 litres water
3 fresh tarragon sprigs
2 fresh basil sprigs

Heat the olive oil in a large pan and sauté the shallots, garlic and herbs over a medium heat until soft. Turn up the heat and add the carrots, celery, fennel, lemon zest, and star anise. Continue to cook, stirring occasionally, until the vegetables are softened and starting to brown. Add the vermouth and wine, and reduce by half. Put in the fish bones and water, bring to the boil and simmer for 10 minutes, then remove from the heat. Add the tarragon and basil, and allow to cool. When the stock reaches room temperature, strain through a colander and then through a double layer of muslin. Chill until needed. Be sure to use this stock within 2 days; alternatively, store in the freezer where it will keep for up to 4 weeks.

SHELLFISH STOCK AND ICE FILTERED SHELLFISH STOCK

Makes about 3 litres

2 kg raw seafood shells, such as clam, crab, langoustine or lobster
200 ml extra virgin olive oil
150 g carrots, chopped
150 g leeks, chopped
100 g celery, chopped
200 g shallots, chopped
15 garlic cloves, finely chopped
½ bunch fresh thyme sprigs
5 g fresh tarragon sprigs
2 bay leaves
2 star anise
20 pink peppercorns
300 ml white wine
50 ml Pernod
50 ml brandy
1.5 litres fish stock (page 286)
1.5 litres chicken stock (page 285)
1.5 litres water
1 lemon, sliced
100 g fresh green herbs, such as tarragon, chervil and flat-leaf parsley

Preheat the oven to 180°C and roast the seafood shells for 20 minutes until golden. Heat the vegetable oil in a stockpot and caramelise the vegetables until golden, then add the herbs and spices. Cover with the alcohol and reduce by half, then pour in the stocks and water, and cook for 40 minutes. Remove from the heat and add the lemon with the mixed herbs, then allow to sit for 1 hour. Strain through a colander and then through a double layer of muslin into a clean pan. Reduce to 3 litres. Freeze in a shallow tray lined with clingfilm overnight or until solid. Then turn out into a muslin-lined perforated tray, resting on top of another tray. Allow to defrost slowly in the fridge – you should have a clear ice filtered shellfish stock.

LOBSTER SAUCE

Add a little thickener, a pinch at a time, to lobster stock (above) until slightly thickened. Use as required.

SEASONED FLOUR

Makes 250 g

100 g cornflour
100 g plain flour
15 g salt
2 g ground nutmeg
2 g cayenne pepper
3 g ground black pepper
8 g ground coriander
6 g ground black cumin

Combine all the ingredients in a bowl and mix well. Use as required.

SEMI-DRIED TOMATO STRIPS/CONFIT TOMATO

Makes 8 portions

4 ripe plum tomatoes
20–30 ml extra virgin olive oil
½ tsp salt
1 tsp sugar
½ tsp fresh thyme leaves, finely chopped

Blanch the tomatoes for 1 minute in a pan of boiling water, then transfer to a bowl of iced water. When cold, peel, quarter and deseed the tomatoes, then put into a bowl with the oil, salt, sugar and thyme. Mix thoroughly, then spread on a tray and dry in a dehydrator or low oven at 80°C for 3 hours, until semi-dried with an intense flavour. Cut into 4 mm strips.

SMOKED DUCK FAT

To make smoked duck fat, take the skins off duck legs and smoke over a medium heat for 10 minutes, then melt the skins in a pan.

SMOKED POTATO

Makes 150 g

2 potatoes, Rooster, scrubbed

Boil the potatoes in a pan of boiling salted water until tender. Drain, and when cool enough to handle, take off the skins. Smoke the peeled potatoes over wood chips for 8–10 minutes, then pass the potatoes through a tamis or drum sieve. Use as required.

COOKED SMOKED POTATO SLICES

Makes 10 portions

200 g small baby new potatoes, scrubbed
25 g butter

Boil the small baby potatoes in a pan of salted water until cooked. Cool and peel off the skins. Smoke over wood chips for 7–8 minutes, then thinly slice. To serve, melt the butter in a frying pan and add the smoked potato slices, allowing to just warm through. Drain on kitchen paper and season with salt and white pepper.

TAPENADE

Makes 180 g

100 g black olives, stoned
40 g rinsed capers
20 g anchovies, drained from olive oil
4 tbsp virgin olive oil

Finely chop the olives, capers and anchovies. Add the oil to form a tapenade paste.

TARRAGON VINEGAR REDUCTION

Makes 400 ml

200 g fresh tarragon sprigs
150 g shallots, sliced or roughly chopped
1 litre white wine vinegar
2 bay leaves
5 g black peppercorns

Put the sliced shallots, vinegar, bay leaves and peppercorns into a pan and bring to a boil, and continue to boil until the liquid is reduced by half. Add the fresh tarragon to the pot, continuing to simmer for 5 minutes. Allow to cool and cover. This reduction will keep for weeks in the fridge, simply strain it off the tarragon and shallots as needed.

CURED PRESSED FOIE GRAS TERRINE

Makes 600 g

600 g lobe foie gras (glossary)
12 g Maldon sea salt
12 g table salt
25 g sugar
65 ml Tokaji (glossary) or sweet white wine

Bring the foie gras to room temperature and, using a pair of tweezers, remove all the veins. Mix the salt and sugar together. In a tray just large enough to hold the foie gras in a single layer, put half the salt and sugar mixture, and pour over half of the Tokaji, ensuring it is evenly spread. Place the foie gras in the tray and put the rest of the salt, sugar and Tokaji marinade on top, again ensuring that it is evenly spread. Chill for 4 hours to marinate. Heat a water bath to 55°C. Lightly oil a rectangular terrine mould. (We use a Le Creuset no. 32 terrine mould 8 × 6 × 29 cm that is 5 cm deep.) Line the terrine mould with a double layer of clingfilm, leaving enough spare to fold over the top of the finished terrine. Drain the excess marinade from the foie gras and vacuum pack it, then cook in the water bath for 6 minutes or until just cooked. Open the vacuum pack bag and put the foie gras into a steamer tray or colander with fine holes, being careful not to break up the liver. Pack the foie gras into the terrine mould, ensuring no gaps are left. Cover with a lid and put a weight on top, then leave overnight to cool and set. When ready, take the foie gras out of the mould and either vacuum pack or wrap it well. This freezes very well for up to 3–4 weeks if required.

YEAST-COOKED BACON

Makes about 300 g

10 g fresh yeast
300 g piece smoked bacon

Crumble the yeast and spread over the surface of the bacon. Vacuum pack the bacon and yeast, and cook in a water bath at 85°C for 4 hours. Chill, then cut into thin slices. Keep wrapped in clingfilm or vacuum packed in the fridge for up to 1 week.

WHITE PUDDING

Makes 2 white pudding sausages

100 g shallots, finely chopped
5 tbsp vegetable oil
2 slices white bread
150 ml cream
200 g veal sweetbreads
75 ml white wine vinegar
2 litres water
2 tsp salt
100 g chicken livers, free range or organic
1 kg pork belly, cut into 2.5 cm dice
2 g Lucky Duck spice mix
1 g each ground coriander and cumin
2 g salt
130 g smoked bacon, diced
125 g pinhead oats
70 g porridge oats
60 g foie gras (glossary), cut into 1 cm dice
120 g lardo di colonnata (glossary), diced
2 eggs
75 mm sausage skins (glossary)

Preheat a steam oven to 80°C. Sweat the shallots in 2 tablespoons of the oil until soft but not coloured. Meanwhile soak the bread in the cream. Boil the vinegar and water in a large pan with two teaspoons of salt. Blanch the sweetbreads for 1 minute and then transfer to a bowl of iced water to cool completely. Peel off the outer membrane and discard, then chop into smaller pieces. Heat a little of the oil in a sauté pan and sauté the sweetbread pieces until caramelised. Transfer to a bowl and add the chicken livers to the pan, adding a little more oil if necessary, and cook until caramelised, making sure they are still rare on the inside. Mix the pork belly in a bowl with the Lucky Duck spice mix, coriander, cumin and 2 g of salt. Wipe out the pan and add the rest of the oil and fry the seasoned pork belly in batches until well caramelised. Allow to cool. Using a mincer, mince all the ingredients together, mixing well to combine. Fry off a small patty to check the seasoning and adjust if necessary. Using a sausage maker, fill the skins and tie off tightly. Cook in the oven on 100 per cent steam for 50 minutes until the sausages have a core temperature of 73°C when probed. Cool quickly in an ice bath or blast chiller. Chill for up to 2–3 days. They also freeze well.

SWEET

SPICED BREAD CROÛTONS

Makes 8 portions

8 cm frozen spiced bread log (page 264)

icing sugar, to dust

Preheat the oven to 170°C. Slice the frozen bread lengthways on a slicing machine to a 0.5 mm thickness. Line a baking tray with greaseproof paper and put 8 slices of the bread on the tray. Sprinkle with just enough icing sugar to cover each one, then cook for 7 minutes to caramelise the sugar. Cool on a wire rack, then transfer to a plastic container until needed. Break each portion in half to serve.

DRIED STRAWBERRY PIECES

Makes 50 g

200 g strawberries

Hull the strawberries and cut into slices. Spread on a tray and place in a dehydrator at 55°C for 5–6 hours until dried. Store in an airtight container and use as required.

BROWN SODA BREAD CRUMB OR POWDER

Makes 50 g

4–5 slices old brown soda bread (page 263)

Dry the slices of soda bread overnight in a preheated oven at 50°C. When dry, blend in a blender to a crumb or fine powder. Store in an airtight container and use as required.

ORANGE POWDER

Makes about 50 g

1 orange

Wash and scrub the orange in cold water. Then peel the orange with a peeler, trying to avoid peeling any of the white pith. Dry the peel on a piece of kitchen paper. Leave overnight or for 12 hours in the oven at a low temperature of 60°C. The next day, blend the dried peel to a fine powder in a blender. Store in an airtight container for up to 5 days.

GINGERBREAD CRUMB OR POWDER

Makes 550 g

75 ml milk

62 g unsalted butter

62 g light muscovado sugar

62 g golden syrup

62 g treacle

112 g plain flour

20 g ground ginger

2 g bread soda

1 small egg

Preheat the oven to 155°C. Heat the milk, butter, sugar, syrup and treacle in a pan until smooth, stirring occasionally. When the mixture reaches 45°C, mix in the flour, ginger and bread soda, and then whisk in the egg and mix until smooth. Pour the mixture into a 550 g lined loaf tin and bake for 45 minutes or until a wooden skewer comes out clean. Leave in the tin for 5 minutes and then turn out onto a wire rack and leave to cool completely. Reduce the oven temperature to 60°C. Cut the gingerbread into cubes and spread out on a tray in the oven to dry overnight. Leave to cool, then blend in a food processor to a crumb or fine powder. Keep in an airtight container until needed or this can be frozen.

IRISH OAT BISCUITS OR CRUMB

Makes 30 biscuits

100 g demerara sugar

100 g plain flour

100 g rolled oats

4 g salt

100 g unsalted butter, diced and well chilled

Place all the ingredients, except the butter, into a KitchenAid with a paddle attachment and mix on a medium speed. Add the butter in 3 stages and mix until it resembles granola. Chill for 1 hour. Preheat the oven to 160°C and cook the biscuits for approximately 10–12 minutes until golden brown. Crush to a rough crumb and cool then store in an airtight container.

CARAMELISED RASPBERRY SAUCE

Makes about 100 ml

50 g caster sugar

50 g raspberry purée

Caramelise the sugar in a heavy-based pan, undisturbed, until it starts to turn a deep, rich caramel colour. Add the raspberry purée to the caramel and cook for another few minutes, stirring with a wooden spoon to dissolve all the sugar. Strain through a fine chinois and chill for 1 hour, then transfer to a squeezy bottle and store in the fridge until needed.

LEMON OR BERGAMOT PURÉE

This is made with unwaxed lemons. However, if you only want to make lemon purée, it is fine to use regular lemons. In the restaurant we use Bergamot lemon purée in the desserts and lemon purée in the savoury dishes.

Makes about 200 ml

150 g sugar

300 ml water

4 Bergamot lemons (this can also be made with regular lemons

2 star anise

4 allspice berries

Place the sugar in a pan with the water and bring to the boil, stirring to dissolve. Allow to cool. Cut the lemons in half and juice them, then pass the juice through a chinois and simmer to reduce by 80 per cent. Blanch the lemon skins with the pith on 2–3 times in boiling water. Vacuum pack the lemon skins with the pith, star anise, allspice berries and stock syrup, and cook in a water bath at 85°C for 12 hours. Drain the lemon skins and purée in a blender with enough of the reduced lemon juice to make a smooth purée. Pass through a fine chinois. This will keep for 1 week in the fridge and it also freezes well.

ABSORBIT SEE ALSO MALTODEXTRIN POWDER
Natural starches from tapioca, which is odour and taste-free. They can be used to turn any oil into a powder. Artisan Foods or Redmond Fine Foods

AGAR AGAR POWDER
A gelling agent extracted from seaweed. It needs to reach a temperature of 85°C before melting and it sets at 30–40°C. Artisan Foods or Redmond Fine Foods

AIR DRIED CURED PORK LOIN
Air drying is a method of curing meat which intensifies the flavour without drying out the meat. It is usually hung for 8 months and then smoked for 12 hours. Fingal Ferguson, Gubbeen Smokehouse

APPLE BALSAMIC CIDER VINEGAR
A balsamic vinegar made from apples. David Llewellyn

APPLE SUGAR SYRUP
A natural apple sugar syrup made from pure apple. Highbank Farm, Kilkenny

BEE POLLEN
Pollen of bees melts on heating. It is commercially available. La Rousse Foods

BERGAMOT HONEY
The honey from bees that feed on the Bergamot lemon flower. It has a strong scent of Bergamot lemon. Al di La.

BLACKBERRY PURÉE
High quality, frozen commercial purée from the Capfruit purée range. Redmond Fine Foods

BLACK TRUFFLE VINEGAR
Vinegar made from black truffles. La Rousse Foods

BONITO POWDER
A powder made from bonito tuna flakes. From our Japanese supplier

BONITO RICE WINE VINEGAR
A vinegar made from rice wine and bonito. From our Japanese supplier

BORAGE FLOWER
Also known as a starflower, it is an annual herb native to the Mediterranean region. Pat Clarke of A Growing Pleasure, through La Rousse Foods

BURREN WILD MUSTARD
A wholegrain mustard made in the Burren, Co. Clare. It is widely available but any good quality wholegrain mustard will do, such as Dalkey Island.

CALAMANSI VINEGAR
This vinegar is made from an aromatic citrus fruit from south Asia which resembles a lime and has a flavour in between a tangerine and kumquat. Vom Fass, UK, info@vomfass.net

CHASSELAS GRAPES
A fragrant and mildly sweet white grape variety grown all over the world.

CHERRY PURÉE
High quality, frozen commercial purée from the Capfruit purée range. Redmond Fine Foods

CLARIFIED BUTTER
Melting butter allows the components to separate. Some solids float to the surface and are skimmed off; the remainder of the milk solids sink to the bottom and are left behind when the remaining butter is poured off.

COCOA BUTTER
Edible vegetable fat extracted from the cocoa bean. La Rousse Foods

COCO DE PAIMPOL BEANS
A fresh white bean from the Paimpol region of France. Artisan Foods

COCONUT PURÉE
High quality, frozen commercial purée from the Capfruit purée range. Redmond Fine Foods

COFFEE ESSENCE
A thick, concentrated liquid coffee. La Rousse Foods or Odaios Foods

COLD PRESSED ORGANIC RAPESEED OIL
Supplied directly by Kitty Colchester, Drumeen Farm, Kilkenny

CRANBERRY JELLY
Made from fresh cranberries but is commercially available.

CREAMED HORSERADISH
We buy good quality horseradish that has been already puréed or grated.

CURED PORK JOWL ALSO KNOWN AS GUANCIALE
This is most often an un-smoked Italian sausage prepared with pig's jowl or cheeks. Fingal Ferguson, Gubbeen Smokehouse

DEHYDRATED SOY GRANULES
Granules of soya sauce made by freeze drying the soy. From our Japanese supplier

ESPELETTE PEPPER
A variety of chilli pepper that is cultivated in the French commune of Espelette, Pyrénées-Atlantiques. Sheridans Cheesemongers or most good delicatessens

FENNEL FRONDS
The delicate leaves of the fennel plant. Pat Clarke, A Growing Pleasure

FENNEL POLLEN
The dried, yellow pollen flower of the fennel plant with a strong, aniseed flavour. Redmond Fine Foods

FEUILLETINE
Fine crumbled biscuit. Cacao Barry, Barry Callebaut, France

FIG PURÉE
High quality, frozen commercial purée from the Capfruit purée range. Redmond Fine Foods

FOIE GRAS
Goose liver, or duck liver, which is very often used, works well too. La Rousse Foods

FONDANT
Literally means 'melting' from the French verb se fondre (to melt) and is usually applied to desserts.

GINGER GEL
A thick, honey-like liquid made from fresh stem ginger. Artisan Foods

GOLD LEAF GELATINE
Gelatine made from gold leaf. Pallas Foods

GREEN SAFFRON SPICES
Spices available from Arun Kapil's Green Saffron spice company based in Cork and now available almost nationwide.

HONDASHI STOCK
Dashi is a primary stock usually made from kelp (konbu) and tuna flakes (bonito). From our Japanese supplier

HONDASHI TAPIOCA FLOUR
Available from Asian supermarkets

HY-FOAMER
This is a water soluble foaming agent and egg white substitute which makes easy and stable foams. Redmond Fine Foods or MSK-Ingredients

ICEWINE VERJUS
Juice from unripened, green grapes which have been frozen while still on the vine and processed without fermentation so there is no alcohol content. Redmond Fine Foods

INVERTED SUGAR
Also called trimoline, it is a cross between glucose and fructose. It is sweeter and its products tend to retain moisture and are less prone to crystallisation. Artisan Foods or Redmond Fine Foods

JAPANESE SPICES, TOGARASHI SHICHIMI
Toasted white sesame, toasted sea vegetable, black sesame, desiccated orange, sansho and hemp. From Green Saffron

KAPPA
A powdered thickening agent extracted from carrageen seaweed. Carrageen moss can also be used. Artisan Foods or Redmond Fine Foods

LARDO DI COLONNATA
This is a high quality, cured Italian pork fat. Artisan Foods or La Rousse Foods

LECITHIN
Used in cooking as an emulsifier. Artisan Foods

LEMON BALM
Bushy, perennial, Old World mint with small white or yellowish flowers and fragrant lemon flavored leaves. Caterway

LEMON VERBENA
A shrub of the verbena, the lemon scented leaves are used as flavouring. Caterway

LIQUID BARLEY MALT EXTRACT AND LIQUID BARLEY MALT
Malt extract is the liquid obtained when barley grains are mashed in water and the resultant solution sieved and the water evaporated. Coopers Irish Barley Malt Extract

LIQUID SQUID INK
Commercially available in a sachet.

LUCKY DUCK SPICE MIX
Juniper berry, black cardamom, star anise, cloves, cubeb pepper, ginger, desiccated orange. From Green Saffron

MALT MULTI SEED FLOUR
Made by Dove and available from good commercial stockists.

MALTODEXTRIN POWDER SEE ALSO ABSORBIT
Natural starches from tapioca, which is odour and taste-free. They can be used to turn any oil into a powder. Artisan Foods or Redmond Fine Foods

METHOCEL
A gelling agent capable of making hot jellies. We use it for our dehydrated lemonade. Artisan Foods or Redmond Fine Foods

MICRO HERBS
Really small but concentrated herbs artisan grown in Ireland, considerably more nutritionally dense than their adult vegetable counterparts. Pat Clarke, A Growing Pleasure

MILK POWDER
Used in some desserts, this is commercially available.

MIRIN
A kind of rice wine similar to saké but with a lower alcohol content and higher sugar content. An essential condiment used in Japanese cuisine. From our Japanese supplier

MONK'S BEARD
A thin green vegetable from the chicory family, commonly grown in Italy. Al di La

MORTEAU SAUSAGE
Strongly flavoured and dense sausage from the Morteau region of France, smoked in traditional pyramidal chimneys called tuyés. Artisan Foods or La Rousse Foods

MUSTARD FRUITS
Whole candied fruits preserved in a mustard flavoured syrup, traditionally served as a condiment. Al di La

NEPALESE PEPPER
This has the cold spiciness of a sichuan pepper with remarkable hints of grapefruit. La Rousse Foods

NEUTRAL GLAZE
Sugar, water and glucose compound which makes a clear glaze used for tarts or fruit glazes. Available from most good baking shops.

OKITSU MANDARIN JUICE
Strong and sweet, this is a variety of Japanese mandarin available in September and October. Al di La

ONION POWDER
Onions that have been dried and put into a powdered form, producing a very concentrated flavour. MSK-Ingredients

ORANGE BLOSSOM WATER
A water flavoured with orange blossom, which is extremely floral and strong. Commercially available

PASSION FRUIT PURÉE
High quality, frozen commercial purée from the Capfruit purée range. Redmond Fine Foods

PATA NEGRA FAT
The fat from the pata negra ham. Artisan Foods or Odaios Foods

PÂTE À BRUNE
A dark chocolate coating compound. Cacao Barry, Barry Callebaut, France

PÂTE À GLACE SEE PÂTE À BRUNE

PEAR PURÉE
High quality, frozen commercial purée from the Capfruit purée range. Redmond Fine Foods

PHEASANT SPICE
Fennel, green cardamom, cassia, juniper berry, smoked Spanish paprika. From Green Saffron

PICKLED COURGETTES
High quality Italian courgettes pickled in a vinegar based solution. Al di La

PICKLED GARLIC AND PICKLED GARLIC JUICE
The garlic has been pickled in a vinegar solution for 7 years. We use the pickling liquid as well as the garlic. The Real Olive Company, Cork

PICKLED HEREFORD OX TONGUE
Most butchers should sell you a good quality pickled ox tongue.

PICKLED THISTLE
Made from edible thistle plant, it is related to the artichoke family and tastes mildly similar. Al di La

100% PISTACHIO PASTE
Paste made from pistachios. Commercially available

PRALINE PASTE
Paste made from hazelnuts or almonds and sugar. Commercially available

PRESERVED CAPER FLOWERS
Flowers from the caper plant grown in Sicily. Al di La

PRESERVED ROASTED RED PEPPERS
These peppers are cooked over wood and preserved in grape juice. Sheridans Cheesemongers or any good delicatessen

RASPBERRY PURÉE
High quality, frozen commercial purée from the Capfruit purée range. Redmond Fine Foods

RASPBERRY VINEGAR
Vinegar made from raspberries. Vom Fass, UK, info@vomfass.net

RED CABBAGE SPICE, CLASSIC BRASSIC
Cloves, cumin, juniper berry, ginger, white pepper, desiccated orange and long pepper. From Green Saffron

ROSE SYRUP
Water infused and scented with rose petals.

ROSE WATER ESSENCE
Water infused and scented with rose petals and reduced to concentrate.

SAFFRON FILAMENTS
Strands of saffron. Commercially available

SAFFRON POWDER
Dried and powdered strands of saffron. Commercially available

SALSIFY
A root vegetable similar in appearance to a long, thin parsnip, with creamy white flesh and a thick skin. Caterway

SAMPHIRE
A sea vegetable that grows in coastal areas. Caterway

SARAWAK PEPPER
This is a strong and distinctive black pepper from Malaysia. La Rousse

SAUSAGE SKINS
These are plastic, round moulding skins of different diameters; we use 50 mm. Food Processing Technology Ireland

SMOKED ALMONDS
These almonds have been roasted, hot smoked and then salted. Redmond Fine Foods

SMOKED SALT
Rock salt smoked over wood. From our Japanese supplier

SPICED BEEF SPICE
Cubeb pepper, black pepper, juniper berry, clove, nutmeg, mace and telpatt. From Green Saffron

SUPER NEUTROSE
Made by Louis Francoise, this is a commercial stabiliser used for ice creams and sorbets. It helps aeration and prevents crystallisation; it also slows down melting after serving. Artisan Foods, MSK-Ingredients or La Rousse

TAT SOI LEAVES
The tat soi plant has small, dark green spoon-shaped leaves with a mild mustard flavour. Brendan Guinan, In Season Farm

THICK AND EASY
A food thickener. Available in chemists

THICKENER/MAIZENA
A starch powder made from corn, used to thicken hot liquids. Pallas Foods

TOKAJI
Sweet wines from the Tokaji region in Hungary.

TRUFFLE JUICE
A juice made from truffle. Al di La

VADOUVAN SPICE
A spice blend that is a derivative of an Indian curry blend with French influence. Odaios, La Rousse or Redmond Fine Foods

VELVET PIOPPINO MUSHROOMS
A long stemmed, black topped mushroom variety. Ballyhoura Mushrooms

WHITE TRUFFLE HONEY
Honey infused with white truffle. Artisan Foods

WHITE TRUFFLE OIL
Oil infused with white truffle. Commercially available

XANTHAN POWDER
A stabiliser added to hot or cold liquids allowing them to thicken without heat and without affecting their taste or colour. Artisan Foods or MSK-Ingredients

YELLOW PECTIN
A slow hardening pectin used for gelation of a substance that is rich in sugars. La Rousse

YUZU JUICE
The juice of the aromatic citrus yuzu fruit. From our Japanese supplier

YUZU SALT
Salt made from the aromatic citrus fruit called yuzu, mainly found in east Asia. From our Japanese supplier

INGREDIENTS	SUPPLIER NAME	COMPANY NAME	WEBSITE	PHONE NUMBER	ADDRESS
Seaweeds	Manus McGonagle	Quality Sea Veg	www.Qualityseaveg.ie	+353 (0) 74 9542159	Cloughglass, Burtonport, Co. Donegal
Double cream, crème fraîche	Alan and Valerie Kingston	Glenilen Farm Ltd	www.Glenilenfarm.com	+353 (0) 28 31179	Glenilen Farm, Drimoleague, Co. Cork
Apple balsamic cider vinegar, Elstar apples	David Llewellyn	Llewellyn's Orchard	www.Llewellynsorchard.ie	+353 (0) 87 2843879	Quickpenny Road, Lusk, Co. Dublin
Smoked venison	Ed Hick	J. Hick & Sons	www.hicks.ie	+353 (0) 1 2842700	Rear 15A, George's St Upper, Dún Laoghaire, Co. Dublin
Spiced beef	Tom Durcan	Tom Durcan Meats Ltd	www.tomdurcanmeats.ie	+353 (0) 21 4279141	Unit 11, Princes Street, Cork
Cultivated mushrooms	Mark and Lucy Cribbin	Ballyhoura Mountain Mushrooms	www.ballyhouramushrooms.ie	+353 (0) 86 8100808 or +353 (0) 87 6494119	Ballinalacken, Ballylanders, Co. Limerick
Smoked bacon, charcuterie	Fingal Ferguson	Gubbeen Smokehouse	www.gubbeen.com	+353 (0) 28 27824	Schull, Co. Cork
Sweetcorn	David Burne	Richmount Farm	N/a	+353 (0) 87 8316688	Richmount, Carrickboy, Co. Longford
Buffalo mozzarella, ricotta	Toby Simmonds	Toons Bridge Dairy	www.therealoliveco.com/toonsbridge	N/a	Toons Bridge Dairy, Macroom, Co. Cork
Greek feta, olives	Brendan O'Mahony	The Real Olive Company	www.therealoliveco.com	+353 (0) 1 6725822 or +353 (0) 86 1709342	53 Arbour Hill, Stoneybatter, Dublin 7
Heritage potatoes	Dermot Carey	None	N/a	+353 (0) 87 2286145	N/a
Italian produce, including mustard essence, pickled courgettes, caper cream, caper flowers, caper sprouts, truffle juice, monks beard, broccoli rabé, pickled thistle	Mario Fontana	Al di La	N/a	+353 (0) 86 8722237	8 Seafield Road, Blackrock, Dublin
Organic cold pressed rapeseed oil	Kitty Colchester	Second Nature Oils	www.secondnatureoils.com	+353 (0) 87 9265423	Second Nature Drumeen Farm, The Islands, Urlingford, Co. Kilkenny
Apple sugar	Julie Calder-Potts	Highbank Orchards	www.highbankorchards.com	+353 (0) 56 7729918	Highbank Organic Farm, Cuffesgrange, Co. Kilkenny
Black pudding	Jack McCarthy	McCarthy's of Kanturk	www.jackmccarthy.ie	+353 (0) 29 50178	Main Street, Kanturk, Co. Cork
Butter, buttermilk	Seamus Mulligan	Cuinneog Ltd	www.cuinneog.com	+353 (0) 94 9031425	Shraheen's, Balla, Castlebar, Co. Mayo
White truffle honey, truffle oil, coco de paimpol, lardo di colonnata, garlic sausage, agar agar, grelot onions	Simon Kilcoyne	Artisan Foods Ltd	www.artisanfoods.ie	+353 (0) 1 6204984	38–39 Canal Walk, Park West, Dublin 12
Pork	Pat O'Doherty	O'Doherty's Fine Meats	www.blackbacon.com	+44 (0) 28 6632 2152	Belmore Street, Enniskillen, Co. Fermanagh, Northern Ireland
Goose	Mary and Tony Walsh	Kilkenny Free Range	www.kilkennyfreerange.com	+353 (0) 87 6439979/ +353 (0) 56 7763426	Shellumstrath, Kilkenny
Micro herbs, edible flowers, asparagus, strawberries	Pat Clarke	A Growing Pleasure	N/a	+353 (0) 86 2332361	N/a
Aberdeen Angus beef	Maurice Kettyle	Kettyle Irish Foods	www.kettyleirishfoods.com	+44 (0) 28 6772 3777	Manderwood Business Park, Lisnaskea, Co. Fermanagh, Northern Ireland, BT92 0FS
Peas and broad beans	Rose O'Sullivan	Spring Cottage	N/a	+353 (0) 86 8243719	Parke, Kinnegad, Co. Westmeath
Cheese (Milleens)	Norman, Veronica and Quinlan Steele	Milleens Cheese Ltd	www.milleenscheese.com	+353 (0) 27 74079	Milleens, Eyeries, Beara, Co. Cork
Cheese	Helen Finnegan	Knockdrinna Farmhouse Cheese	www.knockdrinna.com	+353 (0) 56 7728446	Stoneyford, Co. Kilkenny

INGREDIENTS	SUPPLIER NAME	COMPANY NAME	WEBSITE	PHONE NUMBER	ADDRESS
Spices such as Sarawak pepper, Lucky Duck spice mix, dried rose petals, black cumin	Arun Kapil	Green Saffron	www.greensaffron.com	+353 (0) 21 4637960	Unit 16, Knockgriffin, Midleton, Co. Cork
Snipe, pheasant, venison, hare, woodcock	Mick Healy	Wild Irish Game Ltd	www.wildirishgame.ie	+353 (0) 404 46969	Glenmalure, Rathdrum, Co. Wicklow
Onion powder, xanthan powder, hy-foamer		MSK-Ingredients	www.msk-ingredients.com	+44 (0) 1 246412211	PO Box 1592, Dronfield, Sheffield S18 8BR
Greek olives	Andreas Latridis	Hellenic Celtic Trading	www.hct.ie	+353 (0) 1 2959884	Stepaside Village, Co. Dublin
Organic vegetables	Denis Healy	Organic Delights	www.organicdelights.ie	+353 (0) 87 2485826	Talbotstown, Kiltegan, Co. Wicklow
Chocolate producer	Claudio Corallo	C.C.& C. Lda	www.claudiocoralloco	+351 (0) 914951610/ +351 (0) 213862158	Rua Cecília da Sousa n 85, Príncipe Real, Lisbona, Portugal, CP 1200-10
Yuzu salt, black garlic, Japanese apple vinegar, dehydrated soy crystals	Kayo Ashizawa-Rouxel	Nishikidori Market	www.nishikidori-market.com	+33 (0) 240833333	140 rue Georges, Guyverner, zac de l'Acropole, 4415 ANCENIS, France
Flour	Bill Mosse	Kells Wholemeal	www.kellswholemeal.ie	+353 (0) 56 7727399	Bennetsbridge, Kilkenny, Co. Kilkenny
Coolea Gouda	Dick and Sinead Willems	Coolea Farmhouse Cheese Ltd	www.cooleacheese.com	+353 (0) 26 45204	Coolea, Macroom, Co. Cork
Duck	Eugene and Helena Hickey	Skeaghanore West Cork Duck	www.skeaghanoreduck.ie	+353 (0) 28 37428	Skeaghanore, Ballydehob, West Cork
Smoked salmon	Birgitta and Peter Curtin	Burren Smokehouse	www.burrensmokehouse.ie	+353 (0) 65 7074432	Lisdoonvarna, Co. Clare
Lobster	Terry and Martina Butterly	Coastguard Seafoods	N/a	+353 (0) 42 9372527/ +353 (0) 86 8558609	Harbour Road, Annagassan, Co. Louth
Blackface mountain lamb from Achill	Edward Johnston	Caoracla Ltd	www.mountainlamb@caoracla.ie	+353 (0) 98 26006	Lodge Road, Westport, Co. Mayo
Espelette pepper, gold leaf gelatine		La Rousse Foods	www.laroussefoods.ie	+353 (0) 1 6234111	31 Park West, Nangor Road, Dublin 12
T55 flour		Odaios Foods	www.odaiosfoods.com	+353 (0) 1 4691455	11 Magna Drive, Magna Business Park, Citywest, Dublin 24
Cheese	Kevin Sheridan	Sheridans Cheesemongers	www.sheridanscheesemongers.com	+353 (0) 46 9245110	Virginia Road Station, Carnaross, Co. Meath
Cheese	Maja Beaujouan	The Little Cheese Shop	www.thelittlecheeseshop.net	+353 (0) 87 6255788	Kilcummin, Castlegregory, Co. Kerry
Vegetables	Brendan Guinan and Donnacha Donnelly	In Season Farm	N/a	+353 (0) 87 1825177	In Season Farm, Iona, Oldtown, Co. Dublin
Truffles, smoked almonds, icewine verjus, rare breed pork	Rocky and Ian Redmond	Redmond Fine Foods	www.redmondfinefoods.ie	+353 (0) 45 883570/73	Unit F1, Southern Link Business Park, Newbridge Road, Naas, Co. Kildare
Oysters, fish	N/a	Mulloys	www.mulloys.ie	+353 (0) 1 6611222	3 West Pier, Howth, Co. Dublin
Hereford beef	N/a	Hereford Society	www.irishhereford.com	+353 (0) 44 9348855/ +353 (0) 44 9348862	Irish Hereford Breed Society Ltd, Harbour Street, Mullingar, Co. Westmeath
Cockles	Noel O'Riordan	Glenbeigh Shellfish	www.glenbeighshellfish.ie	+353 (0) 66 9768373	Kneelnabrack Lower, Glenbeigh, Co. Kerry
Sausage skins	N/a	Food Processing Technology (Irl) Ltd	www.fpt.ie	+353 (0) 1 4513110	Cookstown Industrial Estate, Belgard Road, Dublin 24
Corned mutton	Alan Murphy	Coughlan Meats	N/a	N/a	Cork English Market
Honey	Eoghan Mac Giolla Coda	Lannléire Honey	www.orielfoodgroup.ie/ lannléire-honey	+353 (0) 41 6861884	Trean, Dunleer, Co. Louth

EQUIPMENT

MOST GOOD KITCHEN SHOPS SHOULD HAVE THESE, BUT ALL ARE AVAILABLE ONLINE.

BLAST CHILLER
Refrigeration unit that brings the temperature of food lower very quickly.

CHINOIS
A conical sieve with an extremely fine mesh. It is used to strain custards, purées, soups and sauces, producing a very smooth texture.

DEHYDRATER
A machine that maintains a constant temperature which is low enough to dry out the food but not discolour or cook it. It is used for berries, herbs, fruit and meringues.

DRUM SIEVE/TAMI
A type of strainer or food mill. We use it mostly as a fine sieving device.

FOAM GUN
A metal container into which liquid is poured and then mixed with nitrous oxide gas via small chargers which fit into the gun. As the liquid is released, the gas mixes with the liquid and the mixture aerates and expands.

GAS CHARGERS
Small chargers containing nitrous oxide which fit into a foam gun. Available from good kitchen shops such as Sweeney O'Rourke or Kitchen Complements.

GRILL DOME
Designed to store heat very efficiently and can cook over long periods as well as quickly. A range of barbecues are available at www.grilldome.ie.

JAPANESE MANDOLIN
A slicer with adjustable blades which slices thinly and uniformly. While there are other versions of these, the Japanese version creates even thinner slices of the foodstuff being sliced.

KITCHENAID
A machine with a fast moving blade which kitchens use to chop or blend, like a robot-coupe.

LE CREUSET NO. 32 TERRINE MOULD
Le Creuset do a range of terrine moulds which are sized according to requirements, available at Le Creuset stockists and online.

MICROPLANE
A collection of very sharp graters which vary in grating size according to requirements. Available at www.microplane.com or at any good kitchen shop.

MOULI
A hand-operated grater designed for grating or puréeing. The device consists of a small metal drum with holes that grate the food and a blade attached to a handle that turns the drum.

MUSLIN BAG
A bag made from muslin through which liquid is strained to ensure a really clear, finished liquid.

OLIVIETTE TOOL
A range of small scoops which can be round or fluted to shape ice cream, sorbet and other soft foods.

PACOJET
This machine is used predominantly for sorbets, purées and ice creams. It enables chefs to 'micro-purée' deep-frozen foods into an ultra-light mousse, cream or sauce without thawing, capturing the natural flavours and nutrients in individual, ready-to-serve portions.

PACOJET CONTAINER
The container that fits into the Pacojet machine and in which the ingredients to be mixed are contained.

PARISIENNE SCOOP
An implement for cutting spheres out of fruit and vegetables.

SILPAT
A non-stick baking mat.

SMOKER
A small unit using woodchips to smoke any foodstuff.

SPIDER
Similar to a large slotted spoon but with a bigger span and web-like drainer.

STEAM OVEN OR STEAMER
Either an oven or electrical steamer that allows the food to cook while steaming as opposed to roasting or frying.

TEMPERATURE PROBE
A probe used to check the core temperature of meat as it cooks.

THERMOMIX
A food blender with a heating element that controls the temperature while mixing, allowing you to cook and purée.

IMPORTANT POINTS TO NOTE

In order to avoid serious injury, extreme care should be taken in following the recipes when particular techniques are required: high temperatures from open flames and deep-frying are serious hazards. When deep-frying, add food carefully and in small quantities to avoid sudden high-volume foaming and splashing.

The temperature of restaurant ovens is generally hotter than domestic ovens and requires no pre-heating. In the restaurant's kitchen there is a cook-to-order system where food is cooked and served within 30 minutes. Where foods are reheated, not cooked to order or cooked at a lower temperature, these foods should be brought to 73°C for longer than 3 minutes at their core temperature to ensure safe consumption and in order to avoid any health issues.

All food should be cooked to 73°C to avoid food poisoning. Children, the elderly and pregnant women are particularly vulnerable to salmonella and botulism, and they should not be served food that has not been thoroughly cooked.

We have not automatically included the seasoning of salt and pepper in each recipe, unless an exact amount is required, as this is very much dependent on personal taste. The seasoning of terrines and sausage meats can present problems as once the dish is cooked it is too late to season it, so we take a small nob of the mixture and fry it in a pan and then check the seasoning before finishing the dish.

It is important to read recipes in their entirety before embarking on the work in hand. The majority of the recipes are complex and have many components and stages. Some may require the use of elements of other stages before the final assembly. Others use specialised equipment which will not be available to the domestic chef.

There are instances where a recipe does not require the full quantity of a certain part, but it can be saved for later use in other dishes. Many of the recipes can be broken down and components made in advance, stored and frozen separately before final assembly. Individual parts can also be made and served as single dishes. We use Thick and Easy when we refer to thickener in the recipes (page 291).

ACKNOWLEDGMENTS

COMPILING A BOOK IS OFTEN DESCRIBED BY PEOPLE AS A JOURNEY, NOW I KNOW WHY. IT FEELS FAR LONGER THAN ELEVEN MONTHS SINCE WE STARTED WORKING ON THIS BOOK. BUT IT WAS NOT A JOURNEY OF ONE PERSON, AND OF COURSE THE JOURNEY WAS MADE SHORTER BY ALL THOSE PEOPLE INVOLVED ALONG THE WAY. PRESENTING TWENTY-ONE YEARS OF WORK FROM CHAPTER ONE, IN A SINGLE PUBLICATION, TOOK A TEAM OF PEOPLE WHO WERE AS DEDICATED TO THE PROJECT AS I WAS, SO IT IS TO THESE PEOPLE THAT I EXTEND MY GRATITUDE.

Gill & Macmillan worked tirelessly to make this dream come true. Every business dealing must have a facilitator and for us this was NICKI HOWARD who, with great vision, took a leap of faith in helping us reflect the quality and restless art that is the daily grind at Chapter One. At no stage did her enthusiasm flag in the pursuit of quality and she understood how important this was to myself and the entire Chapter One team. For this, we thank you.

GRAHAM THEW, the designer, took on a mammoth task and immediately understood the importance of the details. He married the complex text and beautiful photography into pages and pages of smart layouts and tasteful balance.

Then there is the project team who helped me retain my sanity and provided the support that made this journey so enjoyable.

ROSS GOLDEN-BANNON, his strength of leadership on this project was phenomenal. His encouragement, organisation and enormous contribution to all aspects of design and quality went above and beyond the call of duty. Managing a personal project of this nature requires a profound understanding of the subject matter and very few people could have performed this role for us, but he did it with grace, humour and not too much gnashing of teeth! Thank you.

BARRY McCALL, our good natured snapper. If they gave out Michelin stars to photographers, he would have three. We now have a greater appreciation for the word 'inspirational'. Thank you for lifting the team and the project with your creative genius and professionalism.

ORLA BRODERICK, an indefatigable supporter, who I must thank for initially proposing the project and connecting us with our publishers. We drove you mad with the recipe writing, a long and tedious process. As well as a great deal of gratitude, we probably owe you an apology, sorry Orla!

All successful business leaders are only as good as the commitment of their staff. In our case the engine room operators at Chapter One have all worked long hours and put in a massive effort to make our business a success. It is to them that we owe the greatest debt of gratitude. Before them came our original business partner, EAMONN WALSH, who opened the door for myself and MARTIN CORBETT in 1993 and has shown great support for us ever since. Before that there was the original Chapter One restaurant run by the late FRAN MURRIN, whose spirit lives on in the catering company, With Taste, now curated by her brother LARRY MURRIN. We came full circle in 2011 when I worked with Larry's company in catering for the British Royal visit.

ANDY TURNER, my current head chef, made a substantial contribution to helping with this production. Thanks also to ROZ ALLEN who had the serious and unenviable task of compiling all of our recipes. Some other long term past contributors who added significantly to our kitchen were GARRETT BYRNE, CATHAL LEONARD, PETER BYRNE and DARREN HOGARTY.

THE ARTISANS: it is easy to see the world more clearly when you are standing on the shoulders of giants. This aspect of my career has given me the most satisfaction. Getting to know our artisans has been as important as getting to know their produce. There is an emotional exchange expressed by these people whose guiding principle is that passion, not profit, makes the world go round, and you can taste it in their produce. It is a principle that is deeply important to me. There are many artisans mentioned in this book and there are many more again who are not. Space meant we were not able to include everyone; for those who were not included, it doesn't mean we love you any less. Thank you for all your contribution to our success.

We have often heard it said that 'we have the best customers', but in our case it is true. We have been blessed with their continued support and overwhelmed by their loyalty. We feel privileged to have had their custom over the last 20 years. Our sincerest thanks to you all.

Ross Lewis and Martin Corbett
Dublin, August 2013

MARTIN CORBETT, ROSS LEWIS AND EAMONN WALSH.

J

Jameson, George 117
Jerusalem artichokes
  crushed 159–60
  emulsion 28
  roasted 284
john dory, chargrilled 122
Johnston, Edward 129
Jolliffe, Ed 191
juice, fresh bay leaf, sage, tarragon or rocket 279

K

Kapil, Arun 161
kelp, pickled 84–6
Kenny, Wayne 110
Kettyle, Maurice 173
Kingston, Valerie 201

L

lamb
  Achill Island black-faced 127–8
  offal 127–8
  sauce 285
  see also mutton and caper pie
leeks, and cauliflower 136
lemon
  balm jelly 47–8
  butter emulsion 99–100
  chiboust 248–50
  cream 248
  curd 210–12
  gel 248–50
  jelly 246
  and olive oil dressing 33–4
  purée 289
  purée butter sauce 285
  purée dressing 96
lemonade, dehydrated 236–8
lettuce, blanched 84–6
Lewis, Jessica 37
Lewis, Ross xiv, 116, 213, 297
lime
  chantilly 227–9
  curd 215–16
Llewellyn, David 220
lobster 108, 122, 277
  sauce 287
loin of rabbit stuffed with light pata negra farce 130–31
Lynch, John 239

M

McAleese, President Mary 47, 198
McCarthy, Jack 132, 135
Mac Giolla Coda, Eoghan 209

McGonagle, Manus 50, 112–13
mackerel, pickled 60
Madeira
  jelly 69
  jus 279
malted banana cream 251–2
malted seed and treacle biscuits 269
malted vinegar sauce 108
mandarin sorbet 248–50
Manjari chocolate and espresso mousse cake 232–3
mascarpone mousse 202, 242–4
Maxwell, Declan 38, 45
mayonnaise 280
meat jelly 63, 65
meringue
  Italian 248–50
  poached 210–12
Michelin star 117
milk crumb 224
molasses sponge 219
monk's beard 188
mousse
  chicken 280
  chocolate and tarragon 232–3
  espresso 232–3
  feta cheese 18
  hot chocolate 246
  yoghurt and vanilla 198–200
Mulligan, Seamus 107
multi-seed and rapeseed oil bread 263
Murphy, Alan 183
muscovado biscuits 242
mushrooms
  cep 139–40, 151–2
  dried 139, 281
  mushroom consommé 25
  mushroom duxelle 278
  mushroom ketchup 174
  pickled 282
mussels 96, 188
mustard
  cream sauce 180–82
  and quince purée 70–72
  sauce 171–2
  and white truffle honey dressing 278
mutton and caper pie 180–82

N

nougat
  parfait, frozen 227–9
  tuiles 236–8

O

O'Doherty's slow cooked pork 132
Okitsu mandarin sorbet 248–50
onions
  burnt 159–60
  caramelised 264
  grelot 279
  onion bread 264
  onion broth 28
  red onion relish 284
  white onion purée 284
orange
  confit 276
  glaze 177–8
  oil 18
  powder 289
  purée 232–3, 283
  and tarragon gel 232–3
ox tongue 118–20, 171–2
  with sautéed spring lamb sweetbreads 102
oxtail
  braised prime Hereford 78, 80
  soup 78–80
oysters 84–6

P

pain de mie dumplings 171–2
Parmesan cream 277
parsley
  deep-fried roots 277
  fried flat-leaf 279
parsnip
  purée 66, 139–40
  salt baked and crisps 66
passion fruit
  curd, gel and sorbet 236–8
  ganache and jelly 272
  milk chocolates 272
pasta 99
pastry
  puff 202–4
  suet 180–81
pata negra farce 278
peanut tuiles 251–2
pearl barley 132–4
pearl tapioca and Knockdrinna sheep's cheese 30
pears
  cooked in Sauternes 224–6
  pear and horseradish relish 60
  pear ice cream 224–6
  pear purée 224–6
  poached 224, 227–9
  sliced 75–6
  smoked 70–72
peas 105–6
  pea purée 30, 105–6
  pea stock 105–6
peppered sika venison loin 139–40
pheasant
  breast of 159–60
  sauce 285
  stock 286